The Future of Psychoanalysis

The Future of Psychoanalysis

Richard D. Chessick, M.D., Ph.D.

State University of New York Press

Published by
State University of New York Press, Albany

© 2007 State University of New York

For information, address State University of New York Press,
194 Washington Avenue, Suite 305, Albany, NY 12210-2384

Production by Michael Haggett
Marketing by Michael Campochiaro

Library of Congress Cataloging-in-Publication Data

Chessick, Richard D., 1931–
    The future of psychoanalysis / Richard D. Chessick.
       p. cm.
    Includes bibliographical references and index.
    ISBN-13: 978-0-7914-6895-1 (hardcover : alk. paper)
    ISBN-10: 0-7914-6895-X (hardcover : alk. paper) 1. Psychoanalysis.
I. Title.

RC504.C495 2006
616.89'17—dc22

                                                        2005036226

10 9 8 7 6 5 4 3 2 1

To Marcia

*With love and appreciation on
our Golden Wedding Anniversary
and forever after.*

Però, se 'l mondo presente disvia,
in voi è la cagione, in voi si cheggia;

—Dante (Purgatorio XVI: 82–83)

Contents

Preface

Kierkegaard, in *Concluding Unscientific Postscript*, written in 1846, describes his point of departure as a thinker. While he sat one Sunday afternoon in the Frederiksberg Garden in Copenhagen smoking a cigar and turning over a great many things in his mind, he reflected that as yet he had made no career for himself. Everywhere around him he saw men of his age celebrated, establishing themselves as renowned benefactors of mankind. All their efforts were directed at making life easier for the rest of mankind, either materially, by constructing railroads and telegraph lines and so on, or intellectually, by publishing compendiums of universal knowledge. It occurred to him that since everyone everywhere else was engaged in making things easy perhaps someone might be needed to make things hard again. For life might become so easy that people would want the difficult back again, and this might be a career and destiny for him.

In 1955, when I was a bright-eyed and eager young resident in psychiatry, psychoanalysis was considered the basic science of psychiatry and most chairs of departments of psychiatry were held by psychoanalysts. I remember attending with great excitement a packed meeting in Chicago of the American Psychiatric Association, where one of my teachers, the famous neurosurgeon Percival Bailey, gave the keynote address. To my amazement he spent it attacking Freud's writing, citing chapter and verse in an ironical presentation that compared Freud's *Standard Edition* to a religious tract. To me this was the formal beginning of a reaction against psychoanalysis in psychiatry that became a tidal wave as the discovery of numerous psychopharmacological agents took place. Now the international drug corporations took a greater and greater interest in American Psychiatry, sponsoring many symposia, taking out enormous multicolored advertisements in our journals, offering financial grants for research, and becoming prominent at the meetings of the American Psychiatric Association simply out of their great financial capacities. The chairpersons of departments of psychiatry today, as everyone knows, are no longer psychoanalysts but mostly are psychopharmacologists with little or no interest in the unconscious and psychodynamics, although they may give lip service to these concepts.

The next step was the establishment of the horrendous so-called Managed Care, which essentially eliminated psychoanalysis from insurance payments for mental health care. Even Medicare pays for four times weekly sitting-up therapy but will not pay for psychoanalysis. We were told on every side that psychoanalysis was dead and would be essentially a cult practiced by nonmedical personnel. Neurophysiological research showed that one of Freud's main postulates, that the brain seeks a state of rest, is wrong; there is no doubt today that the brain is a stimulus seeking organ.

How did psychoanalysts react to all of this? A small group remained "traditional" in the sense that they still based their work on Freud and Anna Freud's principles of ego psychology, which of course they were quite willing to modify in the light of confirmed neurophysiological findings, but many psychoanalysts rode off madly in all directions. Some formed a group called "neuropsychoanalysis," whatever that is, and others became "intersubjectivists," or at least "relational psychoanalysts," concentrating on the here-and-now interaction between the therapist and patient. In South America psychoanalysis remained popular but has increasingly incorporated Kleinian and Lacanian notions that, to say the least, are speculative and highly controversial. In the United States, Kohut's "self psychology" caught on, at first presented as an extension of ego psychology but then developed by Kohut and his followers into a different direction. The psychoanalysis of schizophrenic patients almost entirely ceased; often when I was called to interview a schizophrenic patient in front of a group of residents, the patient was absolutely stoned on drugs—but was no longer posing a problem on the ward or in society.

All these changes made life easier for psychoanalysts, allowed them to fit better into the mainstream of psychiatry by emphasizing the neurological and the interactional and the "here-and-now" relationship between the patient and the analyst. It sometimes became difficult to distinguish between psychoanalysis and so-called cognitive behavior therapy, the latter now in fashion. In the more than fifty years I have been in practice, I observed these changes at our meetings and in the practices of my colleagues. I have had great empathy for them, as one must make a living and in order to do so must fit into somewhere in the current fashion. The great danger of these changes, however, is that psychoanalysis is in peril of becoming "whatever the psychoanalyst is doing" and of losing its identity and its anchor in the works of Freud. This book is a plea to psychoanalysts to return to Freud, not the circumscribed Freud of Lacan but the Freud of the entire *Standard Edition*, the record of a lifetime of Freud's evolving thought that formed the centerpiece of the training and thinking of psychoanalysts of my generation.

In a series of articles and books, I attempted to make life harder for psychoanalysts. I emphasized the basic stance of Freud—that current behavior and mentation is determined by what has happened in a person's childhood. Each individual develops a set of core fantasies and internalized object relations in the first few years of life, and subsequently views and experiences everything through this intrapsychic core. Here is the psychological origin of the famous "mood" (*Stimmung*) that Heidegger considered always intrinsic to each human being. If the compromise formations involving defences and the core fantasies and early internalized object relations are maladaptive, or if the person has what Gedo (1988) called "apraxias," that person is going to get into trouble. The compulsion to repeat causes each person to construct patterns over and over again in relationships, patterns that can be quite maladaptive and self-defeating. In the psychoanalytic process, if carried out by properly analyzed and trained psychoanalysts utilizing free association and dream interpretation, we invariably observe these patterns emerge in the transference. The personality, gender, appearance, habits, et cetera, of the analyst may trigger one or another of the patterns but, if these features are not neurotic and disruptive, they do not *cause* these patterns. We remain participants in the psychoanalytic process, but our task is as observers and interpreters of these patterns and then to trace them to their childhood origins in fantasies and anxieties and subsequent defenses the ego develops to satisfy what Freud called its "three harsh masters"—the id, the superego, and reality. That, I believe, is what we should be doing, and what gives psychoanalysis its unique identity as a profession.

In the present book, I attempt to establish a future for psychoanalysis by giving it a specific identity firmly based on Freud's work but also complemented by phenomenology, self psychology, object-relations theory, and so on. These are all helpful ways of psychoanalytic listening, but we must not mistake the trees for the forest. A whole variety of cultural and economic pressures, what Sartre called the "practico-inert," stand in the way of psychoanalysts attempting to maintain their professional identity. I am taking a conservative view, placing both the topographic and structural theories of Freud and the work of Anna Freud in the foreground by construing it as the main channel of psychoanalytic listening. I hope not to eliminate the contributions of the other schools but rather to put them in perspective so that the identity of Freud's technique and practice of psychoanalysis does not become diffuse and eventually meaningless, as it now threatens to do. In this book, I describe the various pressures and factors that threaten the very survival and existence of psychoanalysis and I explicate, as well as I can, from personal and clinical psychiatric experience, psychoanalyses I have conducted, and discussions with colleagues, the plight of the psychoanalyst today.

> After the human mind has once despaired of finding truth, everything becomes very much feebler; and the result is that they turn men aside to agreeable discussions and discourses, and a kind of ambling around things, rather than sustain them in the severe path of inquiry.
> —Francis Bacon (*The New Organon*)

Acknowledgments

———————————————

In addition to substantial previously unpublished material, this book contains, in thoroughly revised form, some material from recent papers previously published in *The Journal of the American Academy of Psychoanalysis and Dynamic Psychiatry* (Chessick 2000c, 2000d, 2001a, 2001b, 2001c, 2002a, 2002b, 2002c, 2002d, 2003a, 2003b, 2005b). Grateful acknowledgement is made to *The Journal* for permission to adapt and revise this material, and to the editor of *The Journal*, Dr. Douglas Ingram, for his help and encouragement in the preparation of this book.

Selections from Dante's *The Divine Comedy*, translated by C. H. Sisson, 1980 are reproduced by permission of Pollinger, Ltd., and New Directions for UK, rights and worldwide rights, 9 Staple Inn, Holborn, London, WC1V 7QH; from *Dante: The Divine Comedy: Inferno*, Canto V, 112–114; Canto VII, 70–75; Canto X, 106–108; Canto XV, 82–83; Canto XXVI, 118–120; *Purgatorio*, Canto XX, 10–12; Canto XXVI, 142–147; *Paradiso*, Canto XIII, 118–120; Canto XXII, 133–138, Canto XXVI, 8–9; Canto XXXIII, 139–145. Grateful acknowledgement is made to Pollinger, Ltd. and C. H. Sisson. Acknowledgement is also made to Chicago: Regnery Gateway 1981, the original publisher of *Dante: The Divine Comedy*, translated by Sisson.

My long friendships with local colleagues, as well as many members of the American Academy of Psychoanalysis and Dynamic Psychiatry, have been a primary source of support and encouragement, for which I am grateful to all. I wish to acknowledge with many thanks the invaluable help and effort in the preparation of this book from my assistant of many years, Ms. Elizabeth Grudzien. Finally, none of my work and efforts to contribute to our field would have been possible without the love and patience of my wife Marcia, who has selflessly provided me with over fifty years of marital happiness, for which I am gratefully appreciative and thankful beyond measure.

1

What is Psychoanalysis?

Psychoanalysis can have a scientific foundation, and does have a future, even if it is a procedure in which the investigator has an indissoluble influence on what is being investigated, and the possibility of replication is deeply compromised by the uniqueness of the relationship. Psychoanalytic notions do not readily lend themselves to empirical validation. Yet it has been increasingly recognized in contemporary philosophy of science that these problems are general to all scientific inquiry and they represent the limitations of all science. The fact that it is very difficult to validate psychoanalytic hypotheses is not restricted only to psychoanalysis as a science; witness the plethora of contemporary theories and arguments in such traditional sciences as physics and astrophysics about quantum theory, about the so-called "cosmological constant" and whether it is necessary to postulate an inflationary phase in the origin of the universe, and the curious difficulty of locating proton decay, determining the mass of neutrinos, and finding gravitational waves predicted by the various theories but so far not possible to convincingly demonstrate empirically. Some very elaborate hypotheses such as "string theory" have never produced a single testable prediction. The whole conception of science in the twentieth century has shifted, but it does not follow from this that the data of psychoanalysis any more than the data of any other field, are nothing but the current product of an interaction or a dialogue between patient and analyst. This is true in spite of the current fashion as expressed, for example, by the popularity of Bakhtin's (Emerson 1997) postmodern concepts of dialogue, polyphony, and unfinalizability. This so-called postmodern stance may or may not be valid but it is far from generally accepted and the whole current fashion of postmodernism and hermeneutics remains very poorly defined and highly polemical.

Psychoanalytic theories are not idolized today as they once were, because we now know that all theories tend to filter awareness and promote counter-transference. On the other hand we need theories, for in any science, as Kuhn (1962) in his famous work explained it, there has to be a "stable paradigmatic corpus of notions," a group of core defining ideas. Progress in science involves departures from the prevailing paradigm, but just as science is dead without innovations, so it is lost without its traditions and fundamental body of acquired knowledge. For us, this has been and should continue to be provided by the work of Freud and the psychoanalytic pioneers as summarized in Fenichel's (1945) classic textbook and brought up to date by others. Much of the recent psychoanalytic literature, however, attempts not to modify and correct Freud's paradigm as of course it ought to be done on the basis of new research findings, but to replace it entirely in the name of either making psychoanalysis more of a traditional science or of making it a relationship therapy or a purely hermeneutic exercise. This is a major mistake and, contrary to current fashion, we should retain Freud's basic ideas as our central paradigm and starting point. I strongly disagree with the claim that we are now close to solving the so-called "hard problem" challenge of the mind-brain problem, the problem of how to get from neuronal firings to the qualia of consciousness. This is exactly what stymied Freud, causing him to abandon his "Project for a Scientific Psychology" and develop his metapsychology.

The only way I know of to establish scientific knowledge is by consensual validation from a series of investigators. Indeed, there has been a serious effort by prominent psychoanalysts, especially in last twenty years to establish some areas of confluence. For example, Gabbard (1995) published an important paper delineating the gradual migration in our field away from extreme positions and toward some generally accepted principles, and Wallerstein's (1988) seminal paper "One Psychoanalysis or Many?" was a central topic of discussion at the 1989 International Psychoanalytical Congress. It is easy to criticize psychoanalytic institutions and bureaucracies and many authors (e.g., Gedo 1997) have done so; nobody would disagree that such organizations should fear dogma more than freedom of inquiry, but it is very difficult, human narcissism and group psychology being what it is, to keep such organizations from becoming a conservative force. At the same time, there is a wealth of clinical knowledge and useful theoretical ideas to be found in Freud's pellucid writings that are of foundational value even today. When Kohut was asked what to read after one reads Freud he replied, "Read Freud again."

Psychoanalysis, although containing a significant hermeneutic aspect, is primarily a clinical science. Also, as originally pointed out by the philosopher Paul Ricoeur (1970), it is a new form of investigation, one that combines both hermeneutics and empirical study. Furthermore, it is increasingly a medical science, for we are in the era of great advances in psychopharmacology and it is no longer unusual these days during psychoanalytic treatment that psychopharmacological medications are prescribed. Both the psychic effect of such prescriptions as well as the physiological effects, including the effects of combining psychopharmacologic agents with other particular medications the patient may be taking, have to be considered and evaluated by the analyst or, in situations where the analyst is not a physician, by a consultant psychiatrist. Prescribing necessary medication is not so different from Freud's feeding of the "Rat-Man" or collecting money for the "Wolf-Man," and it carries the same complications for the transference and potential for countertransference enactment. But it is also a countertransference enactment to withhold necessary medication from a patient, entailing needless suffering. Also, the variety of physical symptoms and problems that arise during the course of a long psychoanalysis, in addition to the already ongoing medical problems of those patients who enter psychoanalysis with a psychosomatic disorder, will require experienced medical judgment.

HERMENEUTICS

Ricoeur, in his famous seminal work, *Freud and Philosophy* (1970), said there are two kinds of hermeneutics. The first of these he labels the "hermeneutics of suspicion," represented by the work of Freud, Marx, and Nietzsche, to some extent Feuerbach, and, I would add, Foucault. Their task is demystification and a reduction of "illusions." A crisis of the philosophy of the subject is involved here; these authors point to the lie of consciousness and to consciousness as a lie. For Freud, consciousness expresses the unconscious and sexuality; for Marx, the conscious is formed by economics. In 1888, Nietzsche's last good year, Freud was thirty-two-years-old and deeply immersed in psychoanalytic work on hysteria; he had not yet undertaken his self-analysis. In that year Nietzsche wrote that all philosophy is interpretation, a tearing-off of masks.

Freud built a one-person or solipsistic metapsychological model, his "mental apparatus," out of a two-person dialogue that was dyadic and non-solipsistic. Ricoeur's discussion of Freud's work places great emphasis on dreams as the key to the psychoanalytic focus on the relationship of desire to language. The text of a dream is the manifest dream; owing to repression it is a coded message. The latent dream Ricoeur calls the "primitive speech of desire." Freud used hermeneutics to get from the text of the dream to the primitive speech of desire and the same process is used for decoding neurotic symptoms.

Viewed in this fashion, Freud's crucial question is: "How does desire achieve speech?" This is found as early as in Freud's theory of aphasia. Freud's explanation of aphasia denies the standard brain location theory (Broca's area, for example) and instead conceives of aphasia as a nonlocalized neurological situation in which speech is cut off from the concepts signified by the words. This leads to Freud's (1914a) later use of the connection or lack of connection of "thing-presentations" with "word-presentations" in his theories of neurosis and psychosis. But in Freud there is a contradiction, for in Freud's metapsychology the human remains a "thing," a "psychic apparatus," and this metapsychology is an attempt at a scientific set of quasi-neurological explanations.

The oscillation between a humanistic and a mechanistic view of humans is a well-known hidden tension in Freud's thought (Holt 1973). Even Freud's wish to decode symptoms and dreams implies a value system in its dedicated pursuit of meaning, coherence, and clarity. Freud begins with a simple natural-sciences hydraulic model and ends with a mythology, the "battle of the giants" (Freud 1930, 122), Eros and the death instinct.[1] But when Freud emphasizes only the dismal, neurotic, regressive, and projective aspects of art and religion, he is actually projecting his own pessimism, his own blinders that allow him to see only the negative aspects. Even psychoanalytic code-breaking, even deciphering, even hermeneutics are permeated by one's own fundamental life attitudes. There is no such thing as a study of truth that does not involve the person doing the study. One's own life attitudes are hidden premises in whatever study one makes.

Freud's original idea of psychoanalysis contains two aspects. The first of these involves explanations through the use of forces, or energetics. These are the so-called "economic explanations" that are made, involving dynamic forces playing against each other. The second presents an exegesis of the apparent or manifest through the latent, the classical hermeneutic approach. But psychoanalysis always has to incorporate energetics into hermeneutics in order to make a psychoanalytic interpretation. This is because the distortions that take place, when one goes from the latent to the manifest, occur for a reason; there is a force at work that must be understood to explain why these particular sets of transformations take place. Because of this force, explanations must involve energetics, dynamics, and so on. The earliest conceptions of psychoanalysis, as in *The Interpretation of Dreams*, contain explanations using energetics and explanations using hermeneutics.

The methodological incorporation of hermeneutics and energetics was Freud's crucial epistemological discovery. It represents a new form of investigation, an alternative to investigating the data of clinical psychiatry and the narratives constituting psychoanalysis and psychoanalytic psychotherapy by either standard natural sciences empirical statistical study or by speculative subjective intuitions. The argument that hermeneutics combined with energetics begins a relevant and autonomous intellectual discipline with its own methodology offers an important message for any mental health professional who feels there has to be an alternative in our work to either the inhumane mechanism of hard empirical science on the one hand or a purely speculative philosophy on the other.

But the problem with hermeneutics is that it does not provide any body of convincingly testable propositions. This runs the risk of it being an arcane source of wisdom that generates little evidence that we may proceed to verify. Recognizing this objection, Ricoeur (1977) tried to answer it with his concept that the analytic experience is equivalent to what the epistemology of logical empiricism calls observable measurable data. For Ricoeur, in psychoanalysis there are no facts, there are only narrative reports. But his view ignores the important communications in the patient's nonverbal behavior, the central role of the transference, and the possibility that psychoanalysts, like any group of trained scientists, could check and criticize each other's work. One should not overlook the empirical implications of the phenomena of transference and the observable and predictable unfolding of the psychoanalytic process as conducted by a properly trained psychoanalyst. Through the transference there is a link between Freudian conceptions and natural science so that one cannot, as Ricoeur does, conceive of psychoanalysis solely as hermeneutics and energetics. There are also important natural science phenomena involved in psychoanalysis, which show themselves in the observable behavior of the patient and, above all, in the crucial phenomena of transference. On that point Ricoeur's exegesis has been the most severely criticized by psychoanalysts (Friedman 1976; Holt 1981; Modell 1978; Spence 1982).

THE FIVE-CHANNEL APPROACH
TO PSYCHOANALYTIC LISTENING

I will now briefly review five standpoints or channels (models, perspectives, frameworks) from which we can tune in to the transmission from the patient (Chessick 1992a). Each of them, as is well-known, is based on premises that are currently conflicting and irreconcilable. The first channel was presented by Freud and focuses on the Oedipus complex and more recently, preoedipal longings. It centers on the emergence in a properly conducted psychoanalysis of the need for drive satisfaction in the transference. This enables us to study the patient's conflict in terms of defenses against the instinctual drives and the resulting compromise formations produced by the ego in dealing with its three harsh masters—the superego, the id, and external reality. Freud's fundamental notion of "drives" has come under considerable attack these days, but, as Anna Freud (1988) said, "Psychoanalysis is above all a drive psychology. But for some reason people do not want to have that" (457). Freud's structural theory was developed for the purpose of delineating and explicating unresolved intrapsychic conflicts that lie at the root of the psychoneuroses. At the core of the psyche are the patient's childhood or infantile fantasies which repeat themselves over and over again in the patient's mental life and behavior (Arlow, 1985b). We carefully listen for the derivatives of these fantasies and look for them to be reenacted in the transference. I believe this to be the primary model, the starting point for all psychoanalytic listening.

The second channel utilizes the perspective of object-relations theory for its model. The work of Klein and her analysand Bion focuses on the earliest projective and introjective fantasies of the patient as they appear in the object relatedness manifest in the transference and in the process of projective identification as it occurs in the analytic process. Bion (1963, 1967) emphasized the "toilet function" of the analyst in which the analyst must receive, metabolize, and give back in acceptable form the unacceptable fantasies and affects and expressions of these coming from the patient. Klein (1946) developed the concept of projective identification (defined differently by every author), in which the patient is allowed to place into the analyst whatever representations he or she wishes to place there, with more therapeutic focus on preoedipal fantasies and processes. For Klein, projective identification was also an interactional event in which great pressure is put on the therapist to behave in a manner that corroborates the projection. For Kernberg (1975), aware of Klein's confusion of the intrapsychic and the interactional under one process, it is a very primitive mental event that represents an incomplete projection. A study of projective identification operating in the therapeutic process reveals the patient's earliest internalized object relations and yields data about how the patient as an infant organized these relations into self and object representations and then projected and reintrojected various aspects of these images. Understanding of these processes clarifies the patient's relationships in the present because all such relationships are perceived and reacted to through the filter of these early organized self and object representations.

A third channel, focussing on the patient's being-in-the-world, is the phenomenologic point of view. Here an attempt is made to grasp the facts of the patient's life phenomenologically, without other theoretical preconceptions to organize the data. This approach was emphasized in philosophy by Husserl and then differently by Heidegger, and taken up especially by the pioneer psychoanalysts such as Boss (1963), especially in their effort to understand seriously disturbed and psychotic patients. A corollary of this approach began with Feuerbach and Marx, and was elaborated by thinkers like Fromm, Sartre, and Lacan: society shapes the individual and we can only understand the individual if we understand the society or culture or world in which he or she must continuously live and interact. So, to understand an individual, we must understand that lived state of being-in-the-world which is unique for the situation of each person.

The fourth approach is from self psychology (Kohut 1971, 1977, 1984; reviewed by Chessick 1993), which focuses on the state of the patient's sense of self as it is empathically grasped by the analyst. Important predecessors of this approach were Fairbairn and Winnicott. The latter introduced the notion of the true and the false self that was taken up in detail by R. D. Laing (1969) in his brilliant exposition of schizoid and schizophrenic conditions. Kohut brought the focus on the self into a systematic and elaborate theory; significant alterations in this theory have been offered by Gedo (1979, 1984) and many others. Gedo's establishment of hierarchies of self organization represents a further elaboration and movement away from traditional psychoanalytic metapsychology.

The final approach to organizing the transmission from the patient might be loosely termed the interactive, or relational, or, at its extreme, the intersubjective, focusing on the countertransference of the therapist or, more generally, on the here-and-now factors in the treatment and emphasizing the central role of the analyst's participation. Many of the numerous and conflicting points of view under this rubric have been developed as a response to our increasing understanding, especially in preoedipally damaged patients, of the patient's need for an experience and not just an explanation in the treatment. Gill (1982) emphasized the importance of the therapist's participation in the particular transference manifestations that develop in a given treatment and also focused his interpretations on the here-and-now interaction between patient and therapist. Gill's view is close to Sullivan's (1953) more extreme "interpersonal theory of psychiatry," one in which the therapist both participates in and observes the interaction at the same time. Sullivan's approach suffered from a metapsychological shallowness because of its emphasis on the interactional without sufficient study of the filtering mechanism through which the patient inevitably experiences this interaction. Sullivan's (1947, 1953) concept of parataxic distortion attempts to make up for this, but has not received widespread acceptance. Loewald (1960) was a pioneer in developing the traditional psychoanalytic approach but he also insisted that the patient's experience of the analyst was a major factor in the curative process.

The most complete traditional exposition of the interaction between patient and analyst was offered in a series of papers by Lipton (1977a, 1979, 1983), who restudied Freud's cases in order to demonstrate how significant aspects of the real interaction between the patient and the analyst profoundly affected the data that were presented for psychoanalytic understanding. Freud in his actual practice (often quite sensibly) violated some of his own admonitions published in his (1912a, 1913, 1914c, 1915) papers on technique. Stone (1981) systematized this real interaction under the rubric of the "physicianly vocation" of the analyst and demonstrated compellingly the profound impact of it on the material produced and the process of the treatment itself.

It is likely that Freud's papers on technique were basically aimed at preventing massive acting out by incompletely analyzed or even unanalyzed therapists with their patients, as was common in the early days of psychoanalysis. Freud's admonitions tended, in the middle of the twentieth century in the United States, to become codified into a rigid set of rules that sometimes produced iatrogenic narcissistic manifestations in patients and led to either an impasse in the treatment or a surrender of autonomy by the patient, accompanied by a massive identification with the aggressor analyst; obviously these are unsatisfactory outcomes for a lengthy and expensive treatment.

In the five-channel approach, theoretical orientations or models are being utilized that directly conflict with each other and can not be thought of as complementary because the basic premises that underlie them, both their epistemological foundations as well as their basic assumptions about human nature and its motivations, directly collide. This forces a radical discontinuity as we shift from channel to channel in our receiving instrument, rather than, as we would all prefer to do, sliding back and forth between theoretically consistent positions, or at least complementary positions that are consistent with each other.

The worst mistake a beginner can make at this point in the development of psychoanalytic theory is to assume that in some fashion these five various standpoints can be blended or melded into some supraordinate theory that can generate all of them. Careful examination of the premises of these standpoints reveals that this is simply impossible in our current state of knowledge and we are forced, if we use this shifting of systems, to accept the radical discontinuities. The problem in the human sciences is profound, and some thinkers such as Foucault (1973a, 1973b) have claimed that *in principle* no agreement can ever be reached on a single theoretical model for scientific understanding of all human mentation and behavior.

It may seem to some readers that certain other theoretical approaches or models should be added to these channels; what I am offering here is what has proved in my clinical experience to be of the most value, to be the least speculative (experience-distant), and to generate the least number of arbitrary inferences. The most important requirement of a model is that it be suggested by the very data the patient produces rather than superimposed on the data by experience-distant or arbitrary prior conceptions in the mind of the therapist. This is a relative concept because no theory is truly experience-near, since it is impossible to approach data without some prior conceptions, even in phenomenology. Our only hope is that our conceptions be not too abstract, generalized, and divorced from the specific material, and that they are capable of being validated by a study of how the patient responds to interventions based on them. Of course this is fraught with difficulty, as it is all too human to hear what we wish to hear or infer what we wish to infer.

The hardest part of using this approach is to be willing to keep discontinuous and conflicting models in one's mind, which offends the natural and very dangerous human tendency for a neat, consistent, and holistic theoretical explanation of all material, even if it is wrong. Kant (1781) called this tendency the regulative principle of reasoning, and Freud would have based it on the powerful synthesizing function of the ego. The five-channel approach requires tolerance and flexibility on the part of the therapist as well as a certain maturity, for it is sometimes the unfortunate result of a personal psychoanalysis that the individual becomes a strong and rigid adherent of the particular theoretical orientation or style of one's analyst. Kohut (1984) suggested that the reasons for this are inherent in a psychoanalysis that has incorrectly and prematurely interpreted certain transference manifestations. Since no data available, at present, convincingly and decisively prove any of these theoretical orientations to be the one and only best orientation, uncritical adherence to any one of them would have to be leftover of a misunderstood or unanalyzed transference.

RELATIONAL PSYCHOANALYSIS

Relational psychoanalysis (Mitchell and Aron 1999), an assortment of views involving interpersonal psychiatry, constructivism, perspectivism, relativism, and more specific types of intersubjectivity such as that of Stolorow and Atwood (1992), challenges the concept of objectivity as an analytic ideal but, as Blum (1998) points out, "Acknowledging the relativity and limitation of objectivity does not diminish its analytic importance" (190).

The term "intersubjective field" was introduced by Brandchaft and Stolorow (1984) and by Atwood and Stolorow (1984) to refer to the fact that diagnosis and meaning in a therapy situation are primarily a function of the mutual interchange between the therapist and the patient. The idea of intersubjectivity is introduced in order to contrast it with the classical positivist notion of the neutral realistic and relatively healthy therapist confronting the emotionally disturbed patient and making an objective diagnosis, a concept analogous to the medical evaluation of a patient with a physical disease.

This approach carries the risk of assuming that diagnoses have no objective validity and are simply a function of the intersubjective field. This is clearly wrong since there is now suggestive evidence for biological and constitutional factors that go into the formation of psychopathology. Brandchaft and Stolorow are well aware of this and have been falsely accused of an untenable position. Stolorow, Brandchaft, and Atwood (1987) have developed their position at greater length, shown its relationship to self psychology, and given clinical illustrations of their approach.

An even more radical view has been presented by Natterson (1991), who claims that the idiosyncratic subjectivity of the therapist "is a basic motivational source and structuring influence in the therapeutic process" (223). In this view there must be continuous self-monitoring by the therapist of his or her individual desires, fears and perspectives brought to the treatment situation, inevitably and constantly exerting a shaping and constituting influence on the transference and treatment process. This is beyond countertransference because it is in addition to it, since it is not stirred up simply by the patient's transference or personality, but by a host of other factors in the external life and past history of the therapist.

There is a whole spectrum of approaches in relational psychoanalysis that must be kept in mind. At one end of the spectrum is the theory of Freud, in which analysis of the transference neuroses of the patient is central, and an unobjectionable positive transference is assumed to pervade the background of the treatment and is not necessary to be analyzed. The next variation on this is the idea that the personality or gender of the psychoanalyst determines the sequence in which the transferences appear. As we approach the other extreme of the spectrum we have those who say that what is called transference and countertransference is really the action of two transferences on each other to form an intersubjective field. The analysts that I call intersubjectivists argue that the analysis of this intersubjective field—"what is going on between us"— is central to the analysis. In the more extreme view the patient's childhood is put on a back burner and the implication is very strong that the interpersonal relations in the here and now determine what appear in the therapy, not the transference. At the far end of the spectrum are those who believe that analysts should make self-revelations in an effort to be clear on "what's going on between us." This of course carries the danger of constituting an invitation to exploit the patient in a variety of possible ways. From the Freudian point of view it hopelessly contaminates the transference.

Traditional psychoanalysts believe that "the analysis of transference, rather than its exploitation, is still the hallmark of psychoanalytic treatment" (Schlesinger 2003) and the crucial purpose of the psychoanalytic situation is to make the transference show itself. The patient both tells his or her story and reenacts it and the analyst must split into an objective listener and at the same time a figure in the reenactment. At the extreme other end of the spectrum is the experimentation by Ferenczi (1988), in which the patient and analyst took turns being the analyst and the patient, a procedure which is not formally practiced today but which at times tends to happen when there is an exploitation of the transference by the psychoanalyst.

In this book, I use the term "intersubjectivist" or "extreme intersubjectivist" for those psychoanalysts toward the Ferenczi end of the spectrum. The centerpiece of their approach, the focus on the here and now, tends to place the transference and the childhood experiences of the patient in the background rather than in the foreground where, in my opinion, it belongs. By concentrating on "what's going on between us," enactments, and so on, these psychoanalysts carry their notion of the process of psychoanalysis an increasingly great distance from the ideas of Freud. For example, Aron (1999) states:

> While a focus on the patient's experience of the analyst needs to be central at certain phases of an analysis, there are other times, and perhaps long intervals, when focusing on perceptions of the analyst is intrusive and disruptive. . . . Analysts' continuous interpretations of all material in terms of the patient-relationship, as well as analysts' deliberate efforts to establish themselves as separate subjects, may be rightfully experienced as an impingement stemming from the analysts' own narcissistic needs. (257)

Or, as Chodorow (1999) puts it, "Relational, intersubjective, or two-person psychoanalytic approaches, I sometimes fear, take us away from our equally important investigations and conceptualizations of the unbelievable complexity of the individual psyche and unconscious fantasy and of the goals of psychoanalysis" (127). She concludes, "I believe our criticisms of one-person psychologies may have been overdone" (128). Spezzano (1999) says:

> I would now have to take into account the reasonable concerns about and objections to the most radical deconstructionist, relativistic, and antiempirical attitudes in some postmodern, constructivist, relational, intersubjective, and hermeneutic writings about psychoanalysis. . . . Although the analyst is not a perfect instrument for observing and capturing the affective states of the analysand, nonetheless, what he observes and imperfectly captures does exist. (457)

The problem with the entire group of theories based on the extreme intersubjective approach is that the external object relationship is emphasized at the expense of what in my clinical experience turns out to be far more important, the intrapsychic self and object representations, compromise formations, and fantasies developed in childhood through which all current adult object relations and objects are viewed, represented, experienced, and responded to. The declaration that the transference is primarily shaped in the present ignores the fact that the transference is basically a revival of unconscious infantile conflicts and more or less traumatic experiences and precognitive memories, which have been worked over during infancy into archaic core fantasies (see Arlow 1969a). In a sense, the patient evolves certain fantasies in infancy that include crucial intrapsychic self and object representations that will then emerge in the transference. Therefore the transference primarily represents the regressive repetition and revival of the past through the displacement of and/or projection of the unconscious fantasy objects and relationships of infancy and childhood onto the psychoanalyst.

INTERSUBJECTIVITY

It is very important to make it clear to the reader that I understand there are many forms of relational psychoanalysis and that in every psychoanalysis there is always some discussion of what is going on between the psychoanalyst and the patient and an attempt to analyze enactments, et cetera. However, when one shifts the focus of the psychoanalysis on a relatively consistent basis to the interpersonal interaction between the patient and the psychoanalyst one places the analysis of the transference and the exploration of childhood fantasies and conflicts as they reveal themselves in free association, dreams, and so on, on the back burner. Those forms of relational psychoanalysis that tend to do this I have labeled, in this book, "intersubjectivity" because of their deliberate and sometimes exclusive concentration on the here and now in the relationship. I am not setting up a straw man here; although very few analysts go as far as Ferenczi did, there are many psychoanalysts today who have shifted their practice much in the direction to that end of the spectrum and it is the extremes of this shift which are appearing in the literature and in my clinical work with patients who are consulting me for a second analysis. These extremes, to my mind, represent a different form of psychotherapy than the psychoanalysis that was invented by Freud and which was based on the various clinical and philosophical assumptions that were the foundations of Freud's conceptions. This group of extreme intersubjective psychoanalysts, one that is increasing in influence and proponents today, are discussed in this and later chapters, and I delineate how they affect the future of psychoanalysis.

The debates between traditional and relationist views of psychoanalysis form a subclass of the current unresolved philosophical question of whether there is hope for human knowledge between the Scylla of relativism and the Charybdis of absolutism (Blackburn 2005). Somehow, if psychoanalysis is to have a future, we must steer between these extremes. The point of this book is that we psychoanalysts are drifting today too far toward the Scylla of relativism, perhaps as a reaction to Freud's tendency to the Charybdis of absolutism that became the ossified model of the psychoanalyst in the mid-twentieth century. This endangers the future of psychoanalysis and, as some philosophers (Boudon 2005) have pointed out, can shipwreck "our science" on the rocks of nihilism, chaos, mysticism, and disrepute.

In previous publications (1995a; 1996a), I have pointed out how inter-subjectivity tends to slide over into nihilism. It even challenges all theory construction, for if there is no objective and consensual observation of clinical facts possible, one can not build any theories and test them against clinical data. The point I am making is that regardless of the idiosyncrasies of various analysts, and assuming that the analysts we are paying attention to have received a thorough personal psychoanalysis of their own and therefore are bringing only sliver patient vectors into the treatment, it is possible to accumulate a body of analytic findings which can be checked "against findings with different patients, with different analysts, and in analytic observations and studies outside the analytic situation" (Blum 1998, 194–195). Furthermore, emphasis on the intersubjective, on the here-and-now aspects of the therapy, while certainly having value, can easily represent a flight from the emergence of both the patient's and the therapist's unconscious conflicts and core fantasies.

Although enactments inevitably occur and are sources of understanding countertransference, a powerful debate continues as to whether these enactments and the analyst's unintentional emotional involvement are the most important curative aspects in psychoanalysis. Whitaker and Malone (1953) point out that all psychotherapy involves a therapist and a patient who have what they call both therapist and patient vectors in them that work on the level of the apparent as well as the unconscious relationship between patient and therapist. Therapist vectors are responses to the needs of the immature child part of the other person. Most often the responses of the therapist are therapist vector responses to the patient. At times, however, the patient responds with therapist vector responses to the (we hope) relatively small residual child part of the therapist. Patient vectors are archaic demands for a feeling response from the other person, much as a young child urgently demands response from his or her parents. Clearly, patients will get well only if the patient vectors of the therapist do not make excessive demands on the patient's therapist vectors, but Whitaker and Malone then make a rather startling point. They insist it is vital for successful psychotherapy that the therapist bring in his or her patient vectors along with his or her therapist vectors. They call this a total participation with the patient, a concept also emphasized by Little (1957) as necessary before the analyst's interpretations can be meaningfully heard. Both the analyst and the patient have characterological defenses against such participation, which carries great vulnerability, that must be worked through before effective explorations of the past can begin. The therapist thus expands the frontiers of his or her own emotional growth during the therapy.

If the therapist refuses to participate totally in this fashion, it is experienced by the patient as a severe rejection, or, in self psychology terms, a massive empathic failure of the selfobject, and the therapy is not successful. In a more extreme view, Boesky (1990) states: "If the analyst does not get emotionally involved sooner or later in a manner that he had not intended, the analysis would not proceed to a successful conclusion" (573). It is clear that this becomes an extremely important issue if we agree that, for a psychoanalysis to be successful, some sort of unplanned and spontaneous participation on the part of the analyst is necessary and unavoidable, perhaps arising from unformulated countertransference (Chessick 1999a), or perhaps from a sort of "preconscious attunement" (Kantrowitz 1999), but always requiring "the analyst's self-discipline to preserve the analytic role and keep the treatment safe for both participants" (65).

McLaughlin (1987) describes how "The incessant play of nonverbal activity between patient and analyst actualizes and amplifies the primary verbal data of the psychoanalytic dialogue" (557). Renik (1993) presents the most extreme view of this, claiming that "an analyst's activity, including how an analyst listens and all the various moment-to-moment technical decisions an analyst makes, is constantly determined by his or her individual psychology in ways of which the analyst can become aware only after the fact" (559). In that sense he agrees with Boesky and points out that "*unconscious* personal motivations expressed in action by the analyst are not only unavoidable, but *necessary to the analytic process*" (564).

But it is quite possible that these factors can also impede or defeat an analytic process! For I define the analytic process as occurring in a situation in which the analyst, attempting to be as objective and neutral as he or she possibly can be, and listening and interpreting on multiple channels that shift as the patient's material indicates, facilitates the emergence of transference phenomena that illuminate the patient's infantile core conflicts and fantasies. So Blum (1998) writes, "In the classical tradition, the relatively objective and neutral analyst permits clarification of the patient's fantasy distortions within a grounded rather definitive reality." But, he adds, "If countertransference is intense and intrusive, if the analyst validates or fulfills the patient's fantasies, or if the analyst behaves like the patient's childhood objects . . . then analysis of transference can be impaired" (197). One of the reasons it becomes impaired is that the patient cannot contemplate the transference if it is being enacted in some major fashion through the analyst's countertransference, instead of being identified and interpreted.

Although it is true that patients will hang the transference on various peculiarities of the analyst, I believe the primary source of the transference comes from infantile core fantasies and unconscious archaic psychic structures. The emergence of these in the transference needs to be continuously studied by both the patient and the analyst. The archaic remains a vital and often disruptive or self-defeating primordial force, an active past at any level

of development. The exceptional emphasis by intersubjectivists on the cocreation of both analytic data and the transference loses sight of this central
proposition of Freud's psychoanalysis since, as Blum (1998) explains, "The
current object relationship of the coparticipants takes center stage, and infantile conflicts recede into relative obscurity or unimportance" (199).

I regard psychoanalysis as retaining a scientific core, based on the observation of emergent transference phenomena. As an ideal, it is important for
the analyst to maintain what might be called good-enough objectivity and
good-enough neutrality in order to allow transference manifestations to
emerge, especially the archaic transference manifestations which often have
only a small connection to the idiosyncrasies of the properly analyzed analyst's personality, for example, such archaic fantasies of the analyst as a serene
Buddha, the analyst as a god, as possessing magical powers, as omniscient,
and so forth.

The matter is actually more complicated than I have expressed it here so
far. The phenomena of transference cannot be understood merely by empirical observation, although this is the obvious natural sciences starting point.
There is more to it, however, because in order to achieve a firm and continuing grasp of the transference, the analyst must be able to have and to be motivated to exercise a self-reflective receptive capacity, characterized by a willingness to maintain a state of reverie akin to that advocated by Bion, until certain
unformulated or inarticulate conceptions begin to float across his or her consciousness. These are countertransference manifestations stirred up or placed
in the analyst by the patient's transference, for example, through projective
identification and the patient's need to recreate certain crucial childhood relationships, sometimes playing the role of the parent and sometimes of the
child. So the analyst must always, besides exercising the psychological self-
receptive process, also be silently asking himself or herself what role is being
pressed upon the analyst and how the patient is attempting to use the analyst,
what is expected, what is anticipated, and what is experienced through the filter of the patient's childhood core fantasies and representations.

Bollas (1987) compares this to the mother's capacity to grasp the inarticulate sensations and feelings of the child and transform them into verbal representations that can be mutually considered and negotiated. The capacity to
do this by the analyst also provides the patient with a new and more mature
object for internalization, and hopefully the very process of self-reflection will
be internalized. This capacity is one of the hardest functions to teach candidates. A certain innate talent is required and also a certain psychological
mindedness and comfort with uncertainty, dreams, fantasies, and desires.
Freud (1926) correctly complained that medical training tends to marginalize
this function in order to stress external observation in the study of physical illness, a long and time-honored tradition in medicine. Anyone who has tried to

help new residents in psychiatry grasp these concepts will attest to the truth of Freud's complaint, and I think it explains why contemporary psychiatry clings so tenaciously to a shallow Kraeplinean orientation, a kind of pseudointernal medicine.

Even more unfortunately, there is a trend among analysts today away from this procedure. As Yorke (1995) complains:

> They do not relax and give themselves up to free-floating attention. They do not, for example, find that appropriate associations attuned to those of the patient come readily to mind, that one of the patient's remarks recalls another that gives it fresh meaning, or that a fleeting thought touches something in their own unconscious that points to a deeper or more primitive context than the one which the patient consciously presents, or that a patient's immediate fantasy spontaneously recalls in the analyst's mind something said in a session days or weeks ago. Rather . . . they give the impression of sitting on the edge of their seats as they try to make sense of what the patient tells them. They try to fit it into a theoretical framework and feel vindicated when the "fit" is a good one. (25)

Even Renik (1998), who has been one of the most outspoken advocates of intersubjectivity in the analytic situation, still regards psychoanalysis as a science. This is because he believes we can, although imperfectly, evaluate our interpretations on the basis of their predictive capacity. He writes:

> When I suggest to a patient that he is burdened by irrational guilt feelings, I can see whether his mood improves; or when a patient and I conclude that she no longer needs to be afraid of being more sexually potent than her mother, we can see whether she will begin to be able to have orgasms during intercourse. The circumstances under which psychoanalysts can make predictions can be poorly controlled, and definitive empirical evidence for a psychoanalytic proposition may be very difficult to obtain, but hypotheses-testing via prediction is possible in psychoanalysis. Therefore psychoanalysis is a science. (492–493)

So in spite of the emphasis on intersubjectivity, it does not follow that objectivity is impossible to achieve in clinical psychoanalysis. The fact that there is a testable and predictive value to the meanings that are interpreted in the psychoanalytic process also distinguishes psychoanalysis from pure hermeneutics, where the criteria of valid meaning do not include subsequent empirical experiences and psychological material.

Gabbard (1997) reminds us that there are a whole variety of differing approaches grouped under the loose heading of "intersubjectivity." The danger of intersubjectivity, he points out, is the privileging of the patient's subjectivity. He stresses the importance of the analyst's perspective being different from that of the patient's internal experience and the developmental value of that difference, just as in infant development the subjective object is transformed into an objective object, "one that is partly created by the infant and partly the by-product of the infant's increasing attunement to the *actual* characteristics of the mother as an external object with her own subjectivity" (18).

The heart of the matter goes back to Freud's (1912b) description of how the patient's template is repeated again and again in the transference. As Gabbard (1997) explains:

> Although the analyst's subjectivity influences that template to some degree, there are nevertheless transference patterns that are characteristic of individuals. The patient's intrapsychic conflicts and internal object relations were forged long before entering analysis and will find a way to make themselves known, regardless of the analyst's contribution. (22)

The crucial point is that the early object representations and characteristic processes of object relations that are internalized in the patient's psyche will appear in the analytic process in one sequence or another depending on the subjectivity of the analyst, but they will appear, and will appear in a reanalysis with a different analyst, assuming the psychoanalysts are competent.

THE ANALYST AS A NEW OBJECT

Psychoanalytic technique involves free association, frequency, regularity, recumbency, the analyst's special way of listening, relative neutrality, abstinence, and interventions primarily involving interpretation and analysis of transference. Starting from the current surface of the material and working in increasing depth, we hope for reconstruction of pathogenic experiences or deficits from the past and uncovering the core fantasies and other compromises that were evolved to deal with them. We recognize the powerful effect of the real person of the analyst and the intensity of his or her emotional involvement with the patient over many years, but whereas in psychotherapy this is deliberately utilized along with the transference, in psychoanalysis the transference is hopefully identified and interpreted along with its genetic roots.

The role of a new object experience as constituting the silent power of psychoanalysis, and the relationship as integral to therapeutic change especially with sicker patients has been increasingly recognized. These patients are characterized by unreliability of object constancy, "failure to tame drives or to develop stable defenses, deficiencies in self-esteem, in frustration tolerance, in affect modulation" (Pine 1992, 252), and at times a blurring of reality testing and self and object boundaries. In psychotherapy, supportive elements are moved to the foreground of the interaction, whereas in psychoanalysis the holding environment forms the background. A shifting back and forth may be necessary, depending on the vicissitudes of the patient's state.

After-education is very important in the analytic process, as is the analyst functioning as a new object providing a corrective reparative experience (Loewald 1960) or transformative experience (Bollas 1987). I do not see how this can be avoided, or even that it should be, but it is a genetic fallacy to think that the interchange between the analyst and the patient has the same direct affective impact as the interchange between a caretaker and an infant. Adult affects and object relations are not isomorphic with their infantile precursors because the former are experienced entirely through the schemata of intrapsychic representations and fantasies established during infancy and childhood. Furthermore, the benefits to the patient from experiencing the analyst as calm, collected, tactful, tolerant, and dedicated are clearly not the same as those benefits arising from "the crucial addition of technical neutrality and relatively objective analytic interpretation of unconscious conflict and trauma"(Blum 1998, 201), as this intrapsychic material is regressively revived and even relived in the psychoanalytic process.

Shane, Shane, and Gales (1997) base their theoretical approach to psychoanalysis on the premise that the salutary effects on development of the mother-child interaction can be also produced by the analyst-patient interaction. Recognizing the uncertainty of this premise, they ask: "Can such a significant and far-reaching development take place in an adult or a child through the analytic experience itself, based on understanding, insight, and a living-through relationship with the analyst? We believe it can" (99). But they require of the analyst, if this is to happen, "Availability, concern, positive responsiveness, positive regard, a commitment to the patient's well-being, and an encouraging attitude in regard to all the patient's struggles and conflicts, as well as wishes and desires" (99). This is very nice, but how does it distinguish psychoanalysis from any other form of physician-patient relationship? Sometimes understanding and insight are actually blocked or defended against by various physician-patient enactments, and sometimes the analyst's attempt to be so empathic and actively produce and even report such loving and caring attitudes to the patient can hide countertransference phenomena. The kind of self-revelation recommended by these authors can easily be used in an unconscious collusion to gratify narcissistic and exhibitionistic needs of the analyst, of the patient, or both. For example, in an admittedly extreme view, they recommend that in certain instances, if a patient says "I love you," and you love the patient you should tell the patient so, forming a "nonsexual attachment" in this manner. Freud, of course, would scoff at even the possibility of such an attachment, and he might sarcastically ask how to respond when a patient says "I love you," and you do *not* particularly love the patient. Do you say "I do not love you"? What do you say in the latter situation that is not either a lie or a humiliation for the patient, if you have already conditioned the patient to expect self-revelatory responses? All this is a rerun of the well-known admonitions Freud gave to Ferenczi when the latter tried physical interaction with his patients; how easily one thing leads to another in boundary crossings! Psychoanalysis of this sort can dangerously disintegrate into a kind of hand holding and love therapy, which is often what patients want and which unanalyzed therapists will sometimes provide in order to avoid having to face the patient's or the therapist's rage and negative transferences or countertransferences.

THE DATA OF PSYCHOANALYSIS

There is a dangerous fallacy in the extreme intersubjective as well as those hermeneutic viewpoints that assume the centrality of continual cocreation of the data of psychoanalysis. The notion of "cocreation" shifts our attention away from the patient's ownership of unconscious conflict and archaic fantasy, and moves our focus away from pathogenesis and toward iatrogenesis. Patients enter analysis with character pathology that has developed as a set of compromise formations and defenses against the drives and experiences that produced early infantile conflicts and archaic fantasies. They present these at the onset of analysis, sometimes even from the very first telephone call in making an appointment; these are not created or cocreated in analysis. The centerpiece of psychoanalysis is to uncover and understand the persisting influence of earlier developmental phases and the conflicts and archaic fantasies these have produced, through the regressive revival of them in the analytic process. In so doing, we have to assume that the good enough psychoanalyst has at least an adequate capacity to retain objectivity toward the patient and toward his or her own countertransference. It is this assumption that forms the basis of my contention that Freud's psychoanalysis is primarily a science with a future, that reliable data can be collected over the years by many well-trained analysts working with a variety of patients, and that on the basis of these data reliable theories may be formulated that can then be extrapolated to the treatment of other patients.

In spite of a number of papers by a variety of prominent psychoanalysts attempting to replace Freud's drive theory, it remains an extremely valuable heuristic notion to help us in thinking about our patients and about our unfortunate species in general (Chessick 1996c). It is reassuring that such well known psychoanalysts as André Green and Leo Rangell agree with me about this (see Raymond and Rosbrow-Reich 1997). Yorke (1995) points out that Freud's metapsychological concepts "although capable of modification in the light of fresh clinical and theoretical findings are, in their fundamentals, indispensable. . . . Critics of metapsychology seem to lose sight of the purpose of metapsychological concepts. They are explanatory concepts, means to an end and not ends in themselves" (3, 23). Perhaps it would be important here to clarify Kant's notion of "heuristic principles," as he used them in his (1790) *Critique of Judgement*. This notion was also taken up by Einstein, who called them "heuristic viewpoints," serving the purpose of allowing us to make assertions from which familiar facts could then be deduced. Heuristic viewpoints, for example, drive theory, cannot be directly falsified or proven; their value is in their usefulness in explaining familiar facts, such as the overwhelming human preoccupation with lust and aggression that makes up what Hegel (1840) called the "slaughter bench" of history, "upon which the happiness of nations, the wisdom of states, and the virtues of individuals were sacrificed" (24). Our greatest novelists are our greatest psychologists. Consider this statement by Captain Ahab (Melville 2002):

> What is it, what nameless, inscrutable, unearthly thing is it; what cozening, hidden lord and master, and cruel, remorseless emperor commands me; that against all natural lovings and longings, I so keep pushing and crowding, and jamming myself on all the time; recklessly making me ready to do what in my own proper, natural heart, I durst not so much as dare? (406)

From my point of view, that of the post-Freudian psychoanalyst in what Wallerstein (1995) calls the post-ego-psychological age, the psychoanalyst does indeed regard everything in the mind and even one's character patterns as compromise formations between drives and repressing forces, but he or she is extremely judicious as to which compromise formations require analysis. This is the way deconstructionist and constructionist aspects are combined in any psychoanalytic therapy. The art of therapy is to know what to analyze and what to leave alone, and to develop the proper timing and phrasing of interpretations and other interventions so that the whole experience does not appear to the patient to be coming from a torture chamber and constitute a perpetual humiliation and destruction of self-esteem.

What is currently missing is a genealogical study of why, in certain cultures, certain types of psychoanalytic theories tend to predominate. For example, in South America, Kleinian theories, peppered with the ideas of Lacan, are the current fashion. Lacan's version of Freud swept like a tidal wave over

France a few years ago. In the immediate post-World War II United States, Hartmann's (1958) ego psychology was the fashion. In our current cultural milieu, one of affluence, global capitalism, and extravagant consumerism, a hedonistic and pleasure-oriented culture that emphasizes fast-fast-fast relief and the relativity of all moral and ethical principles, a plurality of theories and schools and various forms of intersubjectivity have come to be the fashionable basis of psychoanalytic theory formation.

There is also an important financial explanation for this, since the more one views psychoanalysis as a form of hermeneutics, the less one needs to view it as a scientific medical discipline, opening the door, as happened in France with the advent of Lacanianism, for everyone to feel free to practice what they call "psychoanalysis". What this has led to is not a flourishing of psychoanalysis but a marginalizing of it in our society, a loss of respect for it, and the provision of an opening for insurance companies to deny payments for analytic treatment. The net result of this has been a disaster for many troubled individuals who need prolonged psychoanalytic therapy and with the advent of so-called managed care no longer have the means to provide it. This situation also entails a loss of reliable and detailed information from the deep analysis of many psychoanalytic cases by highly-qualified psychoanalysts.

The philosopher Adorno (1973) outlined three forms of what he called negative dialectical thinking, which may help us in untangling the difficult problems involved in trying to derive truth from the data of psychoanalysis. One of these forms is what he calls the internal critique. Adorno and the other members of the so-called "Frankfurt School" argue that the Enlightenment was predicated upon an epistemological error, namely the idea that our knowledge can fully capture reality, and understanding can be determinate. They believe this error leads to an impoverishment of rationality and finally to its collapse. It is the kind of error, for example, involved in trying interminably to specify *exactly* what is psychoanalysis and what is not psychoanalysis. Adorno maintains that our representations of reality always entail some level of indeterminacy. We know that conceptual thought is limited, and we also know there is a discrepancy between any concept of something and the object itself, a discrepancy we can understand through the use of what Adorno calls "nonidentity." Nonidentity refers to that part of the concept which does not fit the object and is therefore misguided and superfluous, but it also negates the concept. Conceptual systems such as Freud's drive theory or his tripartite model of the psyche, then, are valuable and indispensable to give us direction and motivation and they are a part of the dialectical process of understanding. They contain what I have called a heuristic value and we cannot do without them. The contradictions that occur between our clinical experience and our conceptual systems are the way in which we get closer to understanding, but we cannot focus as we should on these contradictions if we assume that our conceptual systems are congruent with the whole truth. This is the first form of negative dialectics; it is the contradictions that take us closer to understanding.

Adorno's second form of negative dialectics he calls constellation, in which one attempts to get to a deeper discernment of the object, or the patient in our instance, by emphasizing the shortcomings of a whole variety of differing conceptual systems that are employed by various individuals or schools of thought in their study of the object or patient. This is the epistemological basis of the five-channel theory of psychoanalytic listening reviewed above, in which I propose that we need to listen to patients (and ourselves) on several channels at a time, each of which are based on differing and conflicting conceptual systems, in order to have a better understanding of the patient.

The third form of negative dialectics, close to Kohut's notion of empathy, consists of what Adorno calls mimesis. This is a form of cognition distinct from conceptualization, an attempt to identify with the object, that is, one's self identifying with the other by becoming in imagination like the other. Elsewhere I, have discussed the whole special and controversial issue of empathy as a form of psychoanalytic investigation (1998). There are no clear or set rules for mimesis but rather an indefinite number of imaginative responses. Mimetic identification is neither precise and exhaustive nor fully comprehensible; it is open to continuous interpretation and its meaning is inexhaustible.

I believe our approach to the patient should employ all of these techniques, and when we are able to do so we have a more balanced and appropriate view of the individual who is coming to us because he or she is suffering; who is enslaved to an infantile fantasy life and poor maladaptive childhood compromise formations as well as manifesting what Gedo (1988) calls "apraxias," a lack of certain basic skills in human adaptation. These "apraxias" may be viewed as manifesting themselves in another form of the transference, the interpersonal situation the patient creates with the analyst. Here again, the main contribution comes from the patient, as what Fonagy (1999) calls "procedural memories" are attempted to be reenacted in the relationship with the analyst, sequences of actions and pressures brought upon the analyst, who needs to recognize and interpret these to the patient. But although the personality and theories of the analyst have a role in the appearance of these memories and the way in which they appear, in my opinion it is an error to ignore what the patient is attempting to tell us about the past, which the patient would tell in one form or another regardless of the specific analyst, if given a chance to do so.

It is our task as psychoanalysts to deal with all of this and to not get caught up in two of the cardinal errors that Adorno talks about. These are hypostasis, which occurs because once a theoretical system is developed it is believed that system has fully captured everything about the object and no further thought is needed or evoked; and rigidity, in which a system tends to become fixed. Not long after that, schools are set up, schisms develop, leaders and apostles appear, and we have the psychoanalytic civil wars (Frosch 1991).

Reporting on a discussion of the topic "One Psychoanalysis or Many?," Hanly (1997) summarized Rangell's central proposal as being that, "psychoanalysis as a body of knowledge is . . . an evolving, unitary, coherent, composite theory, whereas contemporary psychoanalytic culture makes it out to be a collection of alternative, inconsistent, but equally viable theories" (485). Theoretical plurality in our field, Rangell is reported to have said, is more a matter of political and bureaucratic matters and is not based on any established scientific validity. A study of these political and bureaucratic matters surely ought to be the subject of a thorough investigation by future scholars.

Hanly asks:

> Why is psychoanalysis so vulnerable to charisma and group identifications? Psychoanalysts, rather like philosophers, seem to adopt theoretical positions for reasons other than the strictly rational ones of fact, logic, and explanation. . . . Is this a consequence of failure to analyze the idealizing transference, so that analysts are exposed to basing their theoretical views on a personal affiliation rather than on clinical observation? (486)

He continues:

> I take Freud's theory to be the core of a unitary psychoanalytic theory . . . I continue to consider Freud's durable theories to be the best empirical hypotheses available for this purpose and, therefore, consider them like any empirical hypotheses to be subject to continuing clinical testing and logical evaluation. The formulation of new explanatory hypotheses in the form of alternative theories is an essential part of this endeavor to improve and develop psychoanalysis. It is the preference for the easy, exhilarating transformation of new and old theories into charismatic ideologies that causes a failure or refusal to engage in this difficult, painstaking work. (488)

I do not think the Enlightenment project is bankrupt. It is in need of some revision, but future human emancipation and freedom still have the best chance of developing through the exercise of reason. It is incorrect to say psychoanalysis in the contemporary world is generally dismissed as a relic of a bygone age. This is somewhat true in the United States where the pharmaceutical corporations, insurance companies, and managed care tyrannies have been able to dominate United States psychiatry, but it is not true in South America, it is not true in continental Europe, and psychoanalysis is currently enjoying exploding interest in Russia and Japan. There has been remarkable growth especially in France, Germany, Italy, Argentina, and Brazil. There are today a number of critics of Freud who are notorious in their hatred of psychoanalysis but Freud has always been viciously attacked by prominent critics ever since his first publications. Psychoanalysis is a threat in a commercialized society in which a quick-fix mentality reigns and a greater premium is placed on conspicuous consumption than on self examination. More generally, as Chasseguet-Smirgel (Raymond and Rosbrow-Reich 1997) puts it, "there exists a struggle against psychoanalysis which is one with the struggle against thought itself. A denial of the unconscious is in keeping with the dehumanized world in which we live" (462).

Certain authors set up a straw man, the so-called orthodox psychoanalyst who dogmatically believes that his work is pure nineteenth-century science, who does not accept the fact that conflicting theories in our field are legitimate because he considers his own theory to be the only "truth," and who does not make any effort to think about his own contributions to the therapeutic material and to reflect on the unsolved problems of psychoanalysis. These authors have missed the general shift in even the most traditional psychoanalytic literature over the past twenty years, in which the most prominent analysts are wrestling with these problems (see Wallerstein 1995). A number of authors (e.g., Pine 1985; Chessick 1992a) have suggested that multiple theories are necessary in psychoanalysis although these theories are epistemologically conflicting. The harsh critics of psychoanalysis have only addressed selected aspects of it and have neglected the contributions of postclassical analysts. But we are all postclassical analysts these days and there are few if any dogmatic Freudians left.

Only the most poorly trained and inadequate psychoanalysts attempt to fit analysands into a Procrustean bed of authoritarian rigidly established psychoanalytic concepts and procedures, fostering compliance. Kohut (1977) would consider this a massive failure of empathy, and he (1984) stated in his posthumously published work that actually the particular theoretical orientation of the analyst is not as important in psychoanalytic healing as is the analyst's capacity to be empathic with what is hurting or narcissistically wounding the patient at any given time, regardless of the language the analyst uses to communicate that empathic understanding to the patient.

The fact that some of the phenomena generated in the analytic process cannot be traditionally scientifically replicated does not demonstrate that psychoanalysis is not a science; it simply demonstrates that like all sciences, psychoanalysis can only provide a limited picture and is subject to the continual process of alteration and modification of Freud's theories over the years as our empirical knowledge grows out of our clinical work. It is very dangerous to the future of psychoanalysis to divorce it from its biological or even quasi-biological roots such as drive theory, to ignore its scientific foundations, and instead to try to characterize psychoanalysis as some sort of purely hermeneutic or intersubjective discipline in which "the focus of therapeutic action goes from an authoritative therapist interpreting the patient's unconscious roots, to a therapist engaging the patient in a kind of corrective emotional experience, involving a mutual resolution and discovery of unconscious interferences in both therapist and patient" (Feinsilver 1999, 281). This postmodern approach runs the serious risk of encouraging a total relativism, subjectivism, cultism, mysticism, and hopelessness about the progress of the field as well as an increasing derogation of it in the mind of the public and a subsequent marginalization of it in our society.

Psychoanalysis is evolving and changing as every science should, while psychotherapy today is riding off madly in all directions in an attempt to bend itself to fit the inhumane demands of managed care and so to stay in business. There are hundreds of forms of psychotherapy, most of them practiced by poorly trained individuals who have only a foggy idea of what they are doing. I believe this is what can be expected of psychotherapy in the future since there are no criteria agreed upon and no certification examinations that one needs to pass in order to call one's self a psychotherapist. Psychoanalysis, however, is and should be much more strict and is continuously making a serious attempt to define itself.

One of my most influential teachers, Franz Alexander, argued that psychoanalysis and psychoanalytically oriented psychotherapy were procedures that gave operational meaning to the motto of the Renaissance humanists: respect for the dignity of the individual. In his (1964) last and posthumous publication, he wrote:

> Psychotherapy aims not only at enabling a person to adjust himself to existing conditions, but also to realize his unique potentials. Never was this aim more difficult and at the same time more essential. Psychoanalysis and psychotherapy in general are among the few still existing remedies against the relentlessly progressing levelization of industrial societies which tend to reduce the individual person to becoming an indistinguishable member of the faceless masses. (243)

Psychoanalysis is no longer a lucrative discipline; most psychoanalysts confess that much of their practice is now taken up by the practice of psychotherapy. Only a small percentage of well-trained psychoanalysts are dedicated enough to confine their treatment to full scale three or four times weekly psychoanalysis, which often requires them to treat patients at very reduced fees since insurance help for such treatment is now almost completely unavailable. It is to this dedicated group of psychoanalysts that we must look for the future development of the discipline as a science, as a legitimate means for scientific exploration of the human psyche that was the guiding vision of Sigmund Freud.

2

Psychoanalysis as Science and Art

What desires do you speak of? he said.

Those, stirred up in sleep, I replied, when the rest of the soul, the rational, conscious, and essential part slumbers, but the wild and savage part, filled with food and wine, springs up and, repelling sleep, seeks to sally forth and satisfy its own instincts. You know that in such a case there is total courage to do anything, as it is released from all shame and all reason. It does not hesitate from attempting to have intercourse with one's mother in imagination or with anyone else, man, god, or beast. It is ready for any bloodstained deed; it abstains from no food, and, in a word, does not leave out any extreme of folly and shamelessness.

Most true, he said.

. . . the point we wish to notice is this, that there exists in every one of us, even in some of us thought to be the most respectable, terrible, wild, and lawless desires, which become manifest in our sleep . . .

—Plato (*Republic* IX:571c–572b)[1]

In this and subsequent chapters I delve into certain fundamentals that underlie the practice and theory of psychoanalysis as I conceive of it. These involve the role of fantasy, creativity, and imagination, as well as the natural science aspect of psychoanalysis. The questions of whether there exists common grounds for psychoanalytic technique, and of what constitutes the philosophical underpinnings of foundationalism and psychoanalytic technique will be addressed. Postmodern objections to all this will be briefly reviewed but in a "politically incorrect" view, I come down firmly on the side of foundationalism, phenomenology and contemporary traditional Freudian psychoanalysis, that is based on Freud and Anna Freud's (1946) ego psychology and utilizing other channels of approach as needed. Finally, I will turn to creativity as manifested in art and psychoanalysis and indicate as evidence for my position how great art offers us a glimpse of foundationalist truth and beauty.

Spillius (2001) points out clearly the difference between the Kleinian and Freudian view of fantasies. (In this book I refer to Freud's use of "fantasy" and to Klein's use of "phantasy" to help distinguish between them.) She writes:

> In Freud's view, although there *are* phantasies in the *system unconscious*, the basic unit of the *system unconscious* is not phantasy but the unconscious instinctual wish. . . . For Klein, on the contrary, unconscious phantasies are the primary unconscious content and dreams are a transformation of it. For Freud, the prime mover, so to speak, is the unconscious wish; dreams and phantasies are both disguised derivatives of it. For Klein the prime mover is unconscious phantasy. (362)

So Klein regards "phantasy" as a basic mental activity which is present in its rudimentary form from birth onwards, and is essential for mental growth even though it can also be used defensively. She thought it was possible to infer the phantasies of infants from her analyses of small children. Spillius explains that Klein's use of phantasy is much wider than Freud's:

> In the Kleinian view, unconscious phantasy is the mainspring, the original and essential content of the unconscious mind. It includes very early forms of infantile thought, but it also includes other forms that emerge later on in development through change in the original phantasies. (364)

Through introjection and projection, argues Klein, a complex phantasy world of self and internal objects is slowly built up, reaching to unconscious depths and of course:

> This notion of internal objects and the internal world was and has continued to be central in Kleinian thought. This internal world is imaginary by the standards of material reality, but possesses what Freud calls "psychic" reality—that is, to the individual concerned it feels real at some level, conscious or unconscious, and it is also real in the sense that it affects his behavior. (365)

Spillius argues that unconscious phantasy is the mainspring of both creativity and destructiveness and, although phantasies affect the perception of external reality, external reality affects phantasies—there is a continual interplay between them. The big objection of Anna Freud and the Freudians to Klein's

work was to the Kleinian conception that "unconscious phantasy is really syn-
onymous with the content of the unconscious mind" (ibid., 369).

Spillius points out that with certain exceptions, especially the work of
Jacob Arlow, there is less attention being paid to unconscious phantasy or to
"the unconscious in general in American psychoanalysis than in British and
Continental analysis" (370) and this decreasing focus on unconscious phantasy
"is even more apparent among self-psychologists, intersubjectivists and relational analysts than among other sorts of American psychoanalyst [sic]" (370).
All of this is part of the trend away from the original conceptions of Freud.

A similar message is given by Freeman (1998), a well-known psychiatrist
and psychoanalyst, who has made careful studies of psychotic patients and has
been the president of the Northern Ireland Association for the Study of Psychoanalysis. He offers important clinical examples in support of Freud's theories and deplores much of current psychoanalytic theorizing. He defends
Freud's classical theories and is much disturbed by the widespread confusion
in the contemporary pluralistic world of psychoanalytic theories.

Freeman has considerable experience with psychotics and there are a lot
of Kleinian interpretations in his book that are offered as alternative possibilities to the standard Freudian structural theory. For our purposes, his main
point is in the distinction he makes between "clinical facts" and "psychoanalytic clinical facts." The latter are created by the patient-analyst interaction
and are not independent of the analyst's theoretical preferences. This is not
Freeman's original idea, but what he calls our attention to are certain clinical
phenomena "that repeatedly appear in the course of psychoanalytic treatment
and that fulfill criteria demanded for clinical facts. These phenomena are neither specific nor unique to the psychoanalytic situation" (3). Among such clinical facts are dreams, parapraxes, "wish fantasies of adolescents and the mas-
turbatory fantasies that owe nothing to the analysis as far as their origins are
concerned" (3). Freeman argues that these recurring phenomena, these "clinical facts," exist independently of a specific observer and provide the foundations for Freud's basic theories. He offers a number of clinical examples from
his extensive experience.

The farther away a theory is from clinical facts, the more speculative and
questionable the theory. For example, Freeman challenges Freud's notion of
the death instinct, a concept I (1992c) have defended, claiming there is an
explanation for the origin of the compulsion to repeat that does not depend
on a theory of the death instinct. He points out a "repetitive tendency" (47)
that occurs in many organic states of brain damage found in various neuro-
logic disorders, and so he considers this tendency to be a fundamental property of mental life. At the same time Freeman explains the importance of
Freud's final instinct theory as a way to explain the difficulties in trying to
treat obsessional neuroses, depressive states, and personality disorders by the

psychoanalytic treatment method. Also, "The theory of an unconscious super-ego suffused with the death instinct offered an explanation for the negative therapeutic reaction" (70).

Freeman is impressed by Steiner's concept of "psychic retreats" (discussed below) as offering a "relief from intolerable anxiety posed by the threat of fragmentation of the self" (109). Freeman does not try to urge us to accept any given theory. What he wants to do is show how Freud's introduction of the theory of the death instinct and the structural approach late in Freud's life represented a change in Freud's thinking because he no longer tried to anchor such concepts in clinical observations as he had in his earlier theorizing. Now he used the new concepts to reinterpret clinical facts.

What Freeman demonstrates quite cogently is that there are clinical facts (in contrast to "psychoanalytic clinical facts") that can be observed in the psychoanalytic process and which are the best validations and starting points for theory formation. This allows psychoanalysis to remain on a natural sciences basis. I have indicated (1988 and chapter 1) how Ricoeur missed this important facet of psychoanalysis when he argued that psychoanalysis was hermeneutics and energetics; I point out that it was quite possible to observe the orderly development of transference in a fashion consistent with the usual methods of observation in the natural sciences. It follows, then, that much of Freud's theorizing is indeed based as in other natural sciences on clinical facts and should be retained unless further clinical facts seem to contradict them. The closer we stay to such facts the more convinced we can become that we have validation of our theories. So far, with the exception of some significant areas such as those of feminine sexuality, religion, and anthropology, Freud's basic observations of the clinical facts have never been refuted.

COMMON GROUNDS OR IRRECONCILABLE DIFFERENCES?

An entire issue of the *Journal of Clinical Psychoanalysis* (vol. 4, no. 4, 1995) is devoted to the study of psychoanalytic technique, asking whether there are common grounds or irreconcilable differences between psychoanalysts in their clinical practice. (Of course there are also many other publications on this controversial topic). In this issue of the *Journal of Clinical Psychoanalysis* Brenner (1995) points out that, "It is the fact that defenses are analyzed rather than overcome in some other way that chiefly distinguishes modern analytic technique from that which preceded it" (421). Richards and Richards (1995a) state, "Our key theoretical constructs are conflict, compromise formation, and unconscious fantasy" (429). They conclude, "We are now living in a world of psychoanalytic theoretical pluralism. Contemporary Freudian psychoanalysis, self psychology, relational psychoanalysis, Kleinianism, and relational psycho-analysis [sic] are models in competition, vying for ascendancy" (435).

It is important to understand that for the Kleinians, as Caper (1995) writes:

> Failure to negotiate the developmental hazards of the first years of life leaves behind a psychotic residue, which must then be disposed of (defended against) at the price of one's ability to negotiate the oedi-pal period. In other words, neurosis is the consequence of one's failure to resolve earlier psychotic anxieties. It is not a question of addressing one or the other; a thorough analysis of the neurotic situation leads naturally to an analysis of the earlier psychotic one, and the analysis of the latter renders possible the resolution of the former. (467)

In their final response to the various papers situated at the end of this issue of the *Journal of Clinical Psychoanalysis*, Richards and Richards (1995b) conclude, "The fundamental principles of modern Freudian theory are foun-dational and comprehensive in the main. The problem, perhaps, is that the development of theoretical pluralism begins with a brief *against* the common ground" (551).

Even within the foundational Freudian approach there is still confusion between what Paniagua (2001) calls the "topographical technique," using the topographical model, and what he calls the more currently accepted structural approach. Paniagua points out that in his opinion (and I agree) the use of the topographical model tends to bypass the patient's ego capacities. In the every-day practice of psychoanalysis, "Topographical and structural concepts have been applied in an unclear way" (671). The tendency to use the topographical technique, maintains Paniagua, rests on the appeal of its simplicity, and the fertile ground that it offers for the analyst's projections that is provided by interpretations. This emphasizes the role of suggestion in the use of topo-graphical technique.

Paniagua gives many examples of the dangers of *ex cathedra* interpreta-tions by analysts using the topographical technique. Even Freud's interpre-tation of the famous dream of the Wolf-Man (Freud 1918) was described by the patient later as a fantasy of Freud's; no memory of the primal scene ever emerged after the interpretation. Just as Freud often did in his clinical work, when following this topographical technique the analyst presents himself or herself as an expert on unconscious feelings and a judge of hidden dynam-ics, and makes interpretations based on this approach. Paniagua insists that such interpretations are a form of countertransferential enactments and carry the danger the analysand will be diverted from the examination of his or her unconscious dynamics, which will force the analyst to rely on positive transference to motivate the patient to accept as accurate and beneficial the analyst's interpretations. So positive transference becomes the vehicle for influencing the analysand's participation, according to Paniagua. He argues that the analyst utilizing the structural approach, however, tries to include the analysand as a coparticipant and stresses the analysand's autonomous ego functions. He insists that the topographical technique tends to reinforce resistance, although it allows the analyst at the same time to practice with a high degree of suggestion.

Steiner (1993) approaches this debate from a Kleinian standpoint. He defines "psychic retreats" as pathological organizations of the personality to which the patient withdraws in order to avoid contact with the analyst and with reality. Such retreats can offer narcissistic and masochistic gratification and when interventions by the therapist threaten this, an impasse in psychoanalysis or psychotherapy develops. The basis of it, according to Steiner, is that the patient does not wish to separate from primitively conceived internal objects and to have to mourn the loss. Instead the patient tries to involve the analyst in creating a sanctuary or a retreat, functioning to avoid ugly reality. Such patients want equilibrium and not emergence or liberation from internal objects, and use words not to communicate but to affect the analyst. The patient is afraid to examine his or her mental processes and attempts to get the analyst to mutually enact something in a regressed replica of the patient's infantile relationships. Steiner's solution is to avoid patient-centered interpretations implying the responsibility of the patient and instead to try to concentrate on the patient's transference and the countertransference in a focus on enactments that he claims allows for optimal detection of psychic retreats.

PHILOSOPHICAL UNDERPINNINGS OF FOUNDATIONALISM

The subject of foundationalism and the debate as to whether it still is useful in our psychoanalytic thinking forces the interested analyst to become aware of certain concepts that have been introduced by various philosophical thinkers in the twentieth century. For example, Gaston Bachelard (1884–1962) possessed detailed knowledge of the history and practice of science and presented a picture of scientific development centered on the notion of the "epistemological break." He pointed out that science requires a break from our common sense experiences and beliefs because it places everyday objects and phenomena under new concepts. Furthermore, scientific progress, said Bachelard, requires breaks from previous scientific conceptions, which can actually become obstacles to our obtaining scientific truth just as much as our common-sense experiences can be such obstacles. This is somewhat similar to Kuhn's (1962) famous book on scientific revolutions that appeared thirty years later.

These epistemological breaks in scientific thought require corresponding revolutions in philosophy. Bachelard attempted to produce new philosophical views in order to replace those he believed were outdated by the progress of science. Of course even though there are sharp epistemological breaks from one scientific world view to another, there is still progress in science because certain specific achievements of past science are preserved as special cases in later theories. But, as Gutting (2001) explains, Bachelard "emphasizes both the active role of the mind in the construction of the scientific concepts with which we describe reality" (88) and views truth as "the result of the mind's 'revision' (*rectification*) by scientific concepts of a world that is already there" (88).

Bachelard believed both technological and imaginative thinking issued from reverie and emotion and culminated in practical expression. Science and poetry he thought, have a common origin accessible only to psychoanalysis. In both his studies of reason and of imagination, he stressed the projective or creative role of mind. In art he conceived of the subject as projecting his or her dream upon the artistic medium and in science he argued that at a level deep in the subject and beyond the immediate object of study by the scientist is the project itself, which is a creative conception of the scientist's imagination.

Georges Canguilhem (1904–1995) improved on Bachelard's work by concentrating on the history of biological and medical sciences rather than physics and chemistry. He maintained there is a "theoretical polyvalence" of concepts, which means that concepts have an ability to function in the context of widely differing theories. According to Gutting (2001):

> For Canguilhem, by contrast, there is a crucial distinction between the interpretation of phenomena (via concepts) and their theoretical explanation. According to him, a given set of concepts provides the preliminary descriptions of a phenomenon that allow the formulation of questions about how to explain it. Different theories (all, however formulated in terms of the same set of basic concepts) will provide competing answers to these questions. (229)

Canguilhem (1994), a contemporary of Sartre and Merleau-Ponty but not nearly as well-known, explains that a concept does not originate only within the framework of a theory. He regards the belief that concepts are theory-determined as a prejudice that can be removed by a study of the history and epistemology of science. He concludes that if a concept originally outlined or formulated in a theory "is subsequently captured by a theory that uses it in a different context or with a different meaning, it does not follow that the concept as used in the original theory is nothing but a meaningless word. Some concepts, such as the reflection and refraction of light, are theoretically polyvalent, that is, capable of being incorporated into both particle theory and wave theory" (181). This theoretical polyvalence of concepts mentioned by Canguilhem is what lies behind the five-channel theory of psychoanalytic listening described in Chapter 1. For all these incompatible theories employ more or less the same basic concepts such as the unconscious, repression, psychodynamics, et cetera.

Canguilhem also introduces the category of "scientific ideology," defined as an intermediary between science and nonscience:

> A scientific ideology . . . is scientific in the sense that it models itself on a successful scientific theory. It is ideological, however, because it makes claims about the world that go beyond what the science contemporary with it is able to establish; it has, in other words, pretensions that are not scientifically grounded. . . . But Canguilhem also sees a positive role for scientific ideologies: they provide an essential, if not entirely responsible, dimension of intellectual adventure, without which many scientific advances would not occur. (Gutting 2001, 231)

I believe one of the greatest contemporary obstacles to accepting foundationalism in psychoanalysis can be explained by employing Sartre's (1976) concept of the *practico-inert*. The *practico-inert* is constituted by the resistance to our projects posed by our physical personal limitations and environmental conditions, the particular historical situation into which we are born, and the innumerable institutions with which we have to contend throughout our life in order to survive. The drift towards fashionable poststructuralism and nonfoundationalism takes place in contemporary intellectual circles based on a failure of nerve, a consequence of the disappointments we have all had to endure in human history over the past hundred and fifty years. It becomes harder and harder these days to maintain that there are indeed at least semipermanent truths and such universals as Beauty and Knowledge in the Platonic sense. It is much easier on a pragmatic basis to go along with the current fads and fashions and slide away from Freud's deep rationalist convictions into a kind of vague and misty notion that the psychoanalytic process is something produced by the interaction of the patient and the doctor, rather than providing a way of uncovering the unconscious fantasy (or phantasy) life of the patient that determines the patient's entire current life situation and his or her perception of other people and the world. Contemporary postmodernism denies Heraclitus's famous observation that "character is fate."

Poststructuralism questions the assumption phenomenologists make, that we can attain deep truths about the human situation. Poststructuralists present a fundamental challenge to the defining intellectual ideal of philosophy since Plato, which is assuming "the possibility of attaining knowledge about the ultimate nature and meaning of human existence" (Gutting 2001, 251).

Today one must choose in one's life orientation and practice between the views of Plato and Freud on the one hand, and the views of Derrida and Foucault on the other. Poststructuralists would characteristically retort to this by labeling it as just another rhetorical false dichotomy.

Compare the postmodern denial of the subject, for example, with the philosophy of that arch-conservative Santayana, who was so popular before World War II. He thought truth was something sacrosanct and independent; he was repelled by pragmatism. He distinguished between two elements of the human mind: reason and spirit. Reason is the part of us that is located in space and time and responsible for the intelligent adaptation of the psyche to its environment. But spirit is detached and immaterial:

> . . . a disinterested observer that could as easily sympathize with entities remote in space and time as with those that were near. . . . On Santayana's conception, spirit has the capacity to intuit the essences of things—their defining character or 'whatness.' . . . While reason might enable an organism to survive and be happy, spirit could only make it dispassionately aware of what is true, good, and beautiful. Without reason one could not live well; without spirit one could not attain clarity, insight, or fundamental integrity. (Singer 2000, 18)

The whole argument between the classical and postmodern views of psychoanalysis boils down to the choice between two possible conceptions of the self (another dichotomy!). One conception is that the self has a core or kernel with some kind of separation from its current experiences so that:

> The events that impinge upon a person change him only in the sense of adding new attributes to his character and making him seem different. The kernel of his being never changes, and it is with this that his real nature is to be identified. Although this core may be hard to discover or find, it amounts to what the individual is 'in his heart'; all the incrustations of his overt development are outer layers that can in principle be stripped away. . . . On the kernel theory one's involvement with other persons, things, or ideals can only be such as to draw out what one really is anyhow. (ibid., 29)

The resemblance of this humanistic position in philosophical anthropology, as it is called, to the psychoanalytic foundationalism of Freud, stressing the instinctual drives and their derivatives at the fixed core of the personality, or to the views of Klein stressing phantasies and their vicissitudes as forming a core of the psyche, is obvious. I delineated these two psychoanalytic views of the fixed core of our personality at the beginning of this chapter.

The other conception of the self denies there is any inner kernel to be identified with one's real nature and makes the individual just the sum total of his or her experiences. So experience *is* the self. This is the point of view of fashionable philosophers today such as Derrida or Foucault who trumpet the "death of man." Man is no longer a subject, he has no kernel, he is created by the milieu. This is the fundamental approach of poststructuralism and of the intersubjectivist and interrelationist approach to psychoanalysis and, as I will argue in chapter 9, it represents a failure of nerve. That is to say, it is a kind of contemporary giving up of the possibility Freud fervently hoped for, that the quiet voice of reason (Freud 1927, 53) would eventually have its say in the affairs of man. It disregards his Platonic conviction that there are certain eternal or at least relatively basic and universal values that make the search for them a worthwhile goal of one's intellectual life (See, for example, the first paragraph of Freud 1930a). In my view, I am coming down firmly on the side of both Freud and phenomenology which share this Platonic conviction, rather than the side of multipluralism, postmodernism, and poststructuralism.

To put it another way, the debate is between empirical third person methodologies or so-called evidence-based therapy and those who would add first person methodologies such as the arts, phenomenology, or creative psychoanalytic introspection as a source for obtaining knowledge of the inner core of a person and of values, and beauty, and truth. Petranker (2001) remarks how "Proponents of each approach tend to marvel that their opponents can be so thick-headed, so downright perverse" (83). Just as the self is reduced to its social interaction experiences at any given time, so consciousness is reduced by third person methodologies such as neurobiology or eliminative materialists to brain chemistry and physiology, a mereological fallacy. Laughlin (2005) has produced a convincing argument, based on the existence of well-known emergent phenomena, against such reductionism.

For Mead (1962), an important predecessor of the intersubjectivists, the self was a social self that formed in two stages. At first, the individual's self is constituted simply by an organization of the attitudes of others toward both the individual and one another in the specific social acts in which the individual participates with them. Then, at the second stage, there is added "an organization of the social attitudes of the generalized other or the social group as a whole to which he belongs" (158). Thus, for Mead, the mind or self is formed by "reflexiveness" from social experience, a view that probably influenced H. S. Sullivan (1953) in forming his "interpersonal school" of psychiatry (Chessick 1974, 1977; Greenberg and Mitchell 1983).

The debate boils down to the question of whether first person methodologies such as contemporary Freudian psychoanalysis or phenomenology can give a convincing account of what is reliable knowledge. These methodologies are based on the foundationalist premise that was first formulated by Plato and assumed by Freud in his faith that reason and his psychoanalytic method could reach objective or scientific basic knowledge of the core of the patient's personality, a core that was formed and fixed in childhood and influenced the rest of the patient's life in a most significant fashion.

CREATIVITY AND THE SEARCH FOR FOUNDATIONS

Because I believe it is a fundamental aspect of psychoanalysis, I turn now to the role of creativity and its origins in the search for the human essence, for truth, and for beauty. Creativity can serve as a way of attenuating individual emotional conflicts, much as other solutions found by the ego and representing compromise formations can do so. There is nothing new about the idea that creative work is similar in its construction and function to the dream, but what is interesting and important is the unanswered question of why it is that certain creative works have universal appeal whereas most creative works are soon forgotten if they are ever recognized at all.

Let me begin with a case history. Robert Louis Stevenson was a very curious character. Bell (1992), his recent biographer, writes that his bizarre childhood nanny was "the first of a group of strong, mature women who were, in their several ways, to dominate R. L. S." (36). He fell intensely in love twice, each time with an older married woman. The second one divorced her husband and married him. Only after that marriage did he produce his great creative works. Stevenson's *The Lantern Bearers And Other Essays* (1988) displays considerable psychological insight with a painstaking preference for the complexities of psychology, and in my opinion this work ranks him as one of the important forerunners of the Freudian approach.

As recently as 1989, a lost story by Robert Louis Stevenson entitled "The Enchantress" (1989) was discovered. What makes it so modern in feeling and unusual for Stevenson is that its dominating personality is a woman, a rather tough-minded feminist living in an age of Victorian romanticism before the turn of the century. This is a remarkable departure from Stevenson's tendency to focus almost exclusively on male characters. The story is rather autobiographical, which is probably why it was not published by Stevenson's heirs, and was written in pencil in 1889 on a ship en route from Hawaii to Samoa. The author's stepson, the son of the older married woman whom Stevenson, at his personal peril, followed all the way from London to California, and who divorced her husband and married him, blocked its publication. He probably considered Stevenson's portrayal of Miss Emmeline Croft, who uses the male for her own purposes, and the surprise ending of the story in which she cons the male con artist, as too depreciatory of his mother to be exposed to the public. I mention this because it shows how Stevenson dealt with his ambivalent conflicts about his very difficult wife also through the sublimatory use of his creative productions.

But I believe that psychohistorical analysis of creative works based on the author's individual conflict situation is insufficient. For example, Stevenson's *Dr. Jekyll and Mr. Hyde*, the theme of two characters, one of whom is a personification of the id and the other a personification of the ego and intellect, is a universal theme in literature. The example I refer to the most in my work with patients is from Shakespeare's *Tempest*, a work of his old age and greatest maturity. This play, which was produced some time early in the seventeenth century, is the shortest play Shakespeare wrote and gives the freest possible reign to his imagination. Caliban, the offspring of a mating of the devil and a witch, has a physique that Shakespeare purposely keeps impossible to visualize. He is a slave of Prospero, who represents the ego and intellect, and he feels a peculiar hatred for this master who has dispossessed him. Prospero has found him impossible to educate and must simply repress him literally underground.

This is an infinitely suggestive play, just as Stevenson's Jekyl and Hyde story is infinitely suggestive and capable of many interpretations; the obvious one would be a similarity to the Prospero/Caliban double. In my opinion, Stevenson displaced his archaic intrapsychic conflict involving his hatred of women and wish to murder them onto the less archaic conflict involving more realistic and perhaps oedipal factors centering around the demise of his father. Remember Shakespeare's depiction of Caliban as being eager to rape and destroy the innocent Miranda and everybody else. Any analysis of creative products always must consider the principle of multidetermination; there are levels of conflict from the most archaic, involving the poisoned breast and the profound longing for the nurturant mother with the accompanying rage and hatred at the disappointment in the mother's preoedipal failures, up the preoedipal and finally the oedipal ladder to the classical Freudian themes involving incest and castration. That is one of the problems with psychohistory, in that it often centers on those themes which are of most interest to the particular psychohistorian. We should never forget that characters like Mr. Hyde or Caliban are cold-blooded killers and/or rapists, and therefore at some level they are manifestations of the deepest and most archaic human themes, perhaps going all the way back to the doubling of Cain and Abel.

The whole matter is made infinitely more complicated by the literary distinction between the use of doubles and of "*Doppelgängers*," even though the terms have identical denotative meaning. Dostoevsky, for example in his problematic second novel, *The Double*, presents a double that is not like the famous *Doppelgänger* of such authors as Kleist or Hoffmann. The German thing is grossly pathological, lurid, and demoniac, whereas Dostoevsky's double is trite, commonplace, and banal. In addition there is the curious phenomenon that in certain forms of epilepsy the aura is characteristically announced by the illusory appearance of a double of the individual.

Dostoevsky's *The Double* is a study of psychosis. The protagonist is essentially paranoid and his double is the image of what the real protagonist (who is named Golyadkin) wishes to be: a free and easy fellow, able to ingratiate himself with his superiors, to toady and fawn, to gambol and frolic, to make himself liked by all and sundry. At the same time Golyadkin's double is subtly unscrupulous, vicious, and depraved; Golyadkin comes to believe that his double is the chief tool of his enemies. As in the Jekyl and Hyde story, Golyadkin is victimized by his double. Just before he is taken to a lunatic asylum he has a momentary hallucination that an endless stream of his doubles are bursting in at every door. This again suggests the aura of epilepsy, and it is well known that Dostoevsky was indeed an epileptic.

Returning to Stevenson, we see in his story how the evil side of man's dual nature eventually triumphs and begins to assert itself constantly; in despair about this, Dr. Jekyl kills himself. It would be easy to read this story as a prophetic description of the twentieth century, in which the evil side of human nature certainly triumphed and led to the mass suicidal psychosis known as war in which millions and millions of people senselessly and uselessly lost their lives. As of this writing, the twenty-first century has opened by continuing the senseless slaughter.

Stevenson worked on his story, which he called a "penny dreadful," with tremendous excitement. The penny dreadful refers to the fact that the story is basically one of romantic adventure and fantasy, of the type currently found in pulp magazines and Sunday supplements. Melanie Klein would say his manic glee was a form of denial, based on Stevenson's fantasy that he was solving his depressive position. Her early theory of artistic creativity was that the creator wishes to rediscover the mother of his or her early days that has been lost. Stevenson's mother is best described, I think, as a flake, a person who was both there and not there. Bell (1992) describes her as "often vapid, absent even when she was present" (22). Klein reported on the tremendous anxiety of children over the child's sadistic desire to destroy the mother and rob the body of its contents. In her view, since the loss of the love object mother is the basic infantile danger situation, the urge to create arises from the impulse to restore and repair the injured object after a fantasied destructive attack.

I believe that all art work is founded on the seething cauldron of the unconscious and in some fashion or other expresses the unconscious of the individual, even though it may at another level either express or defend against childhood traumata. Extremely traumatized individuals, if they have creative ability, may use art work in the service of either expressing or denying or working through the trauma in some form or other, but I think this is a very

limited description of the function of art. It is much better to progress by trying to understand the multiple functions artistic works can serve. Why, for
example, is the contemporary art of Kalho or Bacon considered great art and
viewed by many people in museums whereas the art of some unfortunate
schizophrenic patient is not? Is there not truth in art as Hegel thought that is
expressed through the artist and his or her artistic creation? Why not look at
art in this way, the way of philosophers, rather than simply characterizing art
as a function of the artist's ego attempting to work something through,
whether it be trauma or unconscious conflicts or both?

I agree with Giovacchini (1968) that although there is a phenomenological similarity between the psychic structure and behavior of creative persons
and that of disturbed noncreative or psychotic patients, these similarities are
not so deep and there are important fundamental differences. The fragmented
self of the psychotic may obtain through the artistic product a selfobject that
can contribute to repairing self fragmentation, but the production of art in the
psychotic does not successfully achieve that function. So psychotic individuals
may compulsively create art over and over again, some of it quite interesting
and a lot of it boring and repetitious, but it does not result in an improvement
of the cohesion of their self; rather it is a kind of obsessive attempt at self
repair that always fails. There is no truth in schizophrenic art. This emptiness
in their productions, regardless of the artistic talent displayed, could be a function of organic factors in schizophrenia, nobody knows.

The history of art is replete with shocked public reactions to any changes
in conventional art, including music and poetry as well as the visual arts. The
audience always prefers conventional forms and is offended and shocked by
changes because these changes, in my opinion (borrowed from Foucault), her-
ald changes that are coming or are already embedded in the culture itself.
Above everything, people hate and fear change. I think the public's reaction
to psychotic art is one of indifference and boredom whereas the reaction to
really innovative art by a great artist is at times quite a bit more dramatic (witness the riots that broke out at the premier performance of Stravinsky's magnificent *Rite of Spring*). The reason for this is that great art conveys truth, a
truth that the individual artist may not even be aware that he or she is communicating. When that truth is communicated, the public strongly responds
to it, sometimes with ecstatic aesthetic pleasure, sometimes with rage, sometimes with avoidance and denial, and sometimes with horror and anxiety.

I (1999b) have challenged as being insufficient the traditional psychoanalytic description of creativity that views it as fundamentally involving
regression in the service of the ego. Weisman (1967) pointed out that
repressed id content can reenter the ego for inspirational creative purposes
without ego regression. Alteration from personal enactment to creative
enactment can be ascribed to the dissociative function of ego; the capacity

for dissociation is a predominant feature of ego functioning in the creative process. So the artist has a creative self and a more conventional self. The dissociative function liberates the artist from his or her customary mode of operation and permits emerging drive derived cathexis to new treatment by the ego and the superego.

The true artist is able to perceive relations and images that most of us do not or cannot perceive, truths we may not perceive and can not express. Creativity is an innate capacity, a rare characteristic of certain endowed individuals involving both the tendency and the ability to perhaps playfully take apart and put together again, to break established patterns of relationships and replace them with new ones. Niederland (1976) wrote, "Creativity is a solitary activity. It is usually accompanied by a withdrawal from complex emotional involvements with the external world and the latter's replacement—in the mind—by ideas, projects, fantasies, and personal, artistic, cultural, or religious strivings" (193–194). This is similar to Bush's (1969) depiction of a self-insulating sanctuary that the artist lives in at least for periods of time. Niederland (1976) called this "a walled-off garden away not only from the turbulence and strife of the outer world but also from irksome emotional problems and involvement with people. It is under such circumstances that, in the gifted person, the world of repressed visual, auditory, and kinesthetic memories emerges, which the artist transmutes into the creative act" (193–195).

Mental illness complicates and obscures whatever attempts to communicate itself through a work of art. First, it interferes with and constricts the creative process of the artist in many ways, sometimes even causing the artist to destroy his or her own work entirely. Second, because of the defective aspects of the art work mental illness engenders, it discourages us from tarrying before the work and interferes with our focus and capacity to directly experience the aesthetic phenomena expressed to us through the artist.

It is a great amateur mistake to think that psychopathology is necessary for and always a motivation for the production of great art (Chessick 1999b). Successful creativity actually requires a relatively intact ego; when the individual slides into the unhealthy side of the ego axis, artistic production deteriorates. Inherent genius along with the capacity for sublimation through artistic creativity is required for the production of great art works that are not flawed. The driving force to creativity may be thought of as the universal human need to resolve intrapsychic conflicts (which is the driving force of all solutions, neurotic or healthy) or the universal human need to provide one's self with enhancing selfobjects as a "glue" to insure cohesion of the self (Kohut 1977). The art work itself may form such a selfobject, or the mirroring appreciation of the audience may perform this function. But in the creation of a great art work there is something more we experience, the shining forth of truth, beauty, and Being (Heidegger 1971) in new and unique modes of expression.

To those not yet convinced, here is another example of a foundationalist truth, that of morality. Probably influenced by postmodernism, Isaiah Berlin (1997) distinguished between two kinds of liberty. These are negative liberty (freedom from) and positive liberty (freedom to). The former rests on what Rawls (1970) calls a "thin" theory of the good, those restraints and injustices that make any human life, however conceived, impossible. Ignatieff (2001) points out that it does not prescribe what is a good life or what one should be free to do. He explains:

> The doctrine of human rights is morally universal because it says that all human beings need certain specific freedoms 'from'; it does not go on to define what their freedom 'to' should comprise. In this sense, it is a less prescriptive universalism than the world's religions; it articulates standards of human decency without violating rights of cultural autonomy. (113–114)

To return to the main theme of this chapter, psychoanalysis is basically a creative activity, and as such depends on our sense of objective conviction about the truth of certain values and ideas, about what is beautiful and what is good, and as well on our hard-earned self-knowledge and the gradual acquisition of knowledge of the inner core of our patients. Only then can our interventions have the mutative impact they ought to have. As Pine (2001) remarks:

> In the clinical situation we are highly dependent upon individual talent and the patient-analyst mix, and the entire process is a creative endeavor in essential ways. But creativity of the best sort stems from knowledge, and I believe the effort to hold down all that we have learned in the background of our mind, to be drawn upon when evoked by the clinical moment, will serve us well. (915)

Foundationalism is not just an obsolete pipe dream. It will rise again in the emergence from our current dark age, as it did several times before in human history. And psychoanalysis waits to rise again with it, when our current state of demoralization and failure of nerve reverses itself, as historically it always has done, and our faith in the power of reason and creativity to ascertain what is essential to humans, truth, and beauty is restored.

3

The Psychoanalyst as Translator

A very serious question was raised perhaps first by the philosopher Ludwig Wittgenstein (Monk 1990), who maintained that when attitudes of the most fundamental kind clash, there can be no question of agreement or disagreement, for everything one says or does is interpreted from within those attitudes. He insisted it should not be surprising therefore, that frustration and incomprehension would be predominant on both sides. The late philosopher Hans-Georg Gadamer (Hahn 1997) subsequently posed the issue of whether it is even possible for us to understand the point of view of someone who speaks an entirely different or foreign language. For example, very few of our colleagues in the United States are sophisticatedly fluent in Japanese or Korean or the various languages of India or other countries in Asia. Is it really possible to translate from these languages into the English language without losing a substantial portion of meaning? What has this to do with psychoanalysis? It will soon be obvious!

It is questionable (Waquet 2000) whether the English language is the ideal one for translation. The comparison, for example, of the current universal language, English, with the previous universal language, Latin, is instructive. English is well-known to be the language of international global capitalism and communication, but has no broad system of cultural symbols, a system that made Latin the common and unifying language of Europe for centuries. T. S. Eliot pointed out that Latin releases us from the provinciality of time; there is general agreement that Latin is a fruitful source of intellectual reflection and cultural sophistication. Since the 1960s in the United States, Latin has unfortunately almost disappeared from University curricula and has become relegated to the province of narrow scholarship. This is a great loss to our civilization, and even worse is the almost total lack of educational

43

opportunities in classical Greek, the language in which western civilization was founded, a language filled with an unsurpassed remarkable capacity to express nuances of meaning.

We should never forget that all the concepts in which thinking is formulated stand silhouetted like dark shadows on a wall. That is to say, they work in a one-sided way, predetermining and prejudging our capacity to understand. When we attend carefully to what goes on in the process of undertaking to understand something, we find that we never approach the phenomenon in question with a blank slate. Rather, we always begin with preconceptions or what Gadamer rather unfortunately calls "prejudices"—preliminary expectations of what the phenomenon in question is likely to mean. Our only hope to reach consensus, or "truth," is that through a dialectical back-and-forth process of now consulting the phenomenon in the light of our prejudices, and now revising our prejudices in the light of the phenomenon, genuine understanding can ever emerge.

Every author is positioned in the midst of a culture and a tradition and equivalently every interpreter or member of any audience is also positioned in a culture and a tradition; there may be a great distance in time and culture that separates the speaker and the audience. So our own personal and cultural drives and interests play a central role in our interpretation of either Plato or the *Baghvad Gita*! In fact, thought itself depends on language. All understanding is interpretation and all interpretation takes place in the medium of language which allows the objects to come into words. If we can reach an understanding with our partners in a dialogue, said Gadamer (1991), there will be a fusion of horizons and a transformation into a communion in which we will not remain what we were.

So we are all trapped in the prison house of language. For example, the philosopher Quine (1960) propounded his famous thesis of the indeterminacy of translation. That is to say, different systematic translations of an alien language into one's own language can be equivalent as regards any possible evidence for them, even as regards any possible more fundamental facts. As Quine puts it:

> Manuals for translating one language into another can be set up in divergent ways, all compatible with the totality of speech disposition, yet incompatible with one another. In countless places they will diverge in giving, as their respective translations of a sentence of the one language, sentences of the other language which stand to each other in no plausible sort of equivalence however loose. (27)

Relevance of this situation to contemporary psychoanalytic practice and understanding has been pointed out by Mahony (2001). He explains that a patient may be psychically conceived as an accumulation of translations and the analyst has the complementary role of a translator: "By means of translations the analyst effects a transposition of what is unconscious into consciousness" (837–838). Even the problem of translating Freud, which is the subject of considerable controversy these days, "involves the following three issues: the textual status of the primary sources in German; Freud's magisterial use of the native language; and the nature of the extant and ideal translations of his works" (838). The problem of the polemical discussions concerning extant and ideal translations of Freud's works arises from Freud's "remarkably creative exploitation of the polysemous and other expressive potentials of his native German language" (838). Mahony refers to Strachey's editorial corrections of Freud's texts and mentions, for the record, that Strachey was assisted by Alix Strachey and Alan Tyson in producing the so-called *Standard Edition*, the subsequently redacted English-language version of Freud's work. I now propose to illustrate and demonstrate various aspects of the confusion of tongues that can easily bedevil the psychoanalyst as a translator both in his or her clinical work and attempts to study the works of Freud and other psychoanalytic authors written in a language different than one's own.

CONFUSION DUE CULTURAL DIFFERENCES

For example, can we understand in English the Japanese concept of *amae*? Doi (1993) defines this household Japanese word as signifying what an infant feels when it seeks its mother, but it is also applied to an adult when that person is supposed to entertain a similar feeling of being emotionally close to another. It is a nonverbal feeling and can be conveyed only nonverbally and should be acknowledged in the same way: "Therefore it is not a manifest emotion, but rather a silent emotion" (165).

This is applied by Doi to his discussion of Freud's (1915) well-known paper "Observations on Transference-Love." Doi (1993) asks, "Isn't it possible, then to assume by extrapolation that behind the transference-love of Western adults as well hides the psychology of *amae*?" (168). Freud argues that transference-love should neither be gratified nor suppressed and that there is no model in real life for this kind of behavior and response of the analyst. Doi explains that Freud could not conceive of any other real life model; but the silent acknowledgment of *amae* often happens in real life not only with children but between adults, constituting an important ingredient in any interpersonal relationship. The unavailability of this concept to western thinkers left a gap or an emptiness in Freud's capacity to delineate the optimal response of the analyst to transference-love, a gap which has finally been addressed and perhaps closed to some extent by Kohut's (1977) emphasis on the importance of empathy.

I had one experience of *amae* as a psychiatric resident in the 1950s. At a meeting, I met Dr. Frieda Fromm-Reichmann, renowned for her intuitive ability to work with schizophrenics. As a young psychiatrist who idealized her, I gushed out my appreciation and admiration. Fromm-Reichmann said not a word, but as she moved on she gave me a smile and a friendly wave, a gesture and eidetic image which has stayed with me through my entire professional life. It has also made me very sensitive to the reception of nonverbal gestures and behaviors of patients especially when they just enter or are about to leave my office. Sometimes the entire theme of the session is presented nonverbally as the patient walks through the door at the beginning. Parting gestures often communicate either a commentary on the session or express a theme opposite to or different from the verbal discourse during the session.

CONFUSION DUE TRANSLATION DIFFERENCES

Over the years I spent much time studying Dante's *Divine Comedy* in the Mandelbaum (1982, 1984, 1986) and many other translations, listening to the tape of another translation, examining the Pinsky (1997) translation of the *Inferno* section both in writing and on tape, and thoroughly enjoying the recently published Merwin (2000) translation of the *Purgatorio* section.[1] As an example of what I have discussed above I would like to examine these translations. Dante's poem is essentially a presentation of the medieval theological-philosophical paradigm as presented in the great writings of Thomas Aquinas. (For a detailed discussion of Dante's *Divine Comedy* as an example of a "medieval psychoanalysis" see chapter 6). A nicely presented brief summary of that paradigm is offered by Schwartz (1999), who also points out how "We recreate the past in accordance with the values of our society" (275).

The famous Gustave Doré (1976) illustrations and the remarkable Botticelli sketches[2] are examples of many remarkably disparate attempts by artists to translate Dante's poetry into visual images. Each canto needs to be read with care and with an effort to visualize in the mind's eye the allegorical picture that Dante is offering the reader. There is nothing quite like it in scope and intensity in all of the world's literature.

The problem of translating Dante's *Divine Comedy* is especially difficult because it is written in a type of Italian poetry called *terza rima*, which runs like this: aba, bcb, cdc, ded, et cetera. The lesser variety of sounds in Italian makes for a greater facility and elegance of the rhyme, but to try to follow this scheme in English would produce incredible distortions. There are some translations that try to do it, like those of Shelley but, as Sisson (1981) writes, "Neither he nor, I think, any other translator has carried imitation to

the point to which it must be carried, if there is to be any real claim to follow the rhyme scheme—that is, to find feminine rhymes . . ." (40) and such
efforts to follow the *terza rima* organization in English have been largely
abandoned. Instead, there are simply prose translations and attempts at
verse translations.

To give an example of the extraordinary difficulty in expression from one
language to another in the humanities where metaphor and allegory are
extremely important, I will pick a characteristic section from the *Inferno* and
compare translations. The reader should note that Freud's prose is of a similar almost poetic and metaphorical quality, and similar problems arise in
attempts to translate Freud as many recent authors have pointed out.

Let us take Canto VII, lines 70 *ff*. To Dante's question about the nature
of Dame Fortune or contingency, Virgil firmly responds with the medieval
theological view that it is inscrutable, but she is an angelic being ultimately
willed by God. Here is Sisson's (1981) translation of Virgil's answer:

> He answered: 'How foolish people are!
> How great is the ignorance which strikes them down!
> Now listen to me and take in what I say.
>
> He whose wise dispositions transcend everything,
> Made the heavens and gave intelligences to guide them,
> So that each part shines on other parts' . . . (75)

Compare Sayers's translation (1951):

> Then he: 'Ah witless world! Behold the grand
>   Folly of ignorance! Make thine ear attendant
>   Now on my judgement of her, and understand.
>
> He whose high wisdom's over all transcendent
>   Stretched forth the Heavens, and guiding spirits supplied,
>   So that each part to each part shines resplendent,
> Spreading the light equal on every side' . . . (112)

Sayers appends this note: "This is the first of the series of great discourses
in which Dante gradually unfolds the plan of the spiritual and physical universe. The 'guiding spirits' mentioned here are the celestial intelligences
(angels) who control the heavenly spheres." (115)

Binyon (1961):

> And he to me: 'How heavy the ignorance,
>   O foolish creatures, that on you is laid!

> Hear now my judgement of her governance.
> The wisdom that transcendeth all, and made
>   The heavens and gave them guides to rule them right,
>   So that each splendour should the other aid
> With equal distribution of the light' . . . (38)

His footnote says that the "guides" are "angels, who govern the revolutions of the spheres" (38)

Sinclair, (1959):

And he said to me: 'O foolish creatures, what ignorance is this that besets you! Now I will have thee feed on my judgement of her. He whose wisdom transcends all made the heavens and gave them guides, so that every part shines to every part, dispersing the light equally' . . . (103)

To this Sinclair appends a footnote: "The reference is to the angelic orders controlling the heavens" (105)

White (1948):

> And he to me: 'Creatures what fools you are!
> What monstrous ignorance oppresses you!
> I wish that you should clearly understand
> What I now say. He whose omniscience
> Transcendeth all, the heavens made, and then
> Angels to govern them, so that the light
> Shines equally on each and every part.' (12)

Norton (1941):

And he to me: 'O foolish creatures, how great is that ignorance which harms you! I would have thee now receive my opinion concerning her. He whose wisdom transcends all, made the heavens, and gave them their guides, so that every part shines on every part, distributing equally the light.' (43–44)

Mandelbaum (1982):

> And he to me: 'O unenlightened creatures,
> how deep—the ignorance that hampers you!
> I want you to digest my word on this.

> Who made the heavens and who gave them guides
> was He whose wisdom transcends everything;
> that every part may shine unto the other,
>   He had the light apportioned equally'; ... (63)

Ciardi (1954):

> And he to me: 'O credulous mankind,
>   is there one error that has wooed and lost you?
>   Now listen, and strike error from your mind:
>
> That king whose perfect wisdom transcends all,
>   made the heavens and posted angels on them
>   to guide the eternal light that it might fall
> from every sphere to every sphere the same.' (74)

Pinsky (1997):

> ... He: 'Foolish creatures,
>   How great an ignorance plagues you. May you receive
> My teaching: He who made all of Heaven's features
>   In His transcendent wisdom gave them guides
>   So each part shines on all the others, all nature's
> Illumination apportioned' ... (55–57)

His footnote equates "guides" with intelligences that govern the motion of the heavenly spheres: "These astronomical forces bear some resemblance to angels, and some also to pagan gods: Fortune is a bit of both, it would seem, though she is given her place in the Christian order" (316).

It is clear from comparing these translations that although Dante wrote in simple direct Italian, many translations of *The Divine Comedy* insist on a very fancy presentation that is anything but simple and direct. One can see from an examination of the various translations how enormously different the ambiance of the poetry is in each one of them; the whole tone of the poem is entirely different from one translation to the other. Ezra Pound (1939) wrote that the starting point of creating or appreciating poetry is to remember that language is a means of communication. He said, "To charge language with meaning to the utmost possible degree" there are three "chief means": (1) "throwing the object (fixed or moving) on to the visual imagination," (2) "inducing emotional correlations by the sound and rhythm of the speech," and (3) "inducing both of the effects by stimulating the associations (intellectual or emotional) that have remained in the receiver's consciousness in relation to the actual words or word group employed" (63). Pound named these, respectively, phanopoeia, melopoeia, and logopoeia.

Let us turn now to the translations and translators quoted above (please refer back to each quoted translation as I discuss each translator's conception).

Sisson (1981) emphasizes the importance of Dante's protest and capacity to finally stand back and disengage from his immersion in the petty quarrels that constituted the miserable events of his time. Dante was clearly aware that every person brings within himself or herself things that prevent that person from realizing his or her best aspirations. These, presented in the opening Canto of *Inferno*, are lust (the leopard), pride (the lion) and greed, the frenetic pursuit of money and power (the She-wolf). Sisson's translation is relatively simple and straightforward; available in one volume, it is an easy introduction to Dante's poem.

For Sayers (1951), the magnificence of Dante's poetry has endeared him to the ages and should be stressed above all. This magnificence one has to take on faith unless one is familiar with the Italian. But notice how the Sayers translation soars into a more formal ambiance.

Binyon's (1961) translation in English triple rhyme adheres, or attempts to adhere, to Dante's own meter, the arduous *terza rima*, producing a kind of backward reach into an older English just as Dante's Italian is of an older version.

Sinclair (1959) offers us a prose translation. It is accurate but completely loses the poetry. Furthermore, it is not even as direct as prose can be. So Sinclair sets his own ambiance.

White's (1948) translation is direct, but for some curious reason he includes the term "Transcendeth" that does not fit in the directness of his phrases such as "Creatures what fools you are!"

Norton (1941) seems to have a great deal of difficulty with his own English sentences, that appear to be quite convoluted for no reason. Here again, the old English "thee" is interpolated into a prose translation, whereas inconsistently the word "transcends" is not, as White renders it, offered as "transcendeth."

Mandelbaum's (1982) translation is one of the most popular in use in colleges today. And rightly so, as it is a fairly direct and readable rendering. What it lacks is beauty.

Ciardi (1954) conceives of language as an instrument and he points out that the process of rendering from language to language would be better called a transposition than translation, because, as Ciardi says, "'translation' implies a series of word-for-word equivalents that do not exist across language boundaries any more than piano sounds exist in the violin" (Translator's Note). Ciardi tried to preserve the *gestalt* or total feeling of each canto by trying to present a language as close as possible to Dante's, "which is in essence a sparse, direct, and idiomatic language, distinguishable from prose only in that it transcends every known notion of prose" (ibid.). Although his is an idiosyncratic kind of approach it is quite readable and consistent.

Pinsky's translation is also available on audiotape in a very stirring recitation. I personally found the audiotape recitation much more impressive than trying to read Pinsky's rendering, replete with such fustian phrases as "all nature's/illumination apportioned. . . ."

CONFUSION DUE TRANSLATOR PREJUDICE OR IGNORANCE

Freud's *Interpretation of Dreams* literally explodes with evidence of Freud's astonishing multilingual education, and he (1914b) wrote that his classical learning had brought him "as much consolation as anything else in the struggles of life" (241). Freud is now studied more in other parts of universities than he is in psychology departments and his work remains more acceptable in the field of the humanities than it does in the area of experimental science. This has to do with eristic arguments about the scientific status of psychoanalysis by such critics as Grünbaum (1984), as well as from the obsessive Freud-bashing criticism of certain fanatical individuals. Nevertheless, even after having read and studied Freud many years, it is still an astonishing experience for me to pick up even a questionable new translation of this work, one that overwhelmingly demonstrates Freud's scintillating genius. As Robertson writes in his note on Crick's (1999) translation, "*The Interpretation of Dreams* reflects the professional and domestic life of a highly cultured academic in turn-of-the-century Vienna, not least his trips with his family to the environs of Vienna, to holiday resorts in southern Austria, and to Italy and the Adriatic" (xxxix).

My first reading of *The Interpretation of Dreams* while in college was in the only available English version at the time, translated in 1913 by A. A. Brill (Freud 1900a). He was an Austro-Hungarian follower of Freud who settled in New York and produced an appallingly dull and inaccurate translation (which unfortunately has just been marketed on audiocassettes). In 1953, Strachey translated it to constitute volumes four and five of *The Standard Edition of the Complete Psychological Works of Sigmund Freud*, translating Freud's romantic and literary prose with scientific sounding terminology in order to make his work more acceptable in medical and scientific circles. There is an endless debate about rendering such words as *Seele* by "mind" rather than soul or psyche, et cetera, and about such notorious quasi-medical renderings of words like *Besetzung* as "cathexis" (that Crick replaces by "charge"; I prefer "cathexis"). In addition to these debates there is confusion over Freud's use of "*das Ich*" to represent the figure seen in one's dreams or the dreamer himself or herself, rendered as "the self" by Crick and as "the ego" by Strachey.

Bettelheim (1983) raised many questions about Strachey's translation from the German and there still is considerable controversy on this matter.

Detailed scholarly discussions of the problems of translation may be found in books by Ornston (1992) and Grubrich-Simits (1996). As Grubrich-Simits points out, her study of the earlier drafts of Freud's essays show that he was a painstaking writer who continually wrote, revised, and rewrote, often incorporating suggestions of colleagues as he went along; this dispels the myth that Freud wrote out his papers in their near-final form, as was true of another genius, Bertrand Russell. It is generally agreed that the Strachey translation makes Freud's colloquial, poetic, and humanistic German into a more scientific-sounding and seemingly precise English. For example, slips or mistakes, as they are described in Freud's *Psychopathology of Everyday Life*, are formally and impressively labeled "parapraxes," and of course there is the endless argument about Strachey's translation of what would be literally the "it" and the "I" as the "id" and the "ego." But most of the criticism of Strachey deals with relatively minor issues.

Laplanche (1992) cites Hoffer's statement, "There is no translation without interpretation" (14), but he rejects the sophistry that says "Since every translation is another interpretation why not keep Strachey?" The ideal of translation, John Forrester in the dialogue with Laplanche (1992) claims, is to avoid interpretation and leave the readers with their capacity to interpret. Whether this is possible or not remains highly debatable. Laplanche argues that neologisms become necessary when a term is untranslatable, for example, Freud's use of *nachträglich/Nachträglichkeit*. He writes: "If you look in Strachey or Masson even, you find '*nachträglich*' translated sometimes as 'later,' sometimes as 'belatedly,' sometimes by 'subsequently,' and sometimes by 'in a deferred fashion'" (16). This kind of discussion arose in France because of the controversy over the value of Lacan's translations of Freud in contrast to the translations of Laplanche.

Laplanche also criticizes Bettelheim as not understanding the German philosophical tradition in which "*das Ich*" is a standard concept. It is used, for example, in Kant's *Critique of Pure Reason*. He believes Strachey's translation of it as "the ego" is straightforward and "resonates with all the 19th century translations of German philosophy" (51), in which "*das Ich*" is always translated as "the ego." Laplanche completely agrees with Forrester's view of interpretation as mentioned above, and enlarges on this problem for a French translator because of the French tradition for using *le moi*. He states, "In our translation, we have been taking *le moi* and not *le je* and the explicit reason we give is because of the French tradition for using *le moi*. *Le moi* is also the first person because I say '*moi je*,' and you never say 'ego I.' Also *moi* has to do with something reified, and actually *das Ich*, the ego is reified in Freud" (51).

Are these important changes or do they represent scholastic nit picking among translators? Nothing could offer a greater experience of how much the personality of the translator and the preconceptions of the translator invariably become incorporated into the translation than this exercise in comparison. So, whereas Strachey's translation brings to Freud's dream book a certain "scientific aura," Crick's translation presents it more as a work of humanistic art, worthy of the Goethe prize for literature won by Freud. The differences between the Brill, Strachey, and Crick translations are sometimes subtle and sometimes startling. Freud is fortunate that his magnificent prose and expository skill, unequaled among psychoanalysts, can be rendered into the kind of artistic and rhetorical presentation that some experts claim is more authentic of Freud's style and thinking while others, like myself, remain more comfortable with Strachey's version.

For example, compare Crick's translation, "Naturally I learned very early that passions today can mean sorrow tomorrow" (131) with Strachey's, "And I had early discovered, of course, that passions often lead to sorrow" (Freud 1900, 173). Or compare Crick's:

> The lonely spinster who transfers her affections to animals, the bachelor who becomes a passionate collector, the soldier who defends a strip of coloured cloth, the flag, with his life's blood, the feelings of ecstasy roused in a love affair by a handclasp lingering for a second, the outburst of rage engendered in Othello by a lost handkerchief—these are all examples of psychical displacements which seem to us incontestable. (135)

with Strachey's:

> When a lonely old maid transfers her affection to animals, or a bachelor becomes an enthusiastic collector, when a soldier defends a scrap of coloured cloth—a flag—with his life's blood, when a few seconds' extra pressure in a hand-shake means bliss to a lover, or when, in *Othello*, a lost handkerchief precipitates an outburst of rage—all of these are instances of psychical displacements to which we raise no objection. (Freud 1900, 177)

Read out loud, the subtle differences in these translations become more apparent and the beauty of Freud's prose declares itself almost dramatically in Crick's new version.

Of course the most serious attention to any given translation of Freud's dream book has to come via an inspection of what the translator has done with the famous Chapter VII, "The Psychology of the Dream-Processes," with its well-known diagrams representing Freud's first major venture into speculative metapsychology. Here again, there is a marked difference, and of course the Strachey presentation has a much more scientific sounding and precise quasi-neurological intonation as he translates this speculative hydro-dynamic system envisioned by Freud's superb imagination into English. Take Strachey's:

> But it is quite possible that consciousness of these qualities may introduce in addition a more discriminating regulation, which is even able to oppose the former one, and which perfects the efficiency of the apparatus by enabling it, in contradiction to its original plan, to cathect and work over even what is associated with the release of unpleasure. (S.E. V, 616)

and compare it read out loud with Crick's:

> . . . but it is quite possible that consciousness of these qualities adds a second, and finer, regulation, which can even be at odds with the first, completing the efficiency of the apparatus by enabling it, quite contrary to its original disposition, to submit even what is connected with the release of unpleasure to the processes of energy-charge and revision. (408)

The quasi-scientific cumbersomeness of the Strachey translation slides away into the more mellifluous prose of Crick. But who is right? Here I think the entire controversy has been blown out of proportion, even though a whole new translation of Freud's work is promised because of this controversy and has probably been energized by all these arguments over Strachey's attempt to make Freud acceptable to the scientific community.

It depends on the preconceptions and the expectations of the reader as to which translation will be found most useful and clinically applicable. If one is a literary critic using psychoanalytic approaches to the study of the humanities or an individual with a general education but no special aptitude for science, the Crick and forthcoming Penguin translations will probably be the most appealing. If one is brought up in the tradition of Freud, namely beginning as a neurologist and shifting over into a study of the psychoneuroses while attempting to use quasi-neurological concepts to explain the symptoms of psychoneuroses, the Strachey translation may be more useful or acceptable, especially because a corrected edition of the Strachey translation has now appeared. Freud himself was always torn between his strict nineteenth-century empirical science orientation and training and his intuitive humanistic tendencies; this produced a certain ambiguity in his writing that makes his magnificently crafted descriptions of his clinical work, as he apologetically said, read more like short stories than like the ordinary hospital chart.

AN EXAMPLE OF CONFUSION
ABOUT THE PSYCHE IN CINEMATIC ART

The British philosopher Malcolm Budd (1995), in his book, *Values of Art*, maintains:

> Criticism, in its attempt to establish a work's artistic value, will draw attention to the aesthetic and also the non-aesthetic characteristics upon which its value depends. Since convincing criticism changes or refines your interpretation of a work, and what you are aware of in it, and since these are integral to the way you experience the work, a change of interpretation effects a change in experience. (41)

For example, all we can do with a film that presents us with ambiguity and anxiety is to view it over and over again in the hope, as a Freudian psychoanalyst might say, of forming rationalizations or compromise formations that reduce our anxiety. In the psychoanalytic process, however, in contrast to viewing a film, careful attention to free associations and transference manifestations from the patient as they unfold week after week and month after month afford us genuinely new information and new data as the associational and transference processes move closer and closer to the deep unconscious material, due to a momentum that is largely the product of the psychoanalytic situation. This of course assumes a skilled well-analyzed psychoanalyst, who does not interfere with the unfolding process due to needs of his or her own.

So, as an example, all we can do with a film like *The Double Life of Veronique* is to view it repeatedly and weave the ambiguous material into our own fantasy life (I hope the reader will watch the movie, which can be rented on VHS, before reading this discussion). What we will come up with is to some extent a description of our own fantasy life, much in the order of the Rorschach test. To give one an idea of how great a variety of fantasies can be stirred up by such an extremely enigmatic movie as this one, some critics have claimed that it is primarily a comment on the dislocation felt by Eastern Europeans who in the post-Soviet vacuum suddenly find themselves suffused by Western life. By way of contrast, it has been noted that while in France the critics and movie goers gave the movie rave reviews, finding it insightful, romantic, and sensitive, in Poland, where concerns are often more quotidian, reviewers and spectators alike left the theatres scratching their heads. My own response to this movie, which I also found ambiguous and productive of anxiety, was that it was drawn too much to an extreme, psychologically superficial, and surrealistic. I was impressed with the depressive elements in the theme of the movie rather than the theme of a search for the imago of the mother, but of course these are two sides of the same coin. I was most affected by the music in the movie, which I found to be almost painfully haunting. Actually, the director Kieslowski risks everything in the movie on the power of Zbigniew Preisner's score for orchestra and voices. Just to hear a small portion of the music is inexplicably moving, and the scene in which Veronika dies while singing Preisner's composition at the same time Veroníque is having an orgasm is an aesthetic powerhouse.

Veroníque teaches her class the same music that Veronika sings. The piece, she tells her class, was composed two hundred years ago but discovered only recently. Actually the music was composed by Preisner, a contemporary. In fairness to Kieslowski, I must report that I purchased the soundtrack of the movie on a CD, after having to search for it at great length; listening to the sound track alone does not produce the same ineffable experience that it produces in the movie in the scene where Veronika dies.

The movie deals with the sense of an awful hole at the center of life; Veroníque feels stripped and alone in the world and hungers for a connection, a sense of being attached meaningfully to some other existence. This is a variation on French existentialism and Sartre's gloomy philosophy. Veroníque is indeed obsessed with finding something to complete her self. She looks to music, sex, or love in order to confirm her existence and she ends in a relationship with her father, an ending that Kieslowski revised several times, and which I found particularly contrived.

Kieslowski said that by having the same person play two different persons, he wanted to express a human message, to show that we are all alike and at the same time completely different. He proposed the central idea of the film to be the question of covert communication between two people. It is something you feel without understanding where it comes from, which he thinks we are all capable of experiencing. This is parapsychology, a variation on mystical and surrealist themes, although it contains a hint of *amae*, discussed at the beginning of this chapter. Unfortunately the movie becomes increasingly fanciful, precious, and excessively ambiguous. My impression was that there was something progressively false about it, perhaps because it had been manufactured to meet some kind of financial contract or deadline. About three quarters of the way through the movie it begins to dissolve and the ending leaves one curiously unsatisfied, which is probably why Kieslowski revised it repeatedly. Vincent Canby, in the *New York Times* of May 26, 1991 wrote: "Is 'The Double Life of Veronica' (sic) really 'about' something and if so, what? I'm not at all sure; but in this case, the movie is such a magnificent visual and aural experience that conventional meaning is not terribly important." Even in France many people reported that they loved the movie but then added that they did not really understand it. As another critic, Caryn James, wrote also in the *New York Times* December 8, 1991: "Try to piece the film together like a jigsaw puzzle, try to make it yield some neat message about identity, and nothing will result except frustration . . . the director sometimes seems to be scattering clues and red herrings across two countries and two lives." I also felt there were too many parallels and coincidences, too many mirrors and too many reflections in windows.

Boundary situations represent the crises in human existence in which conflict and its meaning become poignantly and tragically clear. The philosopher-psychiatrist Karl Jaspers (1932a,b,c) emphasizes death, suffering, and struggle or "death, chance, guilt, and the uncertainty of the world" as well as the particular and historical determination of one's particular existence and the relativity of all that seems real, as constituting boundary situations. His three volume work entitled *Philosophy* also develops the concept of transcendence, which is experienced only indirectly through what Jaspers calls "ciphers." The key point of all this for psychoanalysts is that the human being is always more unknowable and indescribable than can be known. Art gives us higher pleasures including those that enable us to improve the way we live our lives, it gives our lives a spiritual dimension, it offers ciphers. Above all, the immersion in the arts offers to make us empathic and civilized. I believe this depressing movie, whether one views it as centered around the actual loss of the mother in reality or around that profound disappointment in the nursing couple that constitutes the root of all psychogenic depression, offers us, in its combination of artistic beauty and remarkable music, a cipher towards getting in touch with something outside of ourselves, what Jaspers called transcendence

CONFUSION DUE TO TRANSLATION
FROM AN INHERENTLY AMBIGUOUS TEXT

I learned to translate classical Greek for the purpose of being able to read the plays of Sophocles and the *Dialogues of Plato* in the original. From this effort it has become clear to me that there are ambiguities in these texts themselves, which lead to differing interpretations of what the author was trying to say. So another confusion of tongues that we must deal with is in the effort to translate into our own language an already ambiguous text written in a foreign language. Perhaps the most blatant contemporary example of this is in the effort to translate the transcripts of Lacan's seminars from his highly sophisticated and punning French into English. I am told that only a French teacher or an expert in the French language can fully appreciate some of the irony and allusions and puns that Lacan employs.

Here is an example from what I consider one of Plato's most important dialogues, one that ought to be carefully studied by psychoanalysts and psychiatrists, the *Symposium*. It is even possible to argue that of all Plato's dialogues, the *Symposium* has the greatest literary and philosophical value and is the most magnificently constructed work of art ever written in the classical Greek language. At any rate, the example is from the speech of Eryximachus, lines 188c6 through 188d3. The classical Greek reads as follows:

ἃ δὴ προστέτακται τῇ μαντικῇ
ἐπισκοπεῖν τοὺς ἐρῶντας καὶ ἰατρεύειν,
καὶ ἔστιν αὖ ἡ μαντικὴ φιλίας θεῶν
καὶ ἀνθρώπων δημιουργὸς τῷ ἐπίστασθαι
τὰ κατὰ ἀνθρώπους ἐρωτικά, ὅσα τείνει
πρὸς θέμιν καὶ εὐσέβειαν.

The physician Eryximachus is speaking of the two loves; I will loosely translate the first as "the other (kind of) love" and the second as "the well ordered love." He warns us of the dangers in following the former and the values for health and happiness in following the latter. He then continues with the Greek passage I will now straightforwardly translate:

What is assigned to the diviner is to know these loves and to heal them. The diviner, by knowing what befits the loves of men, in such a way generates a tendency toward custom and reverence.

Here is the Jowett (1920) translation:

Wherefore the business of divination is to see to these loves and to heal them, and divination is the peacemaker of gods and men, working by a knowledge of the religious or irreligious tendency which exist in human loves. (315)

Here is a more recent translation by Joyce (1961):

It is the diviner's office to be the guide and healer of these Loves, and his art of divination, with its power to distinguish those principles of human love that tend to decency and reverence, is, in fact, the source of concord between god and man. (541)

Here is the latest translation I have, by Benardete (2001):

And so it is, accordingly, that divination is charged with the overseeing and healing of lovers; and divination, in turn, is the craftsman of friendship between gods and human beings, since it has expert knowledge of human erotics, as far as erotics has to do with sacred law and piety. (17)

It is clear from a careful reading of these translations that the emphasis and general meaning both differ sharply in each. The problem here, in contrast to the Dante translations, has to do with the actual Greek text, which uses a number of terms that have multiple meanings and can therefore be put together in several ways depending on the bias or intent of the translator. So we are dealing in this instance now not only with interpretation due to the bias or ignorance of the translator but due to the intrinsic ambiguity of the text.

Some of that ambiguity can be reduced if we consider the context in which the sentences under scrutiny appear. The speaker in this case is Eryximachus, a physician, whose emphasis is not on religion and reverence and the gods but on the healing arts, which he considers based on a certain harmonious combination of various elements supplied by the gods. His orientation is conservative and aims at the preservation of balance and the status quo which he considers a measure of normality; any imbalances in the various forces at work in the human body or psyche represent for Eryximachus disease. The genius of Plato is to follow this conservative speech of Eryximachus with the ironic and sarcastic speech of Aristophanes, who converts this harmonious balance theory into a caricature that subtly makes fun of the stodgy reactionary Eryximachus and his pompous pronouncements. Because of the ambiguities of the text itself, it is clear how the translators each go off in their own direction, a striking example of the confusion of tongues. Who is right and who is wrong?

This is no mere academic matter; it is the same problem we face in the attempt to interpret manifest dream content. The advantage we have as psychoanalysts is that in addition to the general context of what the patient has been saying we also have the patient's free associations to the dream, which, if listened to carefully, can lead us to a more or less accurate representation of what the patient is attempting to communicate. I suggest that the task of the psychoanalyst in listening to either dream or metaphorical or free-association material is similar to the task of the translator who is trying to translate a foreign language, a foreign text using ambiguous terms. Unfortunately the translator of Plato will not have the luxury of asking Plato to elaborate, so that we are forced to do a lot of guesswork and follow the context the best we can. A literal translation of Plato's complex Greek does not solve the problem, it only serves to guide us as to where the translator has gone off in his or her own direction. But it is no more possible to literally translate Plato's Greek and come up with definitively and exclusive meaningful or reliable results than it is to do so with poets and humanists who write even in our own language. Even the denotations are ambiguous in the passage that I have given as an example and the connotations render the whole thing subject to various interpretations.

This unavoidable confusion of tongues is a good demonstration of why the humanistic sciences can never be exact sciences like physics or chemistry; there are no precise quantitative terms that give us indisputable meanings of the basic concepts and metaphors which characterize all adult human communication. And this is consistent with Freud's contention that all human behavior and communication is psychically overdetermined, brimming with multiple meanings and motivations.

4

The Continental Contribution
to Psychoanalysis

This chapter is an introduction to the subject for mental health professionals and others who are interested in the future of psychoanalysis but who are not familiar with phenomenology. Phenomenology, as we use it here, attempts to capture in all its concrete immediacy the intrinsic nature of one's experience, exactly as it occurs to a person and without any embellishment, explanation, extrapolation, interpretation, inference, or attribution to any theory; for example, what it feels like to experience dizziness, grief, hunger, or pain. The term "phenomenology" has been adopted as the name of a practice in which this subjective, immediately given, lived experience is used as a starting point for the construction of ontological theories, epistemology, ethics, and even a theory of the mind by some authors. It began as a contemporary philosophical movement in the work of Brentano, whose seminars were attended by both Freud and Husserl. The latter made it his life's work and then it was expanded and transformed in various directions by such philosophical pioneers as Heidegger, Sartre, Merleau-Ponty, and numerous other thinkers more distant from the phenomenologic movement.

Obviously there is little possibility of objective debate and the provision of reasons, arguments, and explanations within any system which bases itself exclusively on phenomenology, and as a result phenomenologists all too often write in a dogmatic style consisting of numerous assertions about how things are, without any attempt to justify these assertions except through appeal to subjective phenomenological insight. Once the objectives of a phenomenological psychology are clearly understood, there should be no question about the fact that it has essential limitations and that it can not and must not be considered as a rival of scientific research. Its main function is to serve as an ally to the scientific enterprise.

The phenomenologist Merleau-Ponty insisted, and I agree, that the ideas of Hegel are the source of many important philosophical ideas in the second half of the nineteenth century and the first half of the twentieth century, including the work of Marx, Nietzsche, phenomenology, existentialism, and psychoanalysis. For example, Hegel discusses the limits set to the autonomy of self-consciousness, for self consciousness always belongs to a culture in which the human finds himself or herself immersed. From our Western culture springs the aggressiveness of modern science, which always wants to become master over its object by means of a method. But this excludes the mutuality of participation existing between object and subject, an insight that represents the highest point of ancient Greek philosophy and makes possible what the Greeks thought could be our participation in the beautiful, the good, and the just, as well as in the values of communal human life.

In *Book Lambda* of the *Metaphysics* Aristotle describes the Prime Mover as completely autonomous, completely whole, knowing no limit, no obstruction, no illness, no fatigue, no sleep. By comparison, in the case of the human being, all of these limitations are present; this is known as the finitude of the human being. What the philosophers Hegel and Husserl and finally Heidegger were addressing might be labeled the metaphysics of this finitude of the human being.

For the ancient Greeks, the essence of knowledge arises out of the dialogue with and not the mastery of objects. All of this perhaps can help us to understand why Husserl, with his analysis of time-consciousness, and, after him, Heidegger (1962), the author of *Being and Time*, developed a different way in our age of science for contemporary continental philosophy, which in turn much influenced certain contemporary continental psychoanalysts and psychiatrists (for details see Kraus 2001).

Within the presuppositions of modern science, everything is reduced to methods of objectification and testing. Hans-Georg Gadamer, a student of Heidegger, pointed out that the term "*methodos*" in the ancient sense always meant the whole business of working within a certain domain of questions and problems. "Method" in this sense is not a tool for objectifying and dominating something; rather it is a matter of our participating in an association with the things with which we are dealing. This meaning of "method" as "going along with" presupposes that we are already finding ourselves in the middle of the game and can occupy no neutral standpoint—even if we strive very hard for objectivity and put our prejudices at risk.

This sounds like a challenge to the natural sciences and their ideal of objectivity. The human sciences must occupy themselves with quite different tasks than the natural sciences. In the human sciences there is an elementary and self-evident concern, namely, what really matters is the human being's encounter with himself or herself in relation to an "other" different from himself or herself, more of a "taking part" in something. In the human sciences the help of a method will not enable a person to place himself or herself in a determinate relationship to an "other" who has been posited by that person as an object. Jean-Paul Sartre aptly described what is disastrous about the objectifying gaze: in the instant that the other is reduced to an observed object, the mutuality of the gaze is no longer maintained and communication ceases.

So the functions of the natural sciences and the human sciences are fundamentally different; the former behaves in an objectifying way and the latter has to do with participation. This certainly does not mean that objectification and methodical approach have no value in the humanistic and historical disciplines, and of course the cultural sciences do have scientific methods available to them. But we cannot ignore the value of our mutual participation in and our involvement in the tradition and the life of culture in which both we and the individuals whom we study are immersed. Phenomenology evolved into an effort to recognize this important aspect of the human sciences.

WHAT IS PHENOMENOLOGY?

When anyone claims to answer the question "What is phenomenology?," beware, because although phenomenology was first developed by Husserl in 1900, it has been used differently by Heidegger, Sartre, Jaspers, Merleau-Ponty, and many others since that time. So anyone who answers the question "What is phenomenology?" will be telling you what he or she believes it to be, and that is all.

Husserl began this approach in the following manner. A "phenomenon" is whatever appears to us immediately in experience. No "reduction" is permitted, that is, no selecting out of experience of such items as things, objects, sensation, feelings, entities, and so on, since this already assumes classification principles about the world. No DSM-IV is to be allowed in back of the therapist's mind. In this, Husserl believed he had found a new epistemological method, for phenomenologic statements cannot be called empirical since empirical sciences already assume things or entities, out there, for example a "case" of depression, schizophrenia, and so on.

But Husserl wrongly believed that there is such a thing as presuppositionless inquiry in phenomenology, that is to say, an inquiry using no theories, in which one simply describes the phenomena as they present themselves to an unprejudiced view. His basic approach was what he called a phenomenologic stance: just react to what is simply there in immediate experience. This is similar to Bion's impossible command to approach each psychoanalytic session without memory, desire, or understanding. At least one tries to not disconnect, isolate, interpret, or classify aspects of the experience when taking a phenomenologic stance.

A second part of Husserl's method was what he called *Epoche*, or suspension, taken from Stoic philosophy. This "phenomenologic reduction" or "bracketing of being" includes refrainment from judgement about diagnosis, morals or values, causes, background, or the subject (the patient) as separate and different from the objective observer (therapist). Instead, there exists an experiential field in which, for example, the therapist pays special attention to his or her own state of consciousness in the presence of the patient. A clinical example of this was offered at Chestnut Lodge by the psychoanalyst Pao in dealing with schizophrenics, who emphasized what he called "the feel of a schizophrenic," that is to say, a special communal atmosphere created by a schizophrenic patient.

The rest of Husserl's philosophy does not interest us here, because he used it in a fruitless attempt to gain absolute knowledge. But this new method became the principle alternative in one form or another to the empirical study of humans as natural science objects. Such empirical study ignores the vivid immediacy of the lived world of the patient in its effort to abstract out mechanical scientific laws, reducing the person to a thing to be studied, or manipulated, or liquidated, with all this implies for the history of the twentieth century and for the course now taken by medical psychiatry, so totally under the influence of the huge international pharmaceutical corporations.

Husserl's phenomenology, based on the subjective perspective (i.e., the way in which all our experience takes place), emphasizes the web of anticipations involved whenever we experience anything, a web of anticipations that form a horizon or background and of which we are not aware. This is Husserl's notion of fore-meaning or fore-structure and Heidegger leaned heavily on this aspect of Husserl's philosophy, taking over Husserl's phenomenology and calling it "hermeneutics."

For our purposes then, as Kraus (2001) writes in typical continental prose: "The phenomenological-anthropological and daseinsanalytic [see Binswanger 1963] forms of psychiatry attain a special place in the realm of scientific concerns in psychiatry. . . . It is one of their tasks to display the reductionism of empirical-objectivating approaches in order to open up for those sciences . . . new questions and dimensions" (349). Obviously this openness of questioning in the phenomenological approach poses great difficulties in trying to design research and quantification to satisfy the empirically minded DSM IV enthusiasts and the managed care bureaucrats. As he writes, "The diagnostic glossary largely replaces intuitive-eidological acts with the generation of so-called diagnostic criteria and the introduction of algorithmic decision trees" (350). Kraus points out how this ignores what might be called the hermeneutic nature of diagnostic processes "with their acts which are anticipatory-proleptic and retrospective with regard to part and whole" (350). This hermeneutic stance is an important aspect of Gadamer's thought.

Follesdal (2001) points out that hermeneutics shares two important features of the standard scientific or natural sciences method. "(1) setting forth interpretational hypotheses and (2) checking whether they together with our beliefs imply consequences that clash with our material" (375) and he attempts to regard hermeneutics as "the hypothetical-deductive method applied to meaningful material in order to bring out its meaning" (376). Follesdal also emphasizes the hermeneutic circle, in which we go back and forth between the hypothesis and the material until we achieve some kind of fit: "We may find hypotheses that fit in with part of the material, but which have to be revised because they do not fit in with other parts. A good hypothesis must fit the whole material, and so will have to be modified until it provides an interpretation that fits all the parts" (376). There is a clear parallel to the work of the psychoanalyst here. In psychoanalytic practice the material of free associations is used to test interpretive hypotheses, but passages that were originally interpreted in one way come to be interpreted in another as the free associations unfold. As in the natural sciences, we always struggle with what has been known as the theory-ladenness of observation.

CONTINENTAL PSYCHOANALYSIS

Continental psychoanalysts such as Ludwig Binswanger adopted Heidegger's notion of phenomenology, which was based on utilizing Husserl's phenomenologic method to focus on the lived world of the human being (actually a travesty of what Husserl had in mind). Influenced by this, Binswanger (1963) borrowed Heidegger's whole concept of the surrounding world of the living subject in his attempt to interpret the context of the phenomena of his patients. World and self appeared as correlatives in symbiosis, and being human involved a way of moving in a world, as the phenomenologist, Erwin Straus repeatedly emphasized and investigated here, teaching us as a refugee in the United States (Chessick 1999c). Especially in his analyses of dreams, Binswanger argued that dreams showed different ways of living and moving in a characteristic space for that individual dreamer.

Binswanger gave ultimate credit to Heidegger's concept of *Verfallensein*, a kind of decay of the human, and even dedicated his studies of three such modes of decay or failure to Heidegger. The first one of these modes studied by Binswanger is *Verstiegenheit*, which literally means to have lost one's path in climbing a mountain, similar to the situation of Dante to be discussed in chapter 6. The patient has maneuvered himself or herself into a position from which the patient can no longer extricate himself or herself. In the United States we call that "painting yourself into a corner." An example of it would be the disproportion in an individual's mind between the height of the goals aspired to and the level actually accessible through that person's experience and ability. A prime dramatic example is Ibsen's master builder named Solness, who builds structures which he can no longer climb until he falls to his death. The other modes of failure are *Verschrobenheit* or screwiness, where our meanings get mixed up, and *Manieriertheit* or mannerisms, where, because of our inability to reach or actualize our own self, we imitate an impersonal model or an individual outside of ourselves.

The most important implication of this new conception is that for a real understanding of a person, and particularly a mentally sick person, one has to study primarily his or her world, not just his or her biological organism or so-called personality disorder in itself set apart from the world. Actually Binswanger even spoke of several such worlds for the same person, again borrowed from Heidegger: the *Umwelt*, one's nonpersonal environment; the *Mitwelt*, one's social relations to others; and the *Eigenwelt*, one's private world. These terms stand not for separate worlds, but regions within the comprehensive world of the person.

THE ZOLLIKON SEMINARS

Heidegger gave seminars in Zollikon, Switzerland, at the home of the psychoanalyst Medard Boss. Boss invited him to give these seminars after World War II when Heidegger, because of his Nazi sympathies, was not yet allowed to teach in the university in Germany. These were attended by physicians and psychotherapists, pupils and collaborators of Boss, who taught at the university's psychiatric clinic in Zurich, the famous Burghölzle, the place where Carl Jung had worked. During the war, Medard Boss had been a battalion medical officer with a mounted unit of the Swiss army. He had little to do then, and to deal with his boredom he read Heidegger's *Being and Time* (1962). Gradually he realized that this work formulated some fundamentally new unheard-of insights into human existence and its world that might be used in psychotherapy. In 1947, he wrote his first letter to Heidegger, who replied courteously and asked for a small package of chocolate. Eventually they developed a friendship, which resulted in a series of seminars from 1959 to 1969.

At the first seminar, Heidegger drew semicircles on the blackboard to represent one's primary openness to the world and tried for the first time to make psychic disorders comprehensible through the basic concepts that he had presented in *Being and Time*. Medical histories were discussed. An open relationship to the world meant sustaining the present without escaping into the future or past. Heidegger was critical of Freudian psychoanalysis for rendering the relationship between the patient and the patient's world more complicated by the use of what he called contrived theories. He restated his view that most mental diseases can be understood as a disturbance in existing in the patient's world, a failure to sustain an open relationship in the world. For Heidegger, there is no break between sickness and normality. Two issues always intermingled in the Zollikon seminar, the mental illness of individuals and the pathology of modern civilization. That is to say, in the disturbance of the individual, Heidegger recognized the madness of the modern age.

Askay (1999) presents a clever imagined debate between Heidegger and Freud, using as much as possible the actual quotations from their writings even though, of course, these have to be lifted out of context. It is remarkable that Freud and Husserl were contemporaries and completely failed to take notice of each other's work. Askay points out that the same problem of lack of reciprocity occurred involving the work of Freud and Heidegger:

> Although Heidegger was thirty years younger than Freud, they shared the same language, lived relatively close to one another, had been directly influenced by the philosophy of Brentano, had close relationships with some of the same people (e.g., the Swiss existential psychoanalysts, Ludwig Binswanger and Medard Boss), and were both concerned about the emergence of meaning in the world and the development of psychology. (415)

Freud never mentions Heidegger or his work, and except for the Zollikon seminars Heidegger had little to say about Freud. In the Zollikon seminars, however, he spoke directly about his profound disagreement with Freud's approach. In my opinion it was essentially the same as Heidegger's profound disagreements with the arrogant assumptions of natural science, that through science and reason we had the only instrument for finding out about the world. Heidegger's complaints rested heavily on Freud's attempt to base psychoanalysis on a natural science *Weltanschauung* and Freud's hostile comments about philosophy. In a previous publication (1980) I pointed out how Freud shifted from a Cartesian to a Kantian epistemology and actually Freud himself (*Standard Edition*, vol. 14, 171 and vol. 5, 615–616) points out that his work on the unconscious is simply an extension of Kant's philosophy. Kant warned us that our perception is subjectively conditioned and is not identical with the phenomenon perceived just as psychoanalysis warns us that conscious perception is subjectively conditioned by unconscious mental processes originating in childhood.

Askay offers an excellent contrasting explanation by Freud and Heidegger of the clinical example of a woman who "accidentally" leaves her purse behind when she leaves the room of a male acquaintance. Freud of course would explain it as her wish to return there once again, or, using symbolism, as based on the unconscious wish to offer herself sexually to the man. Heidegger, on the other hand, would reject this explanation as a pure hypothesis and would argue that we should describe "leaving behind" phenomenologically. Heidegger would say that there was no unconscious intention. Askay is one of the translators of the *Zollikon Seminars* (Boss 2001) and he quotes Heidegger as follows:

> Precisely because the man whom she visited is not indifferent to her, her departure is such that by leaving she is still present here more than ever. The purse is not present to her at all because she is so totally with the man while she departs. In this kind of departure the purse is left behind because the woman was so much with her friend already during her visit in the room that the bag was not present to her even at that time. Here the 'goingsomewhere' simply does not exist (for her). If the same woman were to depart from someone to whom she was indifferent in order to go shopping in the city, then she would not forget the purse. Rather she would take it with her because the purse is essential for going shopping. (427–428)

Freud of course would consider this a highly oversimplified explanation, one that attempts to disavow the sexual aspect, but for phenomenologists it is characteristic. If it seems strange to the reader, that is because we psychoanalysts are more or less conditioned to think in terms of unconscious motivations and not phenomenological investigations. A chart for the purpose of highlighting this comparison between the so-called "natural sciences" approach in psychiatry and psychoanalysis and the phenomenological-hermeneutic approach used by the Swiss existential psychoanalysts and a number of other prominent investigators, is on page 73.

We are fortunate that the translation of these seminars has now become available in English (Boss 2001). The Zollikon seminar publication is mostly comprised of a review of what went on from 1959 to 1969 in the seminars as described in the notes of Medard Boss. Heidegger stresses in these seminars a number of crucial items for psychoanalysts. He complains about the assertion that brain research is a fundamental science for our knowledge of the human being. He says:

> This assertion implies that the true and real relationship among human beings is a correlation among brain processes. . . . Then, when one is not engaged in research during semester vacation, the aesthetic appreciation of the statue of a god in the Acropolis museum is nothing more than the encounter of the brain process of the beholder with the product of another brain process, that is, the representation of the statue. Nevertheless, if during the vacation one assures oneself that one does not mean it that way, then one lives by double- or

triple-entry bookkeeping. . . . This means that one has become so undemanding regarding thinking and reflecting that such double bookkeeping is no longer considered disturbing, nor is the complete lack of reflection upon this passionately defended science and its necessary limits considered in any way disturbing. (95)

A crucial section of the book in the English edition begins on page 168. Here, Heidegger directly contradicts Freud's notion of the unconscious and interprets the clinical example of a woman who leaves her purse in the room of her boyfriend, in disagreement with Freud's interpretation, as described above. Heidegger's basic complaint is that psychoanalysis sees humans only in what he has called the "mode of fallenness," an absorption in the world guided by idle talk, curiosity, and ambiguity. Familiarity with Heidegger's (1962) basic thought in *Being and Time* would of course be very helpful to the reader; his complaint in the Zollikon seminars is about the objectification in science of the human into some kind of mechanical thing. Freud's metapsychological depiction of human mental functioning, as for example in the famous chapter 7 of Freud's *Interpretation of Dreams*, where it is depicted as a kind of hydraulic mechanism, concerns Heidegger greatly because, as Heidegger sees it, this leaves out an enormous aspect of the human's being-in-the-world. This complementary aspect of studying humans, functioning beside and as an option to or accessory to the natural science approach, is the basic focus of phenomenology. Consistent with Heidegger's complaint, he bemoans the loss of the family doctor; such doctors he regards as part of a dying breed in a modern world where the patient is now treated as an "object" of medical expertise (as the translators point out on page 263n).

Heidegger could not understand what Lacan was trying to do and suggests that Lacan "needs a psychiatrist" (281). In a more serious vein, Heidegger explains that if one wishes to become familiar with Heidegger's work and one is a psychiatrist and not a professional philosopher, one should read first his (1968) book *What Is Called Thinking*, then his (1991) work *The Principle of Reason*, and finally his (1969) *Gelassenheit (Discourse on Thinking)*. I should warn the reader that when I at one time assigned *What Is Called Thinking* to a group of psychiatric residents I had a revolution on my hands. We in American psychiatry are so totally immersed in the empirical scientific milieu that Heidegger appears to be coming from outer space as he presents an entirely different option for our orientation to the study of humans. This is why Heidegger is one of those thinkers whose work, when carefully studied, brings about almost a dizziness, a sense of revelation, in the mind of the serious reader. In spite of all the difficulties of reading and trying to understand his complex German and his highly debatable derivations of the meanings of Greek terms, Heidegger has something unique and different to offer the student who is seriously interested in understanding humans. For that reason, it was very appropriate for Medard Boss to invite Heidegger to a seminar aimed primarily at mental health professionals, and to take notes in order to pass the ambiance and the substance of this seminar down to us.

The English edition has a nice "Afterwords" by the translators (299–336), discussing Heidegger's critique of Freudian psychoanalysis. The translators point out that Heidegger was very impressed with Freud's technique; what he objected to was metapsychology and the scientific *Weltanschaung* that Freud insisted on, because it reduced humans to objects and caused what the translators call "the greatest ontological dyspepsia in Heidegger" (309). They point out that Heidegger's praise of Freud had more to do with his papers on technique, in which "Freud often alluded to the human capacity for free choice, the truth-disclosing and truth-fleeing tendencies of human beings, the capacity for being absorbed into an anonymous group mentality, thereby forfeiting individual distinctiveness, freedom, concomitant responsibility, and so forth" (309).

Heidegger insisted there is a great need for doctors who think and that the field of understanding humans should not be left to scientific technicians or to brain studies. He complained that science does not properly reflect on its preconceptions and prejudices, which limits what science can offer us about human psychology and about what it means to be human and what it means to be. Like many authors he also complained that psychoanalysis should not neglect the danger of the uncritical imposition of theoretical frameworks by therapists on their patients. As the translators point out, Heidegger in phenomenological terminology described this kind of imposition as a kind of leaping in for the Other. This leads to domination of the patient and to the encouragement of dependency, even if this is a tacit kind of domination and remains hidden from the patient.

What the translators correctly regard as crucial in Heidegger's approach to psychotherapy is for the therapist to be open to the very presencing of being through the patient. One must educate oneself in the language of phenomenology and ontology as it is presented by these major contemporary thinkers if one is to rise above the narrow mechanistic and materialistic conception of humans that dominates American psychiatry today and has led to the usurpation of the profession by the international drug companies and managed care organizations. Psychoanalysis must lead the way in the task of liberation from reductive materialism.

LACAN

Continental thinkers have stressed the importance of what they often call the prison house of language. Heavily influenced by Heidegger, they have concluded that our horizon of understanding is limited by our language and furthermore, that often our language expresses aspects of ourselves we had not consciously intended to communicate. The most famous and extreme example of this constitutes the work of Derrida, who in his "deconstruction," a concept borrowed from Heidegger, maintains that every written communication carries within itself the seeds of its own refutation. The emphasis, as depicted by Lacan, is how the unconscious, which Lacan conceives of as structured like a language, expresses itself through the patient's communications. Through the use of hermeneutics Freud discovered how the body itself, as well as the language of neurotic bodily symptoms and the language of neurotic complaints, could "speak" and express aspects of the patient's unconscious and unacceptable wishes. In hermeneutics, the procedure of interpreting all this as Heidegger proposes it, we move in the kind of circle that is not a vicious circle (*circulus vitiosus*), but rather proceed through a series of questions and answers based on the fact that, as Heidegger (Boss 2001) is quoted in the Zollikon seminars, "It is quite possible that I have some knowledge of what I am asking about, but this does not mean that I already know explicitly what I am asking about, that is, in the sense [that I] have made a thematic apprehension and determination" (37). This is also foundational to the psychoanalytic process.

The Hegelian concept of the "Other" or "Otherhood" may confuse some readers, and it appears frequently and is used in multifarious ways in the work of phenomenologists, Heidegger, and Lacan. It represents another individual viewed as one who can become dominated and dependent and separated from the Subject, a person who is viewed by the Subject or observer as a "thing" to be investigated and studied and manipulated. Heidegger's basic complaint in the Zollikon seminars, and that of many other phenomenologists, is that modern science tends to view humans in Otherhood just as we view inanimate objects in the natural world. This approach to inanimate objects in the natural world has led to great scientific accomplishments, but viewing humans in this manner greatly narrows the information available about human being and the human lived world. The purpose of phenomenology and hermeneutics is to widen the scope of our information by introducing a phenomenologic stance on the part of the therapist instead of a stance in which the therapist views himself or herself as a subject or scientist studying an object, the patient, the "Other." For psychiatrists this is a very difficult transition as it goes against many years of rigorous medical training. I believe this is what Freud had in mind when he warned in *The Problem of Lay Analysis* that medical training made it harder to become proficient in psychoanalysis.

I am concerned about the continental concept of "the Lacanian subject" as completely constituted by language and the culture and therefore having no human essence. This is consistent with recent subjectivism and the continental sense, as Lacan puts it, that man is the marionette of his culture. It is in opposition to Marx, who contended that humans were species-beings at their base (implying there is indeed a base or essence to humans) and are distorted in their behavior and constitution by the capitalistic system in which they have to live. The extremely important issue of whether the human being from the very beginning is wholly intersubjectively constituted remains open. Certainly the Greeks did not think so; European continental philosophy has carried us recently in the opposite direction.

SYMPTOMATOLOGY CONTRASTED WITH PHENOMENOLOGY

My reading of the *Zollikon Seminars* was not as productive for me as it seems to have been for Askay, as I found much of it to be repetitious of Heidegger's well known approach to the study of Being and his emphasis on the ontic-ontological difference (see Chessick 1992b). As in the case of Werner Heisenberg (see Cassidy 1992) it is very difficult to separate the unsavory and frankly repellant personal characteristics of Heidegger from his ingenious original contributions to philosophy.

In the *Zollikon Seminars*, which, as stated above, took place after World War II while Heidegger was under instructions that forbade him to occupy an academic position, Heidegger told Medard Boss what he claimed was his only, although often recurring, dream. The dream was that he had to take his school graduation examination again with the same teachers as in the past. It seems clear from his behavior, although we have no associations to the dream, that this amoral man, like Werner Heisenberg, had no sense of ethical principles or empathy for other humans but simply was disappointed in his pathological narcissistic aspirations to be the central figure in a resurgence and revolution in his chosen field as well as the initiator of a worldwide cultural change (Chessick 1995b).

In the case of the phenomenologists, Heidegger was a profound influence on all who followed him and it is imperative that practicing psychoanalysts have at least a basic grasp of this alternative that may serve as a complementary and ancillary tool in one's armamentarium of understanding other human beings.

The following chart has been taken from the work of my friend, Dr. Alfred Kraus of the University of Heidelberg, who kindly gave me permission to use this material, which is not published. I have edited it for the purposes of this chapter. Of course the editing and presentation are my responsibility and Dr. Kraus should not be blamed for my blunders. The practical purpose of this is to try to clarify for the reader the difference between the DSM-IV standard American psychiatric approach and the phenomenologic approach, which in my opinion also forms an important channel for listening to and understanding our psychoanalytic patients.

Symptomatology—(DSM-IV) contrasted with Phenomenology

• reductive; inclusive and exclusive criteria	• holistic; oriented to the patient's being-in-the-world
• "disease"—medical model	• being-ill as a subjective experience
• oriented to the body functions brain, neurotransmitters	• oriented to the person as a subject, to the history of the individual
• symptoms as result of some physical dysfunction	• certain kinds of experience and behavior as expression of a certain relationship to one's self and to the world
• a symptom can be the same element in different disorders	• a symptom has a special quality in each disorder
• diagnostic entity as a serial summing-up using formulas (DSM—IV criteria)	• diagnostic entity as a psychological whole
• stresses consistence and reliability of of diagnosis	• stresses form and personal validity for diagnosis
• excludes subjectivity subjective experience not a criterion	• experiencing individual subject is central; subjective experience is a criterion
• seeks controllable and repeatable change and experiences	• seeks open-ended unpredictable new changes and experiences
• patient as object of investigation, a supplier of data	• patient as active partner in diagnostic and therapeutic process
• investigator conceived of as independent of patient	• investigator dependent on interaction with patient
• active questioning standard psychiatric interview	• let show itself what will show itself
• stresses medication and behavior change	• stresses profound encounter with therapist
• excludes the unconscious not compatible with psychoanalysis	• usually excludes the unconscious but compatible with psychoanalysis
• e.g., a plethora of A.P.A. publications publications	• e.g., *Emotional Illness and Creativity: A Psychoanalytic and Phenomenologic Study* (Chessick 1999b)

An outstanding review of phenomenology has been published by Moran (2000). He points out, and the reader can understand from the above discussion in this chapter, that phenomenology is not a philosophical system but rather a practice in which there is an effort to get at the truth of matters, "to describe *phenomena*, in the broadest sense as whatever appears in the manner in which it appears, that is as it manifests itself to consciousness, to the experiencer" (4). So phenomenology attempts to reject the domination of inquiry by cultural or religious traditions, so-called common sense, and even from science or any externally imposed methods as well as from any historical tradition, dogma, or a priori metaphysical assumptions. In the words of Husserl it is an attempt to direct attention to the things themselves, to revive our contact with the actual lived world and the living human subject.

I have described phenomenological practice (1999b) as also most valuable in the viewing of art works. Moran (2000) explains that, "Following Hegel and Heidegger, Gadamer's paradigm of genuine cultural understanding is always the experience of art" (250). Many phenomenologists appeal to our different ways of approaching art works as paradigmatic for revealing the different modes of the givenness of phenomena. For example, Heidegger conceived of truth as expressing itself in great art works and Merleau-Ponty (1962) gave a detailed account of the experience of looking at Cezanne's paintings. Try it! Cutrofello (2005, 75–79) reviews Merleau-Ponty's emphasis on Cezanne as being one of the painters who reveal the primordial world of perception. That is to say, "Instead of attempting to reconstruct nature as it is for the scientist . . . Cezanne relentlessly strove to paint that more primordial phenomenal nature upon which science is built" (76). Cezanne emphasizes two aspects of nature that are not found in scientific understanding. These are the indeterminacy of our actual perceptions of nature, and that what we see are no isolated qualities such as "redness" and so on, but a complex phenomenon: "It is only by way of a retroactive illusion generated by the habits of objective thought that we learn to draw sharp distinctions among the separable qualia contributed to perception by the various senses" (76). One finds that the mode of givenness emerging from an art work is best approached when assumptions about the world are put out of account.

For the purposes of psychoanalysts, however, it is what Husserl (borrowing from Jaspers 1963) called the "life-world" and the-being-in-the-world of the patient that is really the most important aspect emphasized by phenomenology. In order to understand this one has to understand the impact of the scientific world view on our consciousness. As Moran explains, "Phenomenology has to interrogate the supposedly objective view of the sciences" (12). Husserl saw this objectification or abstraction so fundamental to science as a kind of idealization, a special construction, remote from everyday experience and abstracted from our ordinary experiences. Phenomenologists are inclined to argue that the traditional concepts of subject and objects are philosophical and psychological constructions that distort the true nature of human experience of being in the world. Phenomenologists claim to offer a holistic approach, for example, as in Merleau-Ponty's view, stressing the mediating role of the body. The same approach was emphasized by the phenomenologist Erwin Straus, who could make a deteriorated patient with tertiary syphilis become a person deserving of extremely interested attention, and who repeatedly aroused our interest in patients ordinarily relegated to the back ward of a mental hospital. Merleau-Ponty, who unfortunately died before he could finish his major philosophical work, pointed out that the whole scientific edifice is built upon the life world, and science is always a second-order expression of that world.

PHENOMENOLOGY IN PSYCHOANALYSIS

The greatest value of the practice of phenomenology for psychoanalysts is that it continually provides a focus on the fundamental and inextricable role of subjectivity and consciousness in all knowledge and in descriptions of the world. What this means is that you can not split off the subjective domain from the domain of the natural world, as eliminative materialism has done in its stance on the mind-brain problem. For anyone who practices phenomenology there is a continual reminder of the irreducible subjectivity of consciousness which has an ontological nature of its own and can not be simply reduced in any way shape or form to neurological processes, although neurological processes are of course the base of and necessary for any phenomena of consciousness. Conscious phenomena are an emergent property (Laughlin 2005) of their neurological and biological base. Phenomenology is an attempt to approach this subjectivity in its own right just as in the natural sciences we approach brain functioning, that is to say third person phenomena, by standard empirical methods. Phenomenology reminds us to remain as experience-near as possible in our dealings with our patients and our attempts to understand them.

Franz Brentano (1838–1917) attempted to develop a descriptive psychology which was the first and most important intellectual stimulus for Husserl's development of phenomenology. Freud attended Brentano's lectures between 1874 and 1876 and these were the only philosophy courses Freud took as part of his medical training. As he did for Husserl, I believe Brentano passed also on to Freud a sense of his deep conviction concerning the self-critical and serious life of a philosopher. Brentano also insisted that any worthwhile philosophy must be rigorously scientific and not just speculation and a mixture of arbitrary dogmatic statements. In our field the contrast between these two kinds of philosophy can easily be found in Freud's (1900) *Interpretation of Dreams* if one compares Freud's description of previous wholly speculative theories of dreams with the theory he now proposes to offer. Brentano along with Wilhelm Wundt were considered the founders of the discipline of empirical psychology. This discipline eschewed any metaphysical speculation on the nature of the soul and attempted to study psychological processes completely on their own without raising the issue of the causal physiological processes which produced them and carried them out.

Another important aspect of Husserl's phenomenology was his concept of the horizon, which has to do with the fact that any perceptual act carries with it a horizon of anticipations. So perception is a temporal process; it is oriented toward future experiences and at the same time it is an experience of enduring past experiences. There is even a "horizon of the past," the potential to awake recollections. In his later work Husserl was concerned to explain how the horizons of our experience interrelate so they produce our experience of the world, which led him to emphasis on the actual lived world and how experience generates historical and cultural consciousness. This is especially true in his (1970) final unfinished work on *The Crisis of the European Sciences*. Obviously these horizons are extremely important limiting factors in our understanding and perception of the phenomena presented to us by our patients.

Husserl's concept of the horizon is especially developed in his (1977) Cartesian Meditations. In that work, and in *The Crisis of European Sciences*, Husserl focussed on how scientific consciousness and its guiding principles of rational investigation emerged out of ordinary nontheoretical forms of everyday lived consciousness and its practices. For Husserl the life-world is the world of pretheoretical experience that leads to our interaction with nature and the capacity to develop our own cultural forms.

It was Hans-Georg Gadamer, following Heidegger, who emphasized the essential connection between phenomenology and hermeneutics since both are concerned with describing the process of interpretation, by which meaning emerges. In describing Gadamer's approach, Moran (2000) writes:

> Philosophy, then, is a conversation leading towards mutual understanding, a conversation, furthermore, where this very understanding comes as something genuinely *experienced*. Moreover, the practice of phenomenology is the best way to access properly and describe the *experience of understanding* itself. (249)

This approach should be extremely familiar to anyone who practices psychoanalysis. Gadamer holds that meaning emerges in a dialectic between the patient and the therapist and always arrives beyond the intentions of the speakers. So Gadamer (1989) writes, "A genuine conversation is never the one we wanted to conduct" (383). What Gadamer tried to do is to apply the phenomenologic method to study the very notion of understanding and interpretation itself, a study which is of great significance to psychoanalysts.

Whether Gadamer succeeded in his phenomenologic account that concludes with a kind of transcendental description of the conditions which make understanding possible is an issue beyond the scope of this chapter. Certainly his work deeply influenced the relational school of psychoanalysis, as for example presented by Mitchell (1997). But Gadamer's work is not as relativistic as the thought of intersubjectivists in psychoanalysis. He believed that Husserl was right in viewing understanding as having to take place within our horizon, as mentioned above, but that our horizon can be fused with the horizon of the other person, leading to mutual understanding and agreement in the exploration of truth. This is borrowing from phenomenology, for Gadamer has taken over Husserl's notion of the inner and outer horizons in an act of perception. So Gadamer's hermeneutics, upon which certain psychoanalytic theorists have based so much, is in turn based on Husserl's phenomenology and Heidegger's modification of it. The late professor Gadamer said (personal communication) that he actually had trouble for many years writing out his views because he always felt that Heidegger was looking over his shoulder, and indeed he was a pupil of both Husserl and Heidegger.

Two other famous thinkers in psychology employed phenomenology in their methods. The first of these, Jean-Paul Sartre, was deeply influenced by Husserl's phenomenology in his early work, and even more influenced by his reading of Heidegger's *Being and Time*, but he took the work of Husserl and Heidegger in an entirely different direction than it was intended by their originators. I think Sartre simply presents an artistic insight into the world rather than a formal phenomenologic study, but his insights are of great interest to psychoanalysts. He was a great psychologist and offered what might be called a kind of phenomenologic study of personal betrayal and self-recognition as well as of the dynamics of one's engagement with others. For example, he writes about the experience of being caught as a voyeur, of encountering others in public, of deciding whether or not to have a sexual affair on a date, or whether to become a resistance fighter or stay at home and take care of one's mother. The first volume of Sartre's (1981) *The Family Idiot*, should be mandatory reading for any psychoanalyst. I (1992b; 1999b) have discussed Sartre's retrogressive/progressive method and used his "phenomenological" approach in a clinical study of Ezra Pound and a composite neurotic character named "Barry." But Sartre's (1973) famous work, *Being and Nothingness*, although it is given the title of "Essay on Phenomenological Ontology," is really a traditional kind of speculative metaphysics of the very kind repudiated by the phenomenological tradition prior to Sartre's time. Characteristically, borrowing from Husserl, Sartre himself claimed that *Being and Nothingness* was an eidetic analysis of "bad faith," a situation where a person is denying their true choice or separating their desire from their decision. This is a variation on Heidegger's famous concepts of authenticity and inauthenticity.

Finally, psychoanalysts should keep in mind the phenomenological psychological work of Merleau-Ponty (1962). I agree with Merleau-Ponty's view that Hegel, and the young Marx (1844) who wrote *Economic and Philosophical Manuscripts*, were phenomenologists of concrete social life rather than originators of abstract distant and arid intellectual systems. At one point Merleau-Ponty held the chair of child psychology at the Sorbonne, a position later held by Jean Piaget. Merleau-Ponty was extremely interested in the child's perception of the world; he argued that the very basis of the child's developing sense of self was the encounter with other people and the encounter with language. But Merleau-Ponty thought that even language was grounded in perception, and of special interest to psychoanalysts. He repeatedly emphasized the role of the body in our primordial perception of the world. Merleau-Ponty used Husserlian reduction as a way to lead back to the preverbal basis of our experience, which for him comes from a combination of our perceptual organs with their own particular strengths or weaknesses and the unique structure of our specific bodies. For example, he (1967) analyses the unusual aspects of El Greco's style of art, which has commonly been ascribed to El Greco's astigmatism, an accident of his bodily constitution. His point is that this physical defect was taken up and integrated into El Greco's life as a whole, who transformed it into his well-known style. So our specific life experiences, especially before sophisticated verbal thought has been attained, are formed out of the contingencies of our physical situation and the particular environment into which we thrown at birth. Our task is to somehow integrate all this and make this contingent realm our own.

As Erwin Straus often did, Merleau-Ponty illustrates this by studying people with physical defects. When the physical systems are malfunctioning, only then can we understand their role in the formation of our experience of the world, because when our physical systems are functioning properly they are apparently invisible. For example, ordinarily we are unaware of our cardiac functioning, but anyone who suffers from heart disease such as atrial fibrillation can attest to the profound influence of cardiac dysfunction on one's entire mental state, philosophy, ideation, and preoccupations! He drew on the well known studies of brain damage performed by Kurt Goldstein, whose work also influenced the work of Frieda Fromm-Reichmann. His master work (1962) *The Phenomenology of Perception*, although extremely difficult, will enormously reward the psychoanalyst who studies it with care.

Merleau-Ponty's studies of the nature of human bodily being-in-the-world are an important detailed example of how phenomenology can interact with the natural sciences orientation to provide a more general and complete account of the phenomena that we encounter in our psychoanalytic work. As Hans Georg Gadamer put it, scientific truths do not constitute the whole of truth. The Copernican discovery of the motion of the earth does not negate what represents the truth-for-us of the rising and the setting of the sun.

5

The Secret Life of the Psychoanalyst

Perusing the psychoanalytic literature reveals a scattering of papers hinting that even the best theorists in the various schools of psychoanalysis do not, in the privacy of their offices, meticulously practice as prescribed by their specific theoretical orientation. This leads to a number of problems that perhaps it is time to bring out into the light.

For example, Rangell (1974) points out that as analysts we must justify a treatment that goes on for an indeterminate number of years, and it is not sufficient to excuse it by arguing that the patient would be in a mental hospital without it. He points out, as others have also done, that being in analysis four or five times a week can become a way of life and even a substitute for ordinary life and its responsibilities. It is the obligation of the analyst to prevent this from taking place. Rangell is especially hostile to the Jungians and the Kleinians. He writes: "Jung's mysticism does not belong to rational psychoanalysis. And more within the analytic body today, the interpretations of some about the earliest months of human life survive their absurdity for a while only by their shock effect" (6).

SYNDROME OF THE COMPROMISE OF INTEGRITY

Rangell introduces what he calls "the syndrome of the compromise of integrity." This concept has not received the attention it deserves. For him, it represents a struggle between the ego and the superego that results from a constant baseline tension between them. In the compromise of integrity, the superego is partially sacrificed and the ego may deny or postpone its own interests. According to Rangell, the great enemy of integrity is narcissism. Uncontrollable and unsatisfied narcissism forms the strongest motivation to the compromise of integrity. As Rangell puts it, "Instinctual pressures are then to neuroses as ego interests are to the compromises of integrity" (8) and he feels that "the whole question of the relation between the unconscious and responsibility needs, in my opinion, a searching re-examination" (10).

Rangell further and correctly proclaims that "The analytic attitude is in its very essence the model . . . of relentless incorruptibility" (11), and, "Analysis aims at turning out an honest man" (10). But we all know there is a tremendous pressure all day long from patients that arises from sexual and narcissistic aspects of the patient-analyst interaction, which leads to the temptation to abuse transference and to many other unfortunate phenomena. But, as Curtis (1980) points out, sexual feelings of a male analyst for a beautiful woman patient become a source of difficulty "only in proportion to the amount of infantile motivation contributing to the reaction. Experiences of this sort have led to the saying, 'analysis is an old man's game'" (163). Not only sexuality but aggression can attach a patient to an analyst, since the analyst is the only one who does not retaliate against the patient's sadism; the task of the analyst is to interpret. In addition, aggression can be expressed in sadomasochism along with a strong mix of sexuality! Narcissistic rage, which is never far from the surface in the analytic situation, needs to be transformed in order to avoid serious interpersonal disasters. Here is a call for Kohut's (1971) transformations of narcissism into empathy, wisdom, creativity, a sense of humor, and an acceptance of the transience of life with which every analyst by now should be familiar. Unavoidable narcissistic injuries and the concomitant narcissistic rage must also be transformed into modulated, tamed responses as part of every psychoanalysis.

Where does all this stress and pressure of the "impossible profession" lead? According to Sandler (1983), it leads to the conscious or unconscious conviction of many analysts that they are not doing a proper job of psychoanalysis and that colleagues would criticize them if they knew about it. Sandler believes this comes from the fact that:

> Any analyst worth his salt will adapt to specific patients on the basis of his interaction with those patients. He will modify his approach so that he could get as good as possible a working analytic situation developing. To achieve this, he needs to feel relaxed and informal with his patient to an appropriate degree, and at times he might have to depart quite far from 'standard' technique. He may be very comfortable with this as long as it is private rather than public, especially in view of the tendency for colleagues to criticize and 'supervise' one another in clinical discussions, and the ease with which analytic material can be seen and interpreted in different ways. (38)

He concludes that the result of all this is, "psychoanalysts develop implicit theories, concepts and definitions that differ from the 'official' or 'public' formulations" (43). Furthermore, they are more or less aware this is happening, again, as in the compromise of integrity, leading to a tension between the ego and the superego and often to a sense of guilt and discomfort. Sandler also believes that the instinctual drives always should occupy a central position in our psychoanalytic thinking.

Burnout Syndrome

How does this all end up? It proceeds to what Cooper (1986) calls the "burnout syndrome" in psychoanalysts. As he explains, the life course of many analysts "begins with an excess of curative zeal and proceeds in the latter part of their careers toward excessive therapeutic nihilism. Both are serious handicaps to therapeutic effectiveness" (577). Already in 1986, Cooper clearly realized that the choice of analytic theory by a given analyst is inextricably wrapped up with the analyst's personality and character: "analysts will choose the theory that best fits their character and value systems" (583). I have become extremely sensitive to value systems in my own psychoanalytic work and I often compare and contrast my value system with that of the patient sometimes quietly and sometimes quite openly and consciously to initiate a discussion. But even this technique is a function of my character, which tends to be straightforward as well as meditative and philosophical, so I am of course, as we all do, leading with my predominant suit.

Cooper claims that Kohut's theoretical position appeals to analysts who are eager to interact with their patients and perhaps wish to bypass the rage and instead to examine the enfeebled self. This is a debatable point and I have discussed some of the controversies about self psychology elsewhere (1985). Cooper agrees that one has to more or less do what the rules indicate but he also recognizes one must adapt to the needs of each situation. And it is this that leads the interactionists to argue that psychoanalysis in a sense constitutes a series of enactments which then must be analyzed and carefully understood . . . often after they have taken place. Certainly this is an important aspect of our work, but it is not the central aspect. The elucidation of free associations and dream interpretation are the royal road to the unconscious.

We all know that analysts practice in an extraordinarily isolated situation far from the usual checks and balances of public procedures. They have very little opportunity for the usual rewards present in the healing arts. They see very few patients in contrast to other specialties, have a great emotional investment in each patient which makes them subject to very great disappointment, and they must deliberately limit the kind of rewards they allow themselves in their work. Cooper writes: "In general, we do not receive gifts, we do not become social friends with our patients, and we do not enjoy the atmosphere of continuing idealization from our patients, either in analysis or after it, as most other healers do" (592).

He goes on to describe two manifestations of the burnout syndrome. The masochistic manifestations are represented by the depressed bored angry analyst who is irritated with his or her patients, colleagues, and self. As Cooper says, "Depression is always on the horizon for these analysts, apparent in their lack of pleasure in their patients or in the profession of psychoanalysis" (594). The other aspect of the burnout syndrome is narcissistic pathology. Analysts suffering from this tend to abandon neutrality, attempt to be charismatic, intrude on the patient, give advice and education, and try to get the patient's admiration. They are grossly directive and paternalistic and may use their patients vicariously or even directly to meet their own needs. Cooper says they are "prone to respond with attitudes of superiority and superciliousness, toward both their patients and their colleagues" (596). We all know analysts who egregiously manifest these burnout syndrome characteristics, often without insight into their impact on patients, colleagues, friends, and loved ones.

WHAT ARE PSYCHOANALYSTS SUPPOSED TO WANT?

Psychoanalysis can be conceived of as a shared communal belief system subject to constant revision through clinical experience, a revision that each of us ought to be doing all of the time as a consequence of our individual clinical practice and our communications with our colleagues. We need to understand a lot more about the choice of theoretical systems in psychoanalysis. What determines our choices of models? How do they affect the "data" gathered in the psychoanalytic treatment? How do they affect the psychoanalytic treatment process itself? How does one go about using more than one model in the most efficient and effective manner in our psychoanalytic work? These are questions that should be going through the mind of every analyst as he or she works with every patient.

This leads to the whole question of what psychoanalysts want. Sandler and Dreher (1996) have reviewed the changing aims of psychoanalytic treatment as theories change. For example, Ferenczi advocated a reeducation of the patient's character. Sandler himself hopes for a change of attitude toward inner objects, the adaptation of new solutions, and the capacity to accept back the unacceptable aspects of the self. I much agree with this although it is a somewhat limited object relations approach. Kohut's (1971) depiction of the transformations of narcissism mentioned above offers well known goals, and self psychologists aim in that direction.

Kantrowitz (1996) briefly reviews the various theories of cure, offering appropriate bibliographic references. These include Freud's original ideas that cure was effected (1) by making the unconscious conscious, (2) by the importance of the affective bond with the analyst and (3) by the working through of conflict. For Kantrowitz, the process of therapy may be described as:

> first requiring an analysis of resistance and a making of the unconscious conscious through interpretation, along with the establishment of the affective bond between patient and analyst. Next there is the repeated experience of powerful past relationships in the transference. Gradually, through understanding, explanation, and ever-increasing tolerance for the affect stimulated, a new sense of self and possibilities evolves. (213)

Object relations theory has emphasized the provision of a new object as a model for identification and a facilitator of organization, while self psychology offers the provision of a selfobject to enable the transmuting internalization of self-soothing and to firm up cohesion of the self. Gedo emphasized the acquiring of missing psychological skills and accepting realistic limitations, and a number of important authors have emphasized the value of tension regulation, especially in preoedipally damaged patients.

Relational psychoanalysts have currently focussed on the importance of the here-and-now to explain the crucial factors in the development of the transference In this most recent approach, Hartmann's ego psychology paradigm has been shifted to the relational, the interactional, the interpersonal, and the subjectivistic and constructivist perspectives in the psychoanalytic process. These factors or explanatory concepts are now given an important position alongside of or even superceding the interpretive process. The treatment process is thought to lead by means of repetitive working through via understanding of enactments and of the here and now relationship to insight and desired change.

But the treatment goals for the patient also are inextricably related to the life goals of the analyst. The pressure of the analyst's implicit or explicit value system has an important influence on the whole changing character of the patient and it is not quite accurate to lump all this pressure under the term countertransference. It is better to distinguish between the analyst's characterology, defensive systems, and explicit and implicit value systems, and reserve countertransference to those specific aspects of the analyst's enactments and internal psychic experiences that are related to the presentations from the specific patient with whom he or she is interacting. This is very tricky and still needs many professional symposia for colleagues to discuss it in detail.

Sandler and Dreher (1996) point out that both partners change in a psychoanalysis. Kantrowitz (1996) tried to study this change in detail, claiming that what evolves in the analytic process is not predetermined but is context-dependent. This is debatable. Factors in the patient that stimulate the analyst, she says, are similarities between the patient and the analyst, a quality or characteristic in the patient that is better than the analyst, interpretations patients make of the analyst's countertransference or personality, and an understanding of transference-countertransference enactments. Kantrowitz points out: "As the patient's transference emerges, and focus is placed on the analyst, the analyst has the opportunity to consider what aspects of himself or herself have contributed to the patient's current experience in more subtle ways" (213).

ILLUSTRATION OF AN ANALYST'S "PARTIAL PRIVATE SCHEMATA"

An excellent case example that should be required reading for all analytic candidates is presented by Mayer (1998). She examines what happens in an analysis when public and private theory diverge. She reports about a consultation with a colleague who had become increasingly attracted to a female patient to the point where he was disturbed and frightened by the extent to which he was starting to allow himself to be physically involved with her. She noted that he did impressive analytic work with this patient for two years, had a good understanding of her dynamics, and had channeled this into insight and interpretation. The patient responded well and it seemed that the analyst was describing a treatment "thoroughly in line with a public theory of analytic technique that has characterized mainstream American psychoanalysis for many years. He, as analyst, viewed his analytic function primarily in terms of facilitating his patient's transferences and interpreting both her transferences and resistances to them. He had maintained a conventionally neutral and abstinent stance in the service of accomplishing both these tasks" (161). At the same time, however, another thread in his view of the treatment appeared. Mayer refers to Sandler's concept of "partial private schemata," characterized in this instance by a strong liking for the patient and a particular wish to help her, more care for her than he felt about his other patients. What was remarkable and important was that this unusual extent of caring clearly had been very good for the patient, and this did not fit the analyst's analytic theory!

The dichotomy between what the analyst knew to be the proper analytic approach and his personal emotional involvement of a high intensity with this specific patient produced a feeling of guilt and shame to the point where the analyst ceased to feel like a "real" analyst practicing "real" analysis. The analyst was filled with shame and a feeling of being a fraud. Mayer argues that this conflict was derived rather paradoxically from the analyst's knowledge that his nonneutral, nonabstinent stance had actually been helpful to the patient and her analysis! He was "stuck with a 'partial, private schema' which refused to coexist happily with his public theory of technique" (164). The conflict went underground and as a result started to become expressed as enactment.

Of course it is possible to interpret this in a number of ways; for example, we know little about the inner psyche of this analyst and whether he was suffering from an archaic countertransference, nor do we know why he became so involved with this specific patient. I have mentioned above the important concept of Curtis (1980), maintaining it is only when the infantile roots of the analyst's needs become involved in his sexual interest in the patient that there is a tendency to get into trouble. The point of this particular situation is that we need to become more aware of our value systems and how these value systems express themselves in the privacy of our consulting room, and can do so sometimes in a way that seems to violate our formal psychoanalytic theory. There has to be some kind of capacity in our thinking to bring these aspects of our relationship with the patient into conscious understanding; doing so actually serves as a preventive against boundary violations. Of course the best way to accomplish this is through consultation with a sophisticated senior colleague, but my experience is that consultation frequently does not happen when enactments begin and the analyst begins sliding down the slippery slope of boundary violations.

THE ANALYST'S VALUE SYSTEM
AND GOALS OF TREATMENT

The impossible profession of psychoanalysis is turning out to be even more difficult and complicated then it was envisioned to be by its founder, Sigmund Freud. Certainly Freud did not hesitate to inject his value system rather strenuously into the analytic process and he was rather abrupt and blunt about it. At times he simply dismissed patients because he found them boring, uninteresting, or disreputable. He did not hesitate to lecture and educate and advise. This was easier to do in his era when there was a prevalent middle-class value system generally accepted by everyone in his milieu, in contrast to our present postmodern era that is characterized by a clashing of equivalent contemporary varieties of life styles. It is the responsibility, demanding and stemming from the absolutely necessary honesty and integrity of the psychoanalyst, to bring these value system factors out into the open as part of the psychoanalytic process.

The atmosphere of the psychoanalytic process is importantly established depending on how the psychoanalyst has solved his or her own intrapsychic problems of greed, envy, and the need for gratification from patients and from analytic work. One of the most important measures of this intrapsychic state of the analyst is found in his or her procedure of the setting of analytic fees. Erle (1993) begins a discussion of this by reminding us of the narcissistic mortification and the injury to the analyst's feelings of self-worth at this current time when appropriate analytic cases are so difficult to find. He suggests that patients should not be told they are being given a reduced fee in order to enable them to have analytic treatment because this can lead to serious transference issues. He does not wish the patient to be burdened by the analyst "with the importance of seeing the analyst as someone whose work commands a higher fee than the patient can pay. Neither the patient nor the analyst is 'reduced' or made 'special' by the arrangement" (107). He suggests it is better to tell the patient that the analyst has a fee range and to set the fee at whatever part of that range the patient can afford, with the implication that anything within that range is an appropriate and acceptable fee. This of course makes a great deal of sense and shows some genuine empathy with suffering people.

There is so much disagreement among psychoanalytic approaches today that it has even been suggested that the term "wild analysis" needs to be eliminated (Schaefer 1985). Allison (2000) quotes Orgel as saying at a meeting of the American Psychoanalytic Association, "Every analyst must struggle with his or her own resistances to accomplish successful analytic work" (539). Unfortunately these inner resistances are fortified and strengthened by the current shifting and changing psychoanalytic ambiance in which so many theories conflict, and by the general ambiance of our contemporary postmodern culture itself, where truth seems to be in eclipse along with morality and belief in transcendence. George Orwell (1968) wrote:

> There is some hope that the liberal habit of mind, which thinks of truth as something outside yourself, something to be discovered, and not as something you can make up as you go along will survive. . . . The feeling that the very concept of objective truth is fading out of the world frightens me more than bombs (II., 258–259, III., 88–89).

For example, Ryan (2000) objects to the increasing trend among artists and dramatists to encourage audience participation. Similarly the current plethora of high technology gadgets in our museums shifts the focus from the art product itself onto the recipient or audience for the product. As an illustration of this, the recent "Sensation" exhibit in London in 1997, that was brought to New York in 1999 and stirred up a hornet's nest of excitement, gave the impression that the artists were primarily trying to get a rise out of the audience rather than to express anything in the way of beauty or truth. An enormous foolish and noisy political controversy was the result.

Ryan points out that it was the major contribution of the early Greek thinkers to stand back, contemplate, and reflect on the day-to-day life of the individual and the community rather than to be caught up in the immediacy of existence, in the here-and-now chaos. He writes, "It was the separation of culture from day-to-day life that marked the highest achievement of the civilization of ancient Greece" (160). In order to develop the powers of contemplation, reflection, understanding, and insight there has to be a certain distance between the analyst and the patient just as there has to be a distance between the subject and the object as a work of art or the object to be studied in order to obtain knowledge:

> This critical distance is essential in order to separate the recipient from immediacy and the everyday concerns with which we are all bound up. By entering into a relationship with the object from a point of critical distance, the recipient can begin to form a view that is more than an immediate first impression and is more all-rounded and objective. The more this capacity is exercised, the more balanced becomes the sense of judgment and objectivity. (161)

A derivative of this approach is Anna Freud's contention that the analyst should be equidistant from the patient's ego, superego, and id.

The eclipse of truth, of morality, and of belief in transcendence has been labeled a philosophic disaster by Polanyi (2000). Essentially this consists of the collapse of the philosophic foundations of rationalism: "Universal standards of human behaviour having fallen into philosophic disrepute, various substitutes were put forward in their place" (233). This eclipse of thought and collapse of rationalism has many deleterious consequences for the human species and it leads to the scientific attitude towards humans as expressed, for example, by the famous Stephen Hawking, who viewed humanity as chemical scum on a remote and insignificant planet.

In our postmodern era Heidegger (1977) has referred to the "enframing" (*Ge-stell*) of humans as "things" to be stockpiled, manipulated, and exploited in the age of technology, posing a threat to the future of our species. In enframing, the human is sucked up in a frenzy of disposing, the placing of objects for material use in production. Knowledge supposedly obtained by the subject about objects now becomes replaced by mastery—the power of having something at one's disposal, and so people become objects or things viewed for this purpose. It is the enframing attitude that leads to the holocaust and such contemporary phenomena as ethnic cleansing. Some intersubjectivists seem to be oblivious to the implications of their approach, which brings us back to the beginning of this chapter and the importance of value systems. It makes an enormous difference to a patient whether the analyst feels that all truth is relative and contextually created, a kind of "narrative truth" (Spence 1982), or whether the analyst has some firm convictions about the existence of historical truth, and about what is good, what is valuable, and what is beautiful. As Freud said, what is moral is self-evident. Freud's nineteenth-century view that there are fixed universal self-evident principles of truth and morality is precisely what has collapsed in our contemporary era, and the shift in conceptualizing the psychoanalytic process is primarily a derivative of this contemporary philosophic disaster.

CIVILITY AND "MATURE RELIGIOSITY"

Consider the philosophy of R. G. Collingwood (1939, 1940, 1942, 1946). Collingwood was aware that science had nothing to say on the really fundamental questions of life such as value systems. His notion of metaphysics was that it is an historical science, studying a culture's absolute presuppositions and showing how these change from one set of presuppositions to another. For Collingwood, a civilization is only safe if it believes its own grounding presuppositions. For him, civilization is an activity of the mind, an approximation to an ideal state. He emphasized the possibility of an ideal of universal civility (1942): civility on every kind of occasion, civility under any kind of provocation, civility to every kind of person:

> In this minimal sense the language of civility is one of abstention; it is a virtue of forbearance or restraint, moderation and discipline, a virtue satisfied by *not* doing that which may be offensive, disrespectful or intimidatory. Civility can refer to the ways we respond to the moral demands which are independent of it. (Johnson 1998, 109)

For Collingwood, absolute presuppositions, a subclass of which are what I have referred to as value systems, are not atemporal entities; rather, they are historically bound to their culture. They appear as latent assumptions behind manifest intentions in the predominant texts of a culture, and sometimes need great effort to be extracted. They must be uncovered or excavated in archaeological fashion and this can be done only in retrospect. This is exactly the problem of the hidden value systems behind our psychoanalytic clinical practices.

For Collingwood, civility as an ideal gains its most significance from religion: "The vital warmth at the heart of a civilization is what we call a religion. Religion is the passion which inspires a society to persevere in a certain way of life and to obey the rules which define it" (Johnson 1998, 116). Kernberg (2000a) points out that Freud's faith in the triumph of reason and his belief that morality could arise from reason missed the unconscious primitive aggression and unconscious sexual motivation that infiltrate reason and even determined the entire calamitous history of the twentieth century. Masses of humans can suddenly shift their behavior to sanction social violence and instant mass psychology is created by the media—especially television with its "inevitable regressive potential" (471). For Kernberg:

> Mature religiosity includes an integrated value system that transcends the individual's interest, and has truly universal validity that applies to all human beings. It is a comprehensive and harmonious system, and its fundamental principles are love and respect of others and of the self. It includes a sense of responsibility for this value system that transcends all concrete laws, and expects such a sense of responsibility also on the part of other human beings, but with understanding, compassion, and concern in combination with a sense of universal justice. (472–473)

Kernberg goes on to enlarge on the conception of what he calls a mature religiosity as including such capacities as that for reconciliation, forgiveness, and prohibitions against murder and incest. He concludes:

> Mature religiosity includes the investment of work and creativity as a contribution to the creation of what is good, and the struggle against destructiveness . . . respect for the rights of others, and tolerance for unavoidable envy and greediness without letting them control one's own behavior. (473)

I question whether the term "religiosity" is a good choice in this age of lunatic fundamentalism. I have suggested (1999b) adding to it Jaspers' concept of "ciphers" (1932c) that might point the way to a transcendent basis for "religiosity" as Kernberg has defined it, and differentiate it from dogmatic religious systems and their interminable violent confrontations. We psychoanalysts must understand and emphasize, as Kernberg (2000a) does, "the irreducible nature of the aspiration for a universal ethical system that transcends the rational needs of the individual" (474).

Whether the psychoanalyst likes it or not, there is an implicit value system transmitted to the patient even in his or her diagnostic evaluation and certainly in the everyday interaction of the treatment process. These value systems of the analyst, as those of the patient, are of course compromise formations which the ego develops as it deals in childhood with its three harsh masters—the id, the superego, and the external world. To ignore them is to miss a significant dimension of what is transmitted between patient and analyst over years of intensive exposure to each other. Even Kernberg, in the conclusion to his discussion of the religious experience, emphasizing the psychoanalyst's function of freeing the patient from unconscious conflicts that limit the patient's capability of developing mature religiosity, does not sufficiently recognize the impact of the analyst's own mature religiosity or lack thereof on the patient's subsequent development and change in his or her value system. Although in that sense the analyst is a new object, we must fundamentally view the analyst as a relatively neutral objective observer who does not crucially contribute to the actual formation of the patient's new compromise solutions.

THE REAL PERSON OF THE PSYCHOANALYST

The fundamental techniques of psychoanalysis include free association, frequency, regularity, recumbency, the analyst's general passivity, relative neutrality, abstinence, and confinement to interpretation according to the classical view, as proclaimed, for example, by Gill (1954) in his well-known earlier work (see Gill 1984 for his radical revision of this view). But the trouble with this formulation is that it is too simplistic; we have achieved an increasing recognition of the extreme complexity of the psychoanalytic process. Ferenczi's elevation of the analytic relationship as a central vehicle of therapeutic change to an equal importance alongside Freud's focus on interpretation has gained increasing acceptance in our time. The debate remains unresolved over whether the therapeutic power of psychoanalysis should be attributed to the verbal-interpretive function of the analyst or to the emotionally involved and responsive analyst asserting his analytic powers through all aspects of his affectively intense relationship to the patient, or to some combination of these factors.

Wallerstein (1999) emphasized the transition of psychoanalysis into worldwide theoretical diversity and the dependence of theoretical orientations on local social and cultural factors, a fact that I (1992b, 2000b) have repeatedly referred to in calling for a Nietzschean style genealogical study of what is considered "truth" and of choice of theories among psychoanalysts in various countries. The eminent British psychoanalyst Steiner (1984) also insisted: "Despite the universality of the process of the unconscious, psychoanalysis is considerably influenced by the historical, cultural, and social context in which it is developing" (233). This does not mean these overarching theoretical perspectives have equal status however, since they are not equal in ultimate explanatory power. We hope that eventually there will be greater correspondences between the constructs of the theory and the relationships between the observables in our consulting room.

We are only now beginning to understand the powerful effect of the real person of the analyst, of the intensity of his or her emotional involvement with patient over many years, of the special qualities that inevitably evolve in each individual's analytic situation, and of the use, wittingly or unwittingly, of noninterpretive interventions. This requires the reassessment of our conceptions of analytic abstinence, anonymity, and neutrality. There is a gradually developing consensus that the sicker patient, who suffers from developmental pathology, requires the provision of support, the role of new experience, and, as Gedo (1979) puts it, the correcting of "apraxias," defects in basic social habits of living. This sicker group is characterized by unreliability of object contact or object constancy; failure to tame drives or to develop stable defenses; deficiencies in self-esteem, in frustration tolerance, and in affect modulation; and a blurring of self and object boundaries.

In psychoanalysis the replay of old scenarios, dyadic and triadic including strong negative transferences, is given the greatest opportunity to be manifested and to be successfully interpreted and worked through in the here and now. One way to look at it has been presented by Arlow and Brenner (1988), who describe the psychoanalytic process as one in which interpretations destabilize the equilibrium of forces that are in conflict in the patient's psyche, which leads to a growing awareness and understanding of these conflicts, working through, and new conflict resolution through more adaptive and less self-defeating compromise formations.

Our theories and our personalities always have distorting consequences on whatever appears in the analytic situation, and this is what produces the exceedingly frustrating paradox that all great conflicting theorists in our field have found clinical material in their patients that they believe validates their theories. But in each person there are certain essential patterns that are built into the fabric of the self or, looking at it from a differing theoretical viewpoint, constitute primary ego mechanisms or defense transferences, that will be revealed sooner or later in any well-conducted analysis. There is no doubt that patients gain an enormous amount of knowledge about us as time passes over years of intensive treatment and that it is impossible to maintain strict neutrality. But it *is* possible to maintain relative neutrality and objectivity, and that is very important to understanding the infantile roots of the transference, which is what psychoanalysis is all about.

Pine (1998) points out that "Psychoanalysis is a highly individual activity, shaped by the personal history, character, and professional training of each practitioner and generally modified over time by clinical experience" (33). We are becoming increasingly aware of this fact and moving steadily away from Freud's positivistic nineteenth-century epistemology assuming the psychoanalyst is the neutral detached scientist. As a result of this patients are learning even more directly about our personalities, our compromise formations, and our value systems. Pine recognizes that a whole variety of interventions and enactments go on inevitably during the process of psychoanalysis besides interpretation that have a powerful effect on the patient. The critical task to produce a successful psychoanalysis is to loosen the patient's clinging to internalized parental objects; a wide range of interventions are necessary to do this.

Interpretation alone is not sufficient and in no psychoanalysis do the interventions consist solely of interpretations no matter how hard the analyst attempts to constrict interventions in that fashion. Even the theory-bound effort to restrict all interventions to interpretations gives a strong message about the personality of the analyst to the patient and constitutes, from the patient's point of view, an enactment. It is an enactment that the analyst is producing, whether the analyst is willing to admit it or not. These days such an admission is easier to make and accept than it was forty years ago. As Pine says, "Were we a fly on the wall in any particular analyst's office, we would see highly individualized ways of working that reflect personal style" (67).

Nothing I have written in this chapter is to be interpreted as advocating deliberate self-disclosure. I tend to do this at times with patients in psychotherapy who have been surrounded by parental hypocrisy and denial, for in such patients a modest amount of self-disclosure, as Pine says, "seemed to play an extremely significant and beneficial role at a certain point in the analysis" (79). But this is dangerous ground because it offers a fertile field for the analyst's exhibitionism and the utilization of the patient as a mirroring selfobject for the analyst or even as an analyst for the analyst. Pine agrees with the point of view I have repeatedly expressed when he writes, "the therapeutic action of psychoanalysis derives from various intertwinings of understanding and of the patient-analyst relationship . . . the actuality of the therapeutic impact is endlessly variable—dependent on features of the patient, the analyst, and the pair" (84).

The self psychologist Anna Ornstein (1999) states: "The analyst's theory and personal beliefs are recognized not only as powerfully influencing the reorganization of the structures of the patient's self but as crucial in bringing about analytic change" (386). Ornstein points out that "Self-empathy (self-acceptance) is indeed a crucial development in the analytic process, primarily because it is the acceptance of the 'sick' or 'childish' in oneself that will make pathological behavior based on defensive psychological structures unnecessary" (389). It is inconceivable that this form of self acceptance could develop without an interchange or at least an influence from the analyst's own value system and hopefully mature personality.

THE ANALYST'S UNCONSCIOUS LONGINGS

The matter is made infinitely more complicated by the fact that the analyst has also an unconscious value system which may be contradictory to his or her conscious beliefs. For example, Gabbard (2000) explains that among the set of unconscious longings that leads an analyst into this field is his or her wishing to experience the patient's gratitude for the analyst's hard work and dedication. He says, "Gratitude implies a specific form of object relationship involving a selfless devoted helper and appreciative patient who acknowledges having been helped. This much desired mode of relatedness may be designed to repair internal object relations from the past in which we did not feel properly appreciated and validated. As analysts gain experience, they learn that this sought after form of relatedness may be thwarted at every turn by certain patients" (707). He adds the caveat that some patients may express gratitude in the hope of receiving further benevolent treatment and as a defense against a negative transference. Attempting continual self analysis of one's unconscious value systems is clearly required in the analytic process because, as Gabbard points out, patients who absorb information about our unconscious desires to use other people as selfobjects may either play the role that we desire them to play, interfering with their analysis and their capacity to develop and mature, or deliberately thwart that role for the pleasure of locking us in a sadomasochistic torment situation that goes on forever.

Coen (2000) carries this further by suggesting that "In the face of analytic impasse analysts should consider whether they might temporarily have joined the patient in mutually regressive wishes that have taken them away from more responsible analytic functioning" (785). Here lies an inherent danger in overtly discussing value systems with patients. As Coen points out, the wish to regress involves the wish to return to infantile modes of relatedness, a pathological object relationship that precludes separateness and interferes with healthy competence, growth, and individuation. An example of the mutual regression in the psychoanalytic process would be the wish to participate in a parent-child relationship, which, as already pointed out by Gabbard, can take a familiar sadomasochistic form. Coen writes: "We can consider as regression any wishful movement of the analyst out of the position of thoughtful, focussed attention on the analysand's needs and conflicts to a less differentiated relatedness, much more determined by the analyst's own needs and conflicts" (795).

CLINICAL VIGNETTES

John Ruskin (Batchelor 2000) once said there is no wealth but life, including all its powers of love, joy, and admiration. In outlining a value system he claimed that a person is richest who, having perfected the functions of his or her own life to the utmost, also has the widest helpful influence, both personal and by means of possessions, over the lives of others. This sounds simple, but when one attempts to apply it to the everyday practice of psychoanalysis it quickly becomes very complicated and conflictual. For example, there are suicidal patients who stir up in therapists the feeling that they really should be able to do something to prevent the suicide. In many instances there is really nothing more the therapist can do except hospitalization and it is necessary for a therapist to recognize humbly that when the chips are down there is very little a therapist can do ultimately to keep a patient alive. Many therapists have great problems with this and, as has been studied recently (Goode 2001), there is often very little support among one's colleagues for the therapist whose patient has committed suicide. The damage done to the psyche of the therapist may be quite long lasting.

Beside dealing with the ever-present risk of suicide, which often represents a form of murderous rage against family and/or therapist, there are many other instances where the therapist is called upon to make decisions that immediately reveal his or her conscious or unconscious value system. I wish to present two case vignettes that illustrate this situation from my own practice. The first of these cases was of a thirty-one-year-old woman physician patient who consulted me about ten years ago for severe bulimirexia and compulsive exercising. She had been to a number of institutions in an attempt to alleviate this situation without success and had been essentially given up on by a number of therapists and teams. After several years of intensive psychoanalytic treatment carried out on the couch in standard fashion, these symptoms were almost entirely alleviated and she began a series of sexual affairs, always choosing men who made it clear they did not love her. When each of these affairs disintegrated the patient suffered devastating physical accidents.

I presented this dramatic case in detail elsewhere.[1] What I concentrate on here is the dilemma these accidents present to the analyst. In the first place, they were so devastating that the patient could not work, in one instance for a year and a half, and in another instance for about three months. During these periods she had no funds available to pay for therapy as there was no insurance coverage for psychoanalysis or psychoanalytic therapy available to her. Until that time she had been consistently paying for the treatment out of her earnings and it had seemed that the treatment would be successful.

The accidents totally disrupted the treatment program and rendered her essentially helpless. What was the therapist to do; how was the treatment to continue under these conditions? There were only two alternatives. Either the patient had to discontinue therapy during a crisis in her life because of inability to pay, or funds needed to be found. Perhaps a saintly analyst would have continued to see her three times a week and charge nothing for a year and a half. I felt unable to do that because I was afraid of the resentment it might stir up in me, especially since I had a waiting list of patients who were quite willing and able to pay for psychoanalytic treatment. What I did was to help her to write to every conceivable organization I could find all over the United States, trying to raise money in a grant for her. I was eventually successful in finding a grantor who sponsored one session a week during the year and a half that she was unable to work. I took on this responsibility of finding the grant myself because the patient was so physically incapacitated and had no family support, although she did cooperate with filling out forms, submitting to interviews, et cetera. By means of this grant we were able to maintain a formal contact during the period of her convalescence and rehabilitation.

A year or two later after another disappointing love affair, the patient suffered yet another accident. This time she was incapacitated to the point where she could not leave her home and so it was not even possible to see her *pro bono*! Here I came up with the idea of communicating with her by e-mail and I carried on an extensive e-mail correspondence with her over the period of several months when she could not come into the office. The general feeling I had with this patient was of trying to hang on tenaciously in order to treat someone who was unconsciously determined to destroy herself, in the hope of aborting the self-destruction that was taking place through her lethal tendency to destroy parts of her body through accidents, surgical procedures, and so forth. The treatment was ultimately quite successful,[2] but clearly a value system was presented to this patient that is quite different from that of her family, who long ago decided to have nothing to do with her.

Had I also decided to have nothing to do with her for financial reasons or out of sheer frustration with such a difficult patient, I would have been expressing a different value system, one more congruent with what she had grown used to expect both from her family and, unfortunately, from her medical colleagues and various mental health professionals who previously treated her and abandoned her when she ran out of money. Notice that it does not follow from this that my approach will ultimately have a favorable influence on the outcome of the treatment of other patients. Of course I hope it will! My point is that in such crises the analyst has no choice but to express a value system in one way or another: decisions simply must be made.

Some years later I was consulted by another woman physician in her forties because her behavior and fierce temper had caused her a number of self-defeating disappointments both at work and in her personal relationships. The patient had recently married with great hopes for success in this, her second marriage. But she soon found herself suffering from episodes of rage and depression similar to what she had experienced for many years in her first marriage and other interpersonal relationships. It was apparent this was an excellent marriage with a good prognosis if the patient somehow could express her rage and dysthymia in a less self-defeating way both at work and at home. Here again the analyst is faced with a choice. Clearly the patient needs psychoanalysis because there is severe underlying conflictual character pathology that is ruining her life. At the same time the situation is one of marital crisis in a new marriage which must be immediately addressed or the second marriage will fail with the consequent devastation to the patient's self-esteem in a patient already depressed and feeling despair and hopeless at times. The classical analytic stance of neutrality and abstinence without parameters would undoubtedly have resulted in the latter consequence; the situation was urgent.

Drawing on my experience with the first of the two patients described here I decided to try to interpose a barrier between upsurges in the patient's anger and despair, and her explosive and self-defeating expression of it in her interpersonal relations. I suggested that when she felt enraged or depressed between our three times weekly psychoanalytic sessions she should write all about it immediately and send it to me by e-mail first before she takes any action or makes any decisions. Here again a value system is involved; I deliberately intruded myself into this patient's psychic life at the beginning of the treatment in order to protect her from the consequences of her own character pathology. I felt I could not wait until the unconscious roots of her self-defeating behavior would be uncovered in the transference and through the discussion of her childhood relationships.

Fortunately this patient, like the other one, was educated, articulate, and quite capable of carrying on an e-mail correspondence. Still there were many interesting vicissitudes in this correspondence. The patient, an intelligent woman, in a self-defeating way would occasionally either lose my responses to her e-mail or send her e-mail in such a way that it got misdirected or erased before it came to me. This led to the first major transference phenomena of the treatment, although it took place outside of my office. When I did not receive an e-mail I obviously did not respond, and when I did respond to received e-mails and she lost the response, the result was the same; the patient was convinced that I had double-crossed her by encouraging her to e-mail and then refusing to bother with her. We were able to discuss the roots of this and the transference aspects of it in considerable detail, leading to a major dent in the patient's quasi-paranoid defensiveness, and enabling her to begin to develop a dependent transference and reveal some of the longings and weaknesses that were under her irritable, explosive, and prickly external behavior.

This innovation eventually enabled the patient to get into a more formal psychoanalytically oriented treatment. Otherwise the crises of her marriage would have destroyed the treatment and possibly herself before it even began. The explosions at home were gradually replaced by e-mail and eventually even that became unnecessary as the patient's internal controls strengthened through insight gained by interpretation and exploration of the childhood roots of her insecurity and mistrust. None of this is consistent with traditional psychoanalytic technique, but these patients are not typical psychoanalytic patients, they must be somehow be enabled to enter into the psychoanalytic situation and continue in it. My willingness to allow this patient to e-mail me at any time when she felt threatened internally with a potential explosion was an expression of my willingness to serve her as an accessory ego or selfobject at a time when she was desperately in need of it.

She once wondered why I did not charge for the time spent at the computer with her and she pointed out that if I were a lawyer every one of those minutes would receive billing. I responded this was not how I practiced medicine; I set a fee for the patient's sessions that I feel is fair to that patient and that fee includes whatever is involved in the treatment process. Here again we have the overt and unavoidable expression of a value system. It would not have been unethical, in my opinion, to charge extra for time spent at the computer, but it would have transformed a selfobject service into a fee-for-service procedure that the patient could have then used to verify her paranoid stance and reinforce the malevolent transformation (Sullivan 1953) that had taken place early in her life. As is true with many of our medical colleagues, she was convinced that psychoanalytic psychotherapy simply meant "easy money" for the analyst, who was paid to listen to patients "whining."

My behavior in each of these cases was not calculated and forced; I felt comfortably willing to do what I had to do because I sincerely agree with Ruskin's values as quoted at the beginning of this section. If I had forced myself to do these things it is certain that the irritation and negative countertransference would have eventually been discovered by the patient through various enactments, slips of the tongue, or even, as I have seen in the case of some colleagues who have consulted me, overtly hostile behavior to the patient. So what is being expressed here is not a technique but a value system built into the character of the psychoanalyst that automatically orients him or her toward decisions in the various situations that inevitably arise in every long term treatment process.

We are well-advised, therefore, to consider consciously our value system, to keep trying to analyze the unconscious aspects of our value system, and to hold these always in mind during the treatment process, because one can be sure that the patient is watching this aspect of our personality and experiencing it continuously. To what extent it does or does not influence the therapeutic outcome is not proven, but I can attest from my experience with patients and as a consultant and supervisor that it certainly either facilitates or destroys the development of trust and the patient's willingness to regress in the psychoanalytic situation and take part actively and emotionally in it. It either facilitates or destroys what Freud (1912a) called the unobjectionable positive transference that enables a psychoanalytic procedure to go on without numerous disruptions. The "other component," he writes, "which is admissible to consciousness and unobjectionable, persists and is the vehicle of success in psycho-analysis exactly as it is in other methods of treatment" (105).

This is a more general philosophical statement of Kohut's assertion that the patient's experience of empathy or the lack of it coming from the analyst has a vital role in the patient's capacity to develop a cohesive and functioning self that will enable the patient to withstand the vicissitudes of life and the pressures and stress of deep psychoanalytic investigation. As Nacht (1962) remarked, it is not so much what the analyst says as what he or she *is* that makes the difference. So clearly it is a good idea, therefore, for each of us to know who we are.

These vignettes are not presented to try to instruct my colleagues as to how they ought to behave in such situations, for many possible differences of style and personality exist among analysts as among all people. They are intended primarily to illustrate the kinds of situations that demand decisions from the analyst and make strict technical neutrality impossible, for even neutrality in such situations when strictly observed is a clear expression of the analyst's value system. The decisions that must be made are often very difficult ones that sometimes must be made very quickly, and therefore they have to come from the deep intuitive psyche of the analyst. As such they constitute the most obvious and palpable demonstration to the patient of just what sort of person the analyst is. No long term therapy can be without such incidents.

It is even more complicated! Analysts have both a working ego and a private personal ego, and the value system embedded in their work ego with patients may be different than that in their private personal ego when dealing with loved ones, friends, or colleagues, as we often see demonstrated in the narcissistic behavior of certain "famous" analysts at psychoanalytic meetings! In the reanalysis of even some experienced and successful analysts we are at times shocked to see the discrepancy in these systems. There may be a vertical split or disavowal between their work and personal value systems as well as a horizontal split between their conscious and repressed unconscious value systems. What exists on each side of these splits can be radically different and contradictory. My argument is that when we are confronted with existential decisions during the psychoanalytic process, the conscious or unconscious value systems built into the analyst's private personal ego come to the fore— sometimes quite suddenly—because the decisions that are made affect us quite personally; for example, the decision to take the time and trouble to correspond with a patient, or to write for grants, to deal with an emergency situation, or even to see patients without charge will have definitive personal reverberations in us as well as generating or being the product of unavoidable countertransference phenomena.

In this chapter I have discussed what philosophers formally call subdoxastic aboutness. Subdoxastic states are unconscious states about certain matters that lead to conscious beliefs and conscious experiences. In the field of psychoanalysis Sullivan's (1953) "malevolent transformation" is a simple example of this. We all know how patients who have unconsciously undergone this kind of transformation of beliefs about people often appear more or less openly, depending on how well they are able to hide it, to be paranoid, suspicious, angry, and mistrustful of everybody, with the result that their conscious behavior and attitude alienate people and drive them away, resulting in experiences serving to verify the patients' beliefs.

Psychoanalysts, we hope, are more subtle. Because they operate in a situation where there is little consensual validation and public scrutiny, the temptation to such syndromes as "compromise of integrity" or "partial private schemata" is very strong, leading to enactments that can be damaging to both patient and analyst and ultimately to burnout. It is necessary, therefore, for analysts to keep a careful check on their conscious value systems and beliefs and to maintain continuing self-analysis for the subdoxastic factors that shape such beliefs (for a detailed example see Chessick 1990a). It is not possible to hide this from patients, and we must assume that sooner or later the patient gets to know the analyst pretty well.

Analysts displaying the syndromes mentioned above, which are more subtle than ordinary character pathology such as that which forms the all-too-pervasive narcissistic analyst, may not even be aware they are doing so if they do not maintain a continual self-scrutiny, and if they do not pay close attention to their patients' material. This material, the patients' dreams, free associations, behavior, and enactments in the analytic process, often reflects not only transference but also constitutes a response to the analyst's unconscious and conscious value systems, which in turn are based on the subdoxastic factors that make the analyst the person that he or she is. Some patients may even precipitate crises or other situations that test the analyst's value system and force the analyst to display his or her secret self in immediate decisions that cannot be avoided. This is especially true if the patient is frightened or terribly threatened by factors in the secret self of the analyst. In this situation the patient may behave like a child who knows his or her father or mother is really very angry under a seemingly calm exterior and as a result the child deliberately precipitates a display of that parental anger to get it out on the surface, get it over with, and reduce the child's anxiety.

A continuing self-analytic study of the subdoxastic factors in each individual analyst's theoretical orientation is mandatory. Every theoretical orientation is based on a value system and a set of desires that determine the goals the analyst consciously or unconsciously wishes for the patient to actualize in the treatment process in order for the analyst to feel that he or she has catalyzed a successful treatment.

Further work is needed to distinguish between countertransference in the sense we ordinarily use that concept today, and these subdoxastic factors determining the analyst's theoretical orientation and value systems, as well as a subclass of these factors, the cultural ambiance and background practices that Heidegger (1962), for example, has identified as being crucial in the formation of the analyst's self as well as that of the patient.

6

What Can Modern Psychoanalysts Learn from a Medieval "Psychoanalysis"?

> The spirits in hell may be defined as those whose intellects have not discerned those good things which can truly nourish and fulfill them. That does not necessarily mean that they have lost the intellect itself: on the contrary, hell is full of very intelligent spirits. Often they are learned too, in philosophy and religion, things which should have availed to guide them. But knowledge may lie unused in the back of the mind, and the intellect, nimble though it may be, may be pushed off the track by forces both inside and outside the psyche; and then it gyrates futilely in the void.
>
> —Fergusson (1966, 103–104)

As individuals age, and develop the various ailments that are concomitant to that state, their minds begin to turn toward death and the possibility of a second life after death. Some deal with this by manic denial, carrying on their lives as if they were adolescents, while others turn to more and more fundamentalist religion and even spend many hours in prayer and religious rituals. A somewhat different path is instead to be drawn once more in life to a study of Dante's *Divine Comedy*.[1] This incredible masterpiece cannot really be appreciated without a background in medieval philosophy, the works of Aristotle and Plato, Ptolemaic astronomy, medieval Catholic theology, and a considerable historical background into the minutiae of warring factions and papal squabbles and evils especially in the twelfth and thirteenth centuries. But those who have repeatedly turned to Dante over the years will find themselves richly rewarded. Dante was a very great poet and master of the Italian language and he has a lot to teach psychoanalysts, as do most really great poets and prose writers. Dante is the first medieval author to directly address common problems psychoanalysts still have to grapple with today.

A vast literature has grown up trying to explain the complex theological, philosophical, and psychological allegories that are contained in this incredibly magnificent poem, but adding to that is not the purpose of this chapter. I need to warn the reader, however, before proceeding, that *The Divine Comedy* is addicting! Once one begins to study it, one finds it is almost impossible to stop since there are so many ramifications and implications in every part. There is so much emotional and intellectual appeal in various directions that one is drawn like a magnet to going back to it over and over again during a lifetime. As T. S. Eliot (1950) put it, "If you get nothing out of it at first, you probably never will; but if from your first deciphering of it there comes now and then some direct shock of poetic intensity, nothing but laziness can deaden the desire for fuller and fuller knowledge" (200). Fergusson (1966) explains that the proper way to read *The Divine Comedy* is to "linger over each canto, until one sees its unique life, or action, in every detail" (109).

The purpose of this chapter, however, is to review some of Dante's psychological ideas in *The Divine Comedy*, examine Dante's medieval concept of a cure of the soul, which is extraordinarily similar to the goals of psychoanalysis in its procedures, and to introduce some of the remarkable characters whom Dante portrays in his *Divine Comedy*. For, in addition to everything else, Dante was a psychologist of remarkable perspicuity and almost in spite of himself had a sensitivity and empathy with conflicted and damaged individuals. In fact at times his empathic countertransference clashed with his rigid Catholic superego and this conflict becomes repeatedly manifested in the poem, as I hope to explain and discuss as relevant to contemporary psychoanalysis. I should add that it is not at all sufficient to read the *Inferno*, the most popular section of Dante's poem. Doing only that is like listening to the first movement of a symphony, and one can no more judge Dante's purpose from reading only the *Inferno* then one can understand what will happen in a chess game from just knowing the opening moves. *The Divine Comedy* is an intricately structured masterpiece which rests on the foundation of the *Inferno* but has as its ultimate aim the cure of a troubled soul. The ultimate therapist is Dante himself, just as the patient or troubled soul is also Dante. Under the guidance of Virgil, then Beatrice, and finally St. Bernard, who function as a psychoanalyst might do so today, interpreting and explaining and catalyzing Dante's progress, he rises from immersion in the *Inferno* of hatred and conflict to a sense of harmony and peace, a rise which Dante, like our patients, must ultimately effect for himself.

Dante describes the purpose of the poem as portraying the transition from a state of misery in this life to a state of felicity. It is organized in an extremely complex numerical fashion consisting of one introductory canto and then three sections of thirty-three cantos each written in a rhyme scheme invented by Dante, who seems to have been fascinated with the number three as representing the Holy Trinity. Each three line stanza, as explained in chapter 3, is called a *terzine* (tercets), in which the first and third lines rhyme and the second line rhymes with the first and third of the next tercet, and so forth. The basic metrical unit of the verse is the hendecasyllabic line common in Italian poetry, an eleven syllable line in which the accent falls on the tenth syllable.

The entire action of *The Divine Comedy* takes place in a week on the night of April 17, 1300, the Thursday before Good Friday. Dante finds himself in a dark wood. All the following day he tries to find his way out of the place and at sunset, on the eve of good Friday, he and Virgil enter the gate of hell, descending through hell all that night and all the next day. On Easter Sunday morning, Virgil and Dante emerge at the foot of purgatory and spend three days and three nights climbing the mountain of purgatory. Dante spends six hours at the top of the mountain, the earthly paradise, and is then taken by Beatrice into heavenly paradise at noon on the Wednesday after Easter. At sunset on the Thursday after Easter Dante has his beatific vision and the poem comes to an end. The work is called a "comedy" because the word in his day indicated a pleasant ending after a horrible beginning. Remarkably, Dante had the genius to use the Italian language instead of Latin in writing his poem which, he said, "even women can understand." The adjective "divine" was added to the title later by some sixteenth century editor.

DANTE: HIS LIFE AND TIMES

Dante's view of the universe is Ptolemaic. The social setting is that of the nasty warring city-states of Italy with their powerful arrogant and feuding aristocrats and the political factions that supported them. Arching over all this were the contesting powers of a fading empire and a greedy grasping papacy. The setting of the poem is the year 1300 AD. It was probably begun around 1307 and completed shortly before Dante's death in 1321. It was released posthumously by his sons.

The relationship of Dante to Beatrice is in typical medieval fashion. He first met her when he was nine years old and she was eight, and apparently decided to dedicate his life and work to her even though he did not meet her again until nine years later. This is in the tradition of courtly love, wherein the lover addresses a beloved who is completely out of his reach and with whom marriage is impossible. He wrote many poems in praise of Beatrice during her lifetime. She died, a married woman, at the age of twenty-five, which shattered Dante psychologically.

Dante's mother died when he was five or six years old and his father died when he was twelve, leaving him and his brothers to the care of a stepmother when his father remarried. By adolescence Dante was an orphan. This might account for a certain hunger for parental affection that can be easily noted in *The Divine Comedy*. He probably received the normal education of his day and of his socioeconomic class, but of course his bent must have always been intellectual and literary. He took an early interest in vernacular Italian, lyric poetry, and the Provençal, as demonstrated by his poems of midadolescence. This was a function of his friendship with Guido Calvalcanti, a gifted poet somewhat older than Dante who was responsible for Dante's life-long interest in the combination of philosophy and poetry. While returning from a political errand, Dante died at the age of fifty-six, probably of malaria.

His adolescent poems were under the influence of Calvalcanti, extending to the early 1290's. This was followed by a period of poetry written in praise of Beatrice, culminating with her death in 1293 and the composition of *La Vita Nuova* (The New Life) (Dante 1293). The psychodynamics of this are not hard to see in a young man who lost his mother at an early age. More than a year after her death, he was "consoled" by another lady but eventually returned to a kind of mystical devotion to the dead Beatrice, all beautifully explained in *La Vita Nuova*. But he decided to stop complaining about his own condition and console himself instead by writing poems in praise of Beatrice. This kind of creative activity apparently served as a selfobject for him during the mourning process, which was connected to the earlier mourning process involving the loss of his mother and perhaps even of his father later in his childhood.

His early poems were conventional love poetry but in *La Vita Nuova* there appear a new kind of poems accompanied by his commentary; these intend to convey philosophical ideas and are not just love poems. Later he composed a book called *Convivio* (The Banquet), which contains commentaries on various of his philosophical poems. Some of these are addressed to a lady who is an allegorical figure that stands for philosophy, written under the influence of Boethius's *The Consolation of Philosophy*, a classic work in which the unfortunate Boethius consoled himself for his anxiety and imprisonment. The employment of allegory, using people or events to stand for abstract ideas, such as a debate between characters representing lust and chastity, was very common in medieval literature and runs throughout *The Divine Comedy*.

As Holmes (1980) explains, the *Convivio* presents a view of man and nature and "It is the first of two general statements of a philosophical vision in Dante's writings. The other will be found later in *Paradiso*, the third part of [*The Divine*] *Comedy*, and the comparison of them embraces many of the main elements in Dante's mature intellectual evolution" (29). In the *Paradiso*, the godhead is both the Aristotelian prime mover, the source of all physical motion in the universe, and the source of love. As Beatrice explains, "From that point/Heaven and the whole of nature depend" (*Paradiso*, Canto XXVIII; Sisson 1981, 473). It is the focal point of all time and space. The nine orders of angels move in circles around this point of light. The angels are pure intellects uncorrupted by matter; some of them are the movers of the heavenly spheres and play an important part in the transmission of divine influences to the lower levels of creation.

Dante (see Bergin 1967; Holmes 1980; Ruggiers 1954; Salvadori and Lewis 1968; Taylor and Finley 1997; and Hollander 2001) was a man of his time, and much involved in various, squabbling, local Italian city feuds. Eventually, he was exiled from his native city of Florence, never to return. He became a wanderer in exile and spent the last years of his life in Ravenna, where he is allegedly buried in a modest tomb that has become a minor tourist attraction. His theological ideas were strictly orthodox, the medieval Catholicism of Thomas Aquinas, with reference also to Augustine and Albertus Magnus. In this sense *The Divine Comedy* can be read as a textbook of medieval theology. He displayed a remarkable knowledge of all that was known or believed in his time, and his science resembles that of Aristotle and contains as much scientific error as one also finds in Aristotle. It is important for the reader to know, for example, that at his time it was believed only the northern hemisphere of the earth was inhabited and the southern hemisphere was covered with water except for the mountain of purgatory which was at the antipode of Jerusalem.

Sisson (1981) reminds us that Dante was the first great writer whom we may term *engage*,' that is to say, writes Sisson: "He was the first creative writer of our millennium who took a notable stand with regard to the current moral, religious and political issues of his day, and whose work springs from irreconcilables, when frustration and disappointment are released in the act of creation" (11). Dante abhorred the widespread materialism, the religious cynicism (that he called Epicureanism) claiming the soul does not persist after death, and the political opportunism that disfigured his world and indeed that disfigures our world today. So his arena, as Sisson points out, was "his acute consciousness of the vastness and power of the opposition, and of the profundity and profusion of the rot which he felt he must eradicate—all this made him tremble, and purged him of much of the self-satisfaction and personal vindictiveness to which, wholly human that he was, he might otherwise have fallen a victim" (13).

Sayers (1951) claims that because the personages in the poem are symbolic images in an allegory it is not necessary to trouble too much about the accuracy of Dante's information and judgement, "or waste our time in exclaiming over his arrogance in adjudicating eternal awards and punishments" (15). There are a number of shifts and changes in historical facts and mistatements about his contemporaries that Dante introduces for his own purposes but this is unimportant for appreciation of his masterpiece. Of course the greatest aspect of Dante's work is in his superb poetry, which is largely lost in any translation. One should also keep in mind that Dante was interesting as a politician, a moralist, a theologian, and a piercing intellect (Lewis 2001).

DANTE'S JOURNEY AND MODERN PSYCHOANALYSIS

> Begin therefore; and say to what end
> Your soul is directed, and be assured that
> Your sight has lost its way but is not dead.
> (*Paradiso*, Canto XXVI; Sisson 1981, 463)

There is not space in this book to sketch out the details of Dante's organization of the *Inferno*, *Purgatorio*, and *Paradiso*. I only wish to mention some of the highlights that are of interest to psychoanalysts and to contemporary psychoanalytic practice, beginning with the *Inferno*. We must be prepared to accept the medieval Catholic doctrine that we are responsible and rational beings with free will if we are going to appreciate Dante, or at least to suspend our personal beliefs and enter the world picture of Dante and his time, just as we must do in order to properly understand our patients. The idea that we are the slaves of chance or the environment or the unconscious must be put aside. Postmodern notions about truth being relative and morals culturally contingent are totally foreign to Dante's thought. Good and evil are specific items in the Middle Ages and we are free to choose between them. We can consciously exercise these choices and must do so, and these choices are vitally decisive for our soul for the rest of eternity. So *The Divine Comedy* is precisely the drama of the soul's choice, much analogous to a psychoanalysis being the drama of the choices made by the ego in dealing with its three harsh masters—the id, the superego, and reality. Not all psychoanalysts are comfortable, however, with this contemporary shift of terminology and current postmodern relativism. Menninger (1988), for example, asks "*What Ever Became of Sin?*" and posits a specific category of moral sickness.

In modern psychoanalytic conceptions there exists a similarity to Dante's journey because we assume that once the conflicts from the unconscious are uncovered the ego can resolve these conflicts in a new and more adaptive way; it has the power to make choices and proceeds to do so. Rangell (1989) and others even believe that the unconscious ego decides, as the analysis goes along, about what greater and greater revelations from the id and unconscious superego and ego operations will be permitted to emerge into the analytic process. The inexorable judge, God in *The Divine Comedy*, who punishes and rewards according to the choices that are made, in our modern conception is the success or failure of adaptation, or resultant maladaptation to the culture in which one lives that leads to punishment or reward. So, neurosis can be thought of as a series of choices made by the infantile ego to defend against unbearable anxiety coming from unconscious mental conflicts. These choices are temporary solutions and reduce the anxiety as they are intended to do, but in adult life they become maladaptive and cause a whole host of difficulties in living. This is what Freud had in mind when he said he hoped to change neurotic suffering into everyday misery. By making maladaptive choices in childhood, the neurotic saddles himself or herself with a character structure and/or symptomatology that make everyday misery even worse than it has to be. This is why patients come to us for treatment.

The whole aim of *The Divine Comedy* is to help Dante change the choices he made. He was on the right track, he believed, while he adored Beatrice, but after she became unattainable and finally died he went off the track, immersing himself in a variety of distractions which led him to a classic middle age crisis, the kind of phenomena we see every day in our office today. This is the "dark wood" in which Dante in middle age finds himself miserable and lost.

As explained in chapter 3, Dante was clearly aware that every person brings within himself or herself things that prevent that person from realizing his or her best aspirations. Three beasts block his path in the opening Canto of the *Inferno*, the leopard (lust), the lion (pride), and the she-wolf (greed— the frenetic pursuit of money and power), the latter being the most fatal flaw to an orderly state and to men collectively. Virgil appears and informs him the only way out is to go through the organization of the universe (the psyche) in its three modes: hell, purgatory, and paradise. This will result in his deliverance from his middle age crisis.

THE INFERNO

In our review of Dante's journey we stop first, after the opening cantos, at the beginning of the *Inferno* proper, a beginning of Hell which consists of four divisions: the circles of the incontinent, the tombs of the heretics; the circles of the violent, and the circles of the fraudulent or the malicious. In the first circle we are, after everything totally unpleasant and raucous in the cantos that have gone before, in the presence of illicit love or sexual incontinence. But the episode of Paolo and Francesca, one of the most beautiful, emotional, and famous episodes in *The Divine Comedy*, stands out as an example of Dante's personal and unforeseen tenderness:

> . . . Oh, alas,
> That such sweet thoughts, desires that were so great,
> Should lead them to the misery they are in.
> (*Inferno*, Canto V; Sisson 1981, 68)

says Dante, and he swoons with pity and sadness.

Commentators agree that this is certainly not the purpose of presenting Paolo and Francesca, but one cannot escape a strong affective empathy with these two unfortunate illicit lovers in spite of their "sin." Beatrice, in the *Paradiso*, implies that their worst sin is to be caught infinitely in the mire of bodily and earthly love rather than using it to rise to the transcendent love of God. To our modern eyes, Paolo and Francesca symbolize the fact that we are almost all caught up in an earthly material world; very rarely do we raise our eyes to anything transcendent any more.

As we move along in the circles of the incontinent we pass the gluttonous (including the unfortunate Ciacco: "Ciacco, your exhaustion and distress weigh on me heavily, and call up tears" [*Inferno*, Canto VI; Sisson 1981, 71]), the hoarders, the spendthrifts, the wrathful, and the souls of the sullen—those who took no joy from the earth and all its beauty. We are introduced in Canto VIII to the "bold jack," Filippo Argenti, who today would be called a borderline personality disorder. He was an extremely narcissistic Florentine knight of the Adimari family with a violent temper. But there is an odd reversal in the scene with Filippo Argenti. For here Dante, having shown pity for Francesca and compassion for the gluttonous Ciacco, bursts into rage as soon as he recognizes Argenti, a man of enormous arrogance. This sudden transition in my opinion is best explained by the fact that Dante sees in Argenti his own major fault, one of overinflated self-esteem. In the *Purgatorio* he recognizes that this will require considerable purging before he is ready to enter the blessed realm of paradise. Dante's rage at Filippo portrays one of the first examples of projection of an internalized self-image in literature.

Another place (Canto XIII) where Dante is overwhelmed by pity is in the forest of the suicides. He meets Pier Delle Vigne who had been a chief counselor of Frederick II of Sicily. Pier fell out of favor, was falsely accused of treachery and imprisoned; subsequently, he killed himself. Depending on one's interpretation of the *Inferno*, it is possible to perceive a similarity in the pity Dante felt for Pier Delle Vigne to that he experienced for Francesca or the gluttonous Ciacco in Canto VI, because of the false accusation that precipitated Pier's unfair imprisonment and suicide. Or one can claim that Dante has no pity for the punishment given to Pier for having taken his own life. The latter argument is bolstered by Pier's admission that he was unjust to himself by destroying himself.

So it is increasingly clear that both a "soft" and a "hard" interpretation of Dante's work is possible, causing a sharp rift between different schools of opinion on the poem. The soft interpreters are convinced that Dante sympathized at least with some of the sufferers in hell, thus subverting the whole Christian dogma he presents, while the hard interpreters insist that while Dante wavers he wholeheartedly endorsed every last cruel torture of this unrepentant mass of souls. Pity is introduced again for Jacopo Rusticucci in Canto XVI and in Canto XX of the *Inferno*, where Dante feels so bad about the state of the soothsayers whose heads are twisted completely around that Virgil admonishes him and calls him a fool for crying at their fate.

One of the most interesting contrasts in *The Divine Comedy* is between Francesca of Rimini and Pia Dei Tolomei, a lady of Siena who was murdered by her husband because he unreasonably suspected her of adultery. These are the only two women allowed to speak to Dante directly in *The Divine Comedy* up to and through Canto V of the *Purgatorio*. Pia speaks briefly and Francesca speaks at greater length; this causes "hard" interpreters to draw an unfavorable contrast between them (with which I do not agree). Pity appears again in Canto XIII of the *Purgatorio* when Dante confronts the souls who are purging the sin of envy through having their eyelids stitched shut with iron thread. Here he meets a lady, Sapia of Siena, who reveled in another's grief, enjoying that more than her own happiness, and who now must have this sin punished. This is the second woman who speaks to Dante in the *Purgatorio*.

Returning to the *Inferno*, in the lower Hell named the City of Dis, which contains those who have malevolently and deliberately sinned, we encounter in Canto X another touching episode in which Cavalcante dei Cavalcanti asks Dante for news of his son, misunderstands Dante's lack of answer as meaning that his son is dead, and sinks back anguished into his burning tomb: "He fell down backwards and appeared no more" (Sisson 1981, 87). Dante feels remorse at having misled Cavalcante and tries to inform him indirectly that his son is still alive. So here again in the *Inferno* Dante shows empathy and compassion for a father whose absorbing passion is his fatherly love. Cavalcante's son Guido was a friend of Dante. Once more we are given evidence of the contradiction in Dante between his rigid Catholic beliefs and his natural poetic sensitivity to the suffering of other people, even when the other people are flawed.

The seventh circle contains the souls of the violent. There are three categories: those who are violent against their neighbors, those who are violent against themselves, and the blasphemers who are violent against God. It is curious that sins so different as blasphemy, sodomy, and usury should be lumped together as forms of violence against God but that was the belief in medieval thinking.

In the circle of those who have sinned against God we meet another most remarkable and pathetic figure, Brunetto Latini. He was a tutor revered by Dante, who says to him:

> For my mind is transfixed, and my heart stabbed,
> By the dear, kind, paternal image of you . . .
> (*Inferno*, Canto XV; Sisson 1981, 109)

In one of the most tender and compassionate of all the episodes of the *Inferno*, Latini, a homosexual, in Canto XV implores Dante to read and perhaps speak of his writings (*The Treasure*, an encyclopedic work) "In which I still live, and I ask no more" (Sisson 1981, 110) when he returns to earth. There is a sad tenderness and wistful melancholy about him and their expressions of mutual affection and their last farewell constitute one of the emotional highpoints of *The Divine Comedy*.

The second of the three great circles of lower hell, circle eight in the *Inferno*, swarms with a whole variety of those who have sinned through fraud. The eighth circle of hell is called *Malebolge*, or evil bag. It is divided into ten valleys or bolges and in the eighth valley, that of the evil counsellors, we hear in Canto XXVI the great story of the last voyage of Ulysses, an invention of Dante. In spite of being this deep in the *Inferno*, Ulysses maintains his dignity and does not even make a personal response to Virgil's questioning; he simply tells of his last days as if someone has pushed a button. Ulysses has an insatiable hunger to know all that may be humanly known, which again inclines us to forgive his sin of giving false counsel:

> Consider then the race from which you have sprung:
> You were not made to live like animals,
> But to pursue virtue and know the world.
> (*Inferno*, Canto XXVI; Sisson 1981, 158)

So Dante at once glorifies Ulysses and at the same time condemns him. Here once more appears an unresolved tension in Dante's mind, this time between the human craving to encompass all knowledge and the necessity of the spirit to submit to religious revelation, a not uncommon problem in the Middle Ages.

Canto XXVIII describes the valley in which sowers of discord are punished and it ends with the appearance of Bertrand de Born, a tortured spirit moving slowly. In his life he was a light hearted, gifted, and famous troubadour poet and warrior. He instigated discord between Henry II of England and his son, and so in the *Inferno* he is decapitated, because to divide father and son is equivalent to severing the head from the body, as it was then believed. This seems to ignore Dante's earlier opinion of him, for he is described in Dante's previous writings as a man of generous character as well as an accomplished poet.

The final character in the *Inferno* I find unforgettable is presented in Canto XXXII and XXXIII, almost at the end of the *Inferno* section of Dante's poem. He is the Count Ugolino della Gherardesca, who gnaws eternally on the head of his enemy, Archbishop Ruggeri. He tells a tragic and painful story of his unspeakable grief as a father who must watch his children die of starvation. The Archbishop shut Ugolino and his sons up in a dungeon and allowed them to starve to death, as Dante has Ugolino tell us in an excruciatingly painful narrative, one of the greatest stories of hate in the entire world literature. The *Inferno*, for Dante, represents the purposeless eternal futile rage in the id, what we commonly refer to today as the archaic aggressive drive, seeking destruction as an end in itself for gratification and discharge. The activities in Hell are motivated for the simple purpose of catharsis of the aggressive drive, and have no other purpose or value. Therefore they lead eternally to nothing.

In the final canto of the *Inferno* Dante encounters Satan in the frozen Lake Cocytus, who chews perpetually with his three heads on Judas, Brutus, and Cassius, the arch-traitors of mankind according to Dante. Judas represents man's treason against God, and Brutus and Cassius represent man's treason against the secular government of the world, the Roman Empire. Forming the background of *The Divine Comedy* is Dante's personal involvement in the feud between Guelfs and Ghibellines in Florence, which ended in his exile from that city. The Guelfs wanted constitutional government, shaking off the yoke of the Empire that had so long pervaded Italy, but the Ghibellines upheld the authority of the Emperor and opposed the growing territorial power of the Papacy. The Ghibellines represented the aristocracy and the Guelfs, appealing with Dante to the Pope for support, represented the growing mercantile middle class. Unfortunately the Guelfs were divided among themselves regarding whether the Pope should be brought in for help, and Dante's faction of the Guelfs lost, resulting in his exile. The endless Byzantine Italian feuds pervade *The Divine Comedy*, and Dante places some of his political enemies into the *Inferno*. In that sense Judas represents the Ghibellines and Brutus and Cassius represent the faction of the Guelfs that rejected the pope, expelled Dante, and threatened him with execution if he ever returned to Florence.

So we have passed, in a period of 650 years, from a portrayal of the archaic aggressive drive in the *Inferno* based on a primitive oral-sadistic method of warfare to the point where now we moderns have the technological means to destroy ourselves entirely almost overnight. These stupendous contemporary forces are the same forces as one finds in *The Divine Comedy* except now they are enclosed in a scientific garb and expressed in an explosion of scientific technology. The problems of the psyche that are dealt with in *The Divine Comedy* are the same problems we are dealing with today in our consulting room; only the language is different. This is what accounts for the enduring relevancy of Dante's poem.

THE PURGATORIO

The therapeutic purpose of the *Inferno* section is to allow the troubled Dante to become aware of the primitive sexual and aggressive forces in the id; by bringing them into the light Dante is able to make a better set of choices with respect to the problem of how to deal with these sinister forces in the psyche. In order to do that consistently and successfully he must now proceed to climb the mountain of purgatory. Here the penitents joyfully go about their task of purification; in modern terminology we would say that the patient has now become immersed in the process of psychoanalysis and the highly motivated working-through of his or her conflicts and characterologic difficulties. Another way to put it is that the inhabitants of the *Inferno*, like patients beginning psychoanalysis, often blame their unhappiness, impulsiveness, self destructive behavior and rage on external persons, forces or "chemical imbalances" and genetics, portraying themselves as the victims of such things. As psychoanalysis proceeds, if it is to be successful, the patient gradually begins to understand his or her own role in bringing on misery and suffering. The focus then shifts to attempts to understand one's own unconscious drives and conflicts and, utilizing the transference, achieve a better intrapsychic organization.

The Enlightenment conviction that truths can be found is the foundation stone on which the entire psychoanalytic process rests. I have labelled the search for these truths the great conversation of mankind (1999b) which continues even today in spite of the relativists and those who have suffered from a failure of nerve, to be discussed in chapter 9. It is not surprising there has been a failure of nerve, since the archaic human drives of lust and aggression combined with the technical miracles of modern science threaten the extinction of the human species. Lust, aggression, and greed, the same three "animals" that threaten Dante's imprisonment in a dark wood are still with us. In Dante's poem, God indirectly intervenes to save him, acting through St. Lucia and Beatrice. Virgil is sent to facilitate Dante's ascent to the higher regions and out of his situation in the dark wood. It is doubtful that divine intervention is going to save us now, and that is why Heidegger pessimistically said "Only a God can save us." We will have to save ourselves or perish.

Just as the *Inferno* is suffused with the futile unneutralized chaotic energy of the archaic drives so in the *Purgatorio* there is also much activity, but it is purposeful and in an atmosphere of hope rather than hatred and rage. For Dante humans have free will and there are clear and unmistakable signposts on the journey through life that can be ignored or followed, with the consequence that the journey of life terminates in a dismal swamp or in a relative psychic paradise. A classical example of this has been presented by Kohut (1982), who compares the ending of Homer's *Odyssey* with the ending of Sophocles's *Oedipus Rex*. In the former, the father and son stand side by side helping each other to destroy the evils that have infested their house; in the latter, the son kills the father and commits incest with the mother, resulting in a curse on the house and the destruction of the children. These endings are the consequences of choices made by the fathers about the treatment of their sons while in infancy.

The *Purgatorio* is characterized by music and by the souls of various poets; for Dante the arts have a major role in the purgation of the soul from the influence of the drives. Schopenhauer (1818) many years later offered a similar solution. Because of this the *Purgatorio* is actually more interesting to an educated individual than the grim horrors of the *Inferno*. There is more philosophical discussion and musings about the arts, especially the art of poetry.

In the *Purgatorio* Dante is first sidetracked by music. He meets his old friend Casella and asks for a song, which Casella supplies, beginning by singing a poem of Dante's. The first line of it is "Love that speaks to me in my mind." Dante the author has to bring the conservative Roman Cato into the poem to admonish Dante and the souls who are enjoying this distraction; the general distraction of natural beauty and the arts is presented throughout the *Purgatorio*. In fact the first two friends whom Dante meets in purgatory are Casella the musician and Belacqua, a maker of musical instruments famous for his indolence.

Barbi, in his *Life of Dante* (Ruggiers 1954), suggests that the *Purgatorio* can be understood as a contribution to the glory of art. For example, it presents in one of its circles a new kind of art beyond ordinary human skill that Dante describes as bas-reliefs in which the dead seem dead and the living seem actually alive. He explains that "*The Purgatorio* also contains a great variety of figures and scenes, from Cato and Manfred to Arnaut Daniel and Matelda, from the disembarking of the new spirits to be purified on the bank of the island to the allegorical representation of the earthly Paradise" (78). He points out that the poetry of the *Purgatorio* is more intimate than that of the *Inferno* and it is filled with tender pathos. He reminds us:

How many artists there are in this second canticle: Casella, Belacqua, Sordello, Oderisi, Statius, Bonagiunta, Guido Guinizelli, and Arnaut Daniel. What long discourses are held between Virgil and Statius about art and the creatures they have immortalized, while Dante follows them, listening to the conversations which give him "an intellectual understanding of poetry." (78)

Early in the *Purgatorio* we are introduced to Virgil's fellow Mantuan, Sordello. This troubadour was born near Mantua about 1200 AD and spent most of his later life in Provence. About forty of his poems are extant and written in Provençal. In the *Purgatorio*, he is a solitary and self-absorbed poet, a grave and scornful figure, but also a genius who appreciates Virgil. He triggers a long and passionate series of complaints against Italy by Dante, a steadily mounting crescendo of grief and shame. One of the high points in the *Purgatorio* is the appearance in Canto VIII of two green angels swooping down from heaven. Sordello explains them to be guards against the approach of the serpent during the night. Green is the color of hope and this is the only time in the entire *Divine Comedy* green angels appear. The serpent represents the kinds of evils and temptations that tend to creep in under the bed sheets at night. This episode occurs as Dante and Virgil wait before entering Purgatory proper and while they are mixing with those who have been busy and preoccupied with earthly cares and who now must remain in antepurgatory to reflect and think about what they have missed by being such rabid and predatory global capitalists. Three stars appear in the sky representing faith, hope, and charity, which these souls need especially to contemplate. The same is true of such persons as the CEO of today but getting them to do it, as in the *Purgatorio*, seems to be a task only God can accomplish.

In the *Purgatorio*, Dante has three dreams, one on each of the three nights he spends in purgatory. They all symbolize and interpret something which is happening or about to happen. If one studies the dreams with some care, one can also apply Freud's notion that dreams are expressions of the unconscious, because each of them deals with a problem or a conflict that Dante must overcome in order to proceed along in his "psychoanalysis," for they all involve female figures, and they all are to some degree erotic.

For example, in the first dream (Canto IX), he is being taken up to heaven by an eagle. This heavenly aid in his climbing up purgatory we discover is represented by St. Lucia, who looks after peoples' eyesight. She may be taken as a figure of illuminating grace if one is performing a medieval psychoanalysis or, if one is performing a modern psychoanalysis, Dante's eyesight is being improved and he is getting a clearer and clearer vision of his unconscious mind and the kinds of solutions that his unconscious ego has developed which brought him into trouble in middle age, and must be purged and changed. In the first dream Dante's mind is so absorbed in sensuousness that he thinks being carried to the gates of purgatory in St. Lucia's arms represents an act of sexual violence. This can be interpreted as a reflection of the state of Dante's soul at the time or the reflection of Dante's sexual desire expressed in a dream.

The cornices of Purgatory proper contain the souls of the proud, the envious, the wrathful, the slothful, the covetous, the gluttonous, and the lustful, in that order. The second dream occurs in the cornice of the covetous (Canto XIX). This dream I think may be interpreted as dealing with Dante's narcissism. In it he sees a Siren of antiquity, one who lures mariners to destruction through her song. Originally she appears ugly but his gaze transforms her into a ravishingly beautiful women. Suddenly a lady from heaven appears and warns Virgil, who in the dream tears the clothes of the Siren and exposes the hideous stench that comes from her belly. Without associations one might imagine that this dream deals with Dante's ambivalence towards women, but since this is an allegorical poem, the associations that are offered in the canto have to do with overweaning pride and anger which is hidden by narcissistic pretensions. Avarice, gluttony, and lust appear as a false and enchanting beauty and it is clear that Dante, the dreamer, is still tempted by them and unable to terminate his "psychoanalysis" at this point. Dante notes in Canto XX that the She-wolf or greed is the worst destructive force in social life:

> So curses be upon you, ancient she-wolf,
> Who have more prey than all the other animals
> Because your hunger is bottomless.
> (*Purgatorio*, Canto XX; Sisson 1981, 284)

A remarkable soul is that of Statius, a poet who lived about 45–96 AD whom Dante admired, and who appears on the fifth cornice where the covetous and the profligate are being purged. He seems to form a link between Virgil and Beatrice and here the tender and empathic aspect of the poem is displayed in the relationship between Statius and his master-poet Virgil. Statius, who was both slothful and profligate, has had to serve time in purgatory on two terraces, but now he seems to be allowed to accompany Dante and Virgil on their climb. More poets appear and there is discussion of the new style of poetry praising sexual love as a symbol and manifestation of divine love. In this prolonged discussion there is a gradual integration and acceptance of the role of sexuality in a healthy life. Sex now ceases to be simply a sin and becomes a part of sharing and of transcendence over narcissism and greed, and above all, a road that one may travel to more spiritual pleasures. This strikes me as extremely platonic, analogous to the progression of the discussion that takes place in Plato's *Symposium*.

Other poets appear; one of the most interesting is Arnaut Daniel, an intensely self-conscious poet who was a great craftsman in Provençal poetry. Opinions clash as to the message of his poetry, but there is general agreement that he could produce the most minutely ingenious and metrically resourceful poems. In one of the most beautiful passages in *The Divine Comedy*, Arnaut Daniel tells Dante in Provençal:

> I am Arnaut, who weep and sing as I go;
> Thoughtful now, I see my past folly,
> And I see with joy the day I hope for ahead.
>
> Now I beg you, in the name of that worth
> Which guides you to the top of the stairway,
> Be mindful in good time of my pain.
> (*Purgatorio*, Canto XXVI; Sisson 1981, 315)

In Canto, XXVII, we find the most intense concentration on the fifty-year-old poet Dante himself. He identifies himself with the proud, the angry, and the lustful and presents his third dream, about the biblical Leah and Rachel. Leah is gathering flowers to adorn herself and speaks to Rachel, who sits all day gazing into a mirror at the reflection of her eyes. Leah explains in the dream that she finds her joy in action and her sister delights in contemplation. We are now at a point where Dante is achieving harmony in his psyche, a state where there is room for both adaptive and fruitful activity, as well as contemplation and enjoyment of the beauties of the arts and nature. In this working-through dream of resolution, he has completed this fusion and maturation and freed himself from the raucous disruptions of the id. In modern language, he has achieved a greater capacity for sublimation and therefore his character and behavior are much less maladaptive than they were at the beginning of his journey.

This third dream, in *Purgatorio* Canto XXVII, presages the outgrowing of Virgil, who can no longer guide Dante as he ascends to "home," the goal of Dante's journey. His goal represents the return of the soul to God through the figures of Beatrice and Matelda, (prefigured by Rachel and Leah), culminating in adoration of Beatrice and finally divine revelation leading to the love of God and the unending joy of the beatific vision (for a theological interpretation of all this, see Royal 1999). Virgil leaves Dante with a phrase worthy of the ending of any psychoanalysis: "I crown and miter you lord of yourself" (Musa 1985, 294).

This leads us to the focal point of *The Divine Comedy*, the reunion of Dante and Beatrice at the end of the *Purgatorio*. We are led up to this in a very dramatic fashion all the way from the very beginning of the poem, where we are told Beatrice commissioned Virgil to aid Dante. During the journey Virgil uses her name to spur Dante on when he is afraid. Virgil suggests that Beatrice can answer some of the questions of theology that he is unable to answer. She waits for him in the blessed garden with eyes "bright with bliss"; at that point Virgil disappears.

What is remarkable is that when Beatrice in Canto XXX and XXXI finally greets Dante, it is in a fashion reminiscent of the comic strip portrayal of the husband who has been out too late at night and the wife is waiting for him to bash him with a rolling pin. She gives him a terrific tongue lashing, heaping reproach upon reproach and hammering him into a state of speechless tears and misery. All commentators agree that the figure of Beatrice is extremely complex in *The Divine Comedy* and I do not wish to get into that scholarly dispute here. What is interesting is her energetic love for him, expressing itself in terms of a mixed exasperation and relief. In his middle-age crisis he has been in great danger and through her intercession he is now more or less successfully analyzed and able to engage in an intimate interpersonal relationship, of the kind that all of us need so desperately. Of course, like all good wives she is in part, but only in part, a mother image. Freud (1917) explained how the shadow of the early objects falls on the adult object choices. But she is not simply functioning as a mother here but as a representative of true adult intimate love which, in Dante's poem, can help lead Dante to paradise, or, as we might put it today, to the capacity for love and intimacy that represent mental health. In Dante's terms, paradise implies attaining a perspective on what is truly important in human life.

THE PARADISO

Rage is the keynote of Dante's *Inferno*, hope is the keynote of Dante's *Purgatorio*, and love is the keynote of the spirit of the *Paradiso*. Contemplation, love, and beatitude become central. In the *Paradiso* souls have transcended earthly affection and live for the joy of loving and contemplating God. In medieval theology and in Dante's view that was the extreme salvation for someone caught in a middle-age crisis. In our day and age this conclusion would be rather rare. Yet there is a magnetic attraction one senses in Dante's poetic portrayal of this ascent into the heavens. The poem now becomes increasingly lyrical and religious as we leave the voice of reason and enter into the *Paradiso*, a great music and light presentation, for Dante has now become purified and ready for the stars. The poetry becomes increasingly complex as Dante is taught by means of light, motion, music, and symbols shaping messages for him in some of the spheres as well as dancing in unending circles in others. Dante himself warns the reader at the beginning of Canto II of the *Paradiso* that this is a difficult part of the poem and it certainly is the most symbolic and artistic! Its success depends to a certain degree on whether the reader is able to accept traditional Catholic theology. Dante claims that he has become transhumanized, a state that can not be explained by words and is alluded to in Canto I by the transformation of Glaucus, a figure in mythology who ate a certain herb and was thereby transformed into a sea god. Ciardi (1970a) calls the *Paradiso* "miraculous" (xv), "the summit of all European expression" (xvii)

Another woman, Piccarda Donati, speaks to Dante in Canto III, in a story that I found most puzzling. She was a nun who was violently forced to leave the convent and marry, thus breaking her religious vows against her will. Dante is confused as to why she should be placed at such a low level in paradise for this fact; and we are given a complex theological explanation that I found most unconvincing in contrast to this lady's humility and acceptance of her fate. Here again, a curious tension arises between the poet's inspired presentation of some of these appealing individuals in all three of the realms, and the puzzling harshness, rigidity, and dogmatic fate to which they are condemned by this supposedly all knowing and all loving God. According to the theology one must simply accept all this on faith.

Canto XXI of *Paradiso* is one of the most beautiful and interesting parts of *The Divine Comedy*, taking place in the sphere of Saturn where Beatrice is not allowed to smile (it would consume Dante's mortal senses) and there is no music. It is the sphere of contemplation. Dante sees the famous golden ladder gleaming in the sky and stretching beyond the reaches of his sight, a situation that shifts from contemplation into mystical visions of paradise, a ladder I also found to be a superb metaphor (1999d). The steps of this ladder seem to represent the virtues by which contemplative souls mount upward, or truths that are mastered in the ascent to universal truth; it is a symbol of contemplation. The earth, on the other hand is described as a puny threshing ground that drives us mad through desires to possess as much as we can and to gratify our needs of lust and aggression, a threshing ground metaphor that appears both in Canto XXII and Canto XXVII. As Dante concludes it:

> I turned my eyes back through every one
> Of the seven spheres and saw the globe which looked
> Such a miserable thing that I smiled;
>
> And I recognise that the best opinion about it
> Is that which makes least of it; and the man whose thoughts
> Are elsewhere can truly be called just.
> (*Paradiso*, Canto XXII; Sisson 1981, 449)

As a brief example of the Ptolemaic astronomy that pervades *The Divine Comedy*, the poet embarks at the perfect time for the flight toward heaven. It is when there are four circles joined to three crosses: the line of the equator, the ecliptic of the zodiac, and the horizon intersect at the equinoctial colure. Their intersecting forms the crosses.[2] The entire *Paradiso* is structured on Aristotelian astronomy and on the medieval notions of the spheres of the planets. The spirits in the first three spheres are least sanctified because their virtues contain some taint of earthliness just as those "planets" nearest the earth (the moon, Mercury, and Venus) sometimes come under the shadow of the earth in an eclipse. In these realms the spirits appear indistinctly or like images seen dimly and in the higher regions one cannot distinguish the bodily forms of the spirits and sees them only as bright light.

One of the main tenets of the *Paradiso* is just as relevant today as it was then: Happiness depends on love and it increases with one's understanding. The more one produces happiness for others and can love others, the more one brightens and achieves one's own happiness. Thus patients gradually learn that self-absorption, narcissism, and greed or the concentrated pursuit of happiness leads only to unhappiness. In the *Purgatorio*, as Dante becomes more understanding and mature, Beatrice literally grows brighter and more beautiful as a symbol of this principle. Dante offers many poetic descriptive passages to avoid our experiencing Beatrice simply as a pedantic lecturer. He is clearly eager to confirm her as his beloved and not just as a teacher, so many striking passages praise her beauty and her tenderness toward him; for example see the long lyrical paean to her beauty in Canto XXX.

There is a lengthy discussion in the eighth and ninth cantos, where spirits are assigned because they have too great a devotion to earthly love, regarding the issue of how children from the same parents can turn out so differently. This is the nature-nurture dilemma which has been solved no better today then it was in Dante's time; only the language has ceased to be theological.

In the higher regions of Paradise we arrive first at the sphere of the sun where spirits distinguished for their wisdom abide. Among them in Canto X is an interesting character, Sigier of Brabant, who was an intellectual debater with Thomas Aquinas in Paris in the thirteenth century. Sigier taught truths according to logic; Aquinas rested truth on Church doctrine. Each of us must choose between them. Although vigorous debate opponents, both are in paradise because of their selfless devotion to the discovery of truths, also the most admirable facet of Freud in spite of his foibles and innumerable human limitations.

In the next canto (Canto XI), Dante introduces reflections on the vanity of human pursuits on earth, which seem so trivial compared to the state Dante enjoys in heaven with Beatrice. Unfortunately, the rest of us are still on earth, and this poetic ecstasy does not help us very much. But Canto XIII carries a warning from Thomas Aquinas to all psychoanalysts. He advises us against making hasty conclusions or building up systems upon either misinformation or insufficient evidence:

> Because it often happens that a quick opinion
> Inclines in the wrong direction, and after that
> The intellect is hampered by vanity.
> (*Paradiso*, Canto XIII; Sisson 1981, 408)

As we learn in Canto XIX, reason and science alone cannot penetrate all the riddles of the universe any more, as Dante puts it, than human vision can penetrate the depths of the ocean. There are some problems we simply cannot solve. For contemporary humans, one of the most important of these is the mind-brain problem (discussed in chapter 9), the aporia that is still with us today. But as the *Paradiso* progresses, it becomes increasingly theological and mystical and seems more distant from our present scientific age. Whether this is a good development or not remains highly controversial, as the future of humanity becomes increasingly problematic.

The ending becomes rather sad because, although Beatrice and Dante are in the presence of the *Primum Mobile* or Crystalline Sphere, the base from which all the lower spheres receive the impetus for their emotion and are powered by the force of God's love, Beatrice uses the occasion to explain how greed has taken control over mankind. She insists that men are not vicious by nature and emphasizes the innocence of childhood in a pre-Freudian view, but complains that as people grow older they turn to evil ways. There is the usual religious promise that the future will bring a Messiah or a "light from heaven" that will alter the course of history.

The *Paradiso* ends with a kind of light and sound show containing moving patterns and music and an intense glorification of the beauty of Beatrice. The saints and angels finally appear in their individual incarnate forms. Beatrice now represents revelation, which Dante realizes is necessary in addition to intelligence in order to reach Paradise. He is introduced to a final new "psychoanalyst," St. Bernard, who represents intuition, a third necessary factor. It is quite interesting that St. Bernard was devoted to the role of Mary in Christianity, which has led him to be considered responsible for the great upsurge in the veneration of Mary noted from the later Middle Ages to the present day. Here we are on much more solid ground in conceiving of Mary rather than Beatrice as representing the great mother figure projected into religious belief.

I suggest that the final confrontation between Dante and Mary at the end of the *Paradiso* represents here the successful introjection of a new object, utilizing an object relations explanatory channel (see chapter 1) in psychoanalysis. This intrapsychic object, based on a projection of one's wishes and a fusion of them with the actual physicianly vocation and empathic personality of the psychoanalyst and then internalized, forms at the end of analysis an internal iron rod of being that will sustain the patient long after the analysis is completed. It rarely replaces other malevolent internalized objects as it was once believe to do in the early days of psychoanalysis, but more often exists side by side with them and more or less neutralizes their power over the patient's current life.

T. S. Eliot (1950) thought that the last canto (XXXIII) of the *Paradiso* is "the highest point that poetry has ever reached or ever can reach" (212). It concludes:

> But that was not a flight for my wings:
> Except that my mind was struck by a flash
> In which what it desired came to it.

> At this point high imagination failed;
> But already my desire and my will
> Were being turned like a wheel, all at one speed.

> By the love which moves the sun and other stars.
> (*Paradiso*, Canto XXXIII; Sisson 1981, 499)

So, Fergusson (1966) explains: "*The Divine Comedy* is a complete scale of the *depths* and *heights* of human emotion; that *The Purgatorio* and *Paradiso* are to be read as extensions of the ordinarily very limited human range" (229).

I have provided in this chapter a sort of deconstruction of Dante's *Divine Comedy*, a poem that putatively attempts to raise human vision to transcendent heights and to focus love on the love of God, but that along the way indulges in the very human aspects of pity, compassion, music, poetry, and the other arts, as well as reason and puzzlement. In this sense the poem is also an exposition of the value of the higher human faculties, which contrasts at times rather vividly with the apparently harsh autocratic fates that are assigned to some characters—who do not always seem quite deserving of what is inflicted upon them. Here we have a collision between absolute faith in the judgement of God, and human reason and compassion which sometimes seems to be unable to justify these judgements. In spite of the fact that Dante is trying to adhere to orthodox theology throughout, it is clear that his poetic soul has great difficulty in avoiding the depiction of characters for whom he has a secret sympathy.

For psychoanalysts, the central point of this study of *The Divine Comedy* is to emphasize how Dante, almost in spite of himself, expressed empathy and understanding for a variety of unfortunates either in the *Inferno* or in the *Purgatorio*. Virgil even scolds him for his compassion, arguing that God's justice is always correct and if God is angry at someone and punishes him or her, Dante should also be angry and not compassionate. Dante tries, but he cannot quite manage to do it. Translated into modern terminology, we can learn an important lesson for our clinical work from this report of a medieval "psychoanalysis." This may be summarized as follows: Freud (1912a, 1913, 1914c) proclaimed (although he himself never obeyed) certain rules of psychoanalytic technique, such as his admonition that one must always be opaque to the patient. Rigid adherence to these rules, or to one or another psychoanalytic "school" or theory, must be understood as a form of countertransference and, at worst, a character flaw in the analyst, and will lead to confusion and mixed messages introduced into the psychoanalytic process. One must be able to move comfortably from one orientation or channel of understanding to another as the material of free association and dreams requires it, and to test several channels simultaneously to see which might best fit the material at that point. This will result in maximally effective interpretations presented in a language most understandable to the patient where he or she is residing psychologically at the time.

Each case demands its own approach and its own form(s) or channels of understanding—just as Dante offers us in *The Divine Comedy*. It is because he offers such a perspective, almost in spite of himself, that his poem transcends the medieval mind and becomes relevant to all ages and cultures. As a rule of thumb, when one finds instinctual convictions about how to proceed in conflict with one's theories and set of rules, something is wrong. It is with the greatest trepidation that a well-analysed psychoanalyst should force himself or herself to ignore an instinctual or intuitive feeling of how to respond to a patient because it conflicts with some theoretical principles or official rules of procedure. Such a conflict is a call for further self-analysis, consultation with colleagues, and creative solutions.

7

Freud's Great Discovery

Transference was arguably Freud's greatest discovery. It is the centerpiece of the psychoanalytic process and, along with free association and dream analysis, it is a powerful tool toward the exploration of the patient's unconscious. The state of the transference must be constantly kept in mind by the analyst, because it colors everything the patient says and determines how the patient will hear what the analyst says. Many surprising responses to interpretations and many unexpected enactments and developments in the therapy can only be understood if the analyst is *au fait* regarding the nature and intensity of the transference at any given time.

There has been so much confusion about and obfuscating discussion of the concepts of transference and transference neurosis that it might be worthwhile at this point to review the standard approach to the topic as I understand it and employ it in my psychoanalytic work. I will begin with the basics and then move on to more complex considerations, so readers who are advanced in our field please have patience.

The customary definition of transference is given by Fenichel (1945): "In the transference the patient misunderstands the present in terms of the past; and then instead of remembering the past, he strives, without recognizing the nature of his action, to relive the past and to live it more satisfactorily than he did in his childhood. He 'transfers' the past attitude to the present" (29).

Fundamentally, transference is a form of resistance in which patients defend themselves against remembering and discussing their infantile conflicts by reliving them. It also offers us a vital and unique clinical opportunity to observe and experience derivatives of the past directly and thereby better understand the development of nuclear childhood conflicts. Transference offers the patient the best sense of conviction that the narrative is about his or her life.

The importance of understanding the concept of transference and recogniz-ing its appearance in any form of psychoanalytic therapy is clear. Many authors argue that the basic difference between intensive uncovering psychotherapy and supportive psychotherapy or behavioral or so-called cognitive therapies lies in the way that transference is recognized and dealt with. In my opinion it is the observ-able—and often in a general sense predictable—orderly unfolding of the trans-ference during a well-conducted psychoanalytic psychotherapy that firmly anchors this discipline in the realm of science (Gill 1978).

Greenson (1967) points out that the term "transference" itself may be misleading. It is a singular noun, but transference phenomena are plural, mul-tiple, and diversified. The term "transferences" is grammatically more correct, but the phrase "transference reaction" or transference is customarily used. This is not to be understood as one specific transference only but rather a group of reactions and phenomena typically appearing in intensive psychotherapy and psychoanalysis. Greenson lists five important characteristics denoting a trans-ference reaction. The outstanding trait that overrides all others and is included in all the others is inappropriateness: "It is inappropriateness, in terms of intensity, ambivalence, capriciousness, or tenacity which signals that the trans-ference is at work" (162).

A transference does not just arise in psychoanalysis, but can appear in many kinds of interpersonal situations, and play a very important constructive or destructive role. In psychoanalysis, we usually speak of a positive transfer-ence and a negative transference. A positive transference implies reactions composed predominantly of love in any of its forms or in any of its forerun-ners or derivatives. We consider a positive transference to exist when the patient feels towards the analyst any of the following: love, fondness, trust, amorousness, liking, concern, devotion, admiration, infatuation, passion, hunger, yearning, tenderness, or respect.

In the psychoanalytic process, we often do not worry as much about the appearance of positive transference as we do about the appearance of negative transference. In a negative transference we observe a series of reactions based on the various forms of hate. Negative transference may be expressed as hatred, anger, hostility, mistrust, abhorrence, aversion, loathing, resentment, bitterness, envy, dislike, contempt, or annoyance. It is always present, although it is perhaps surprisingly often much more difficult to uncover negative trans-ference than the manifestations of positive transference. There are many pos-sible reasons for this clinical fact. The two most obvious are that some patients don't like to become aware of transference hate and to express it and that ana-lysts don't particularly enjoy being the object of transference hate and to have to deal with it or be exposed to it.

It is extremely important for the analyst to remain sensitive to subtle manifestations of negative transference at all times and to directly interpret and deal with them. Otherwise a number of unfortunate results may take place. For example, there may be a sudden explosion of previously ignored and accumulated negative transference with an intensity that wrecks the treatment. In some cases the negative transference may not surface in full impact until after the treatment is over—and an apparently grateful patient suddenly becomes a bitter inimical ex-patient, who may even join various antipsychiatry movements, complain to licensure departments, or initiate litigation.

As a general rule of thumb one may say that for psychoanalysis to be successful there will have to be sharp manifestations of both positive and negative transference. To put it another way, if a person wishes to do psychoanalysis he or she must be prepared to be exposed to powerful negative and positive emotional feelings coming from the patient, often on a highly irrational basis. This exposure to such powerful feelings can lead to many mistakes, retreats, and confusions in psychoanalysis if analysts are either not expecting them to appear, not prepared to deal with them, or are so primarily preoccupied with their own needs and problems that they cannot clearly perceive what is going on. There is a strong all-too-human tendency in psychoanalysis to deflect emerging manifestations of powerful erotic or negative transferences by various forms of interventions, such as making a joke, extra kindnesses, and so forth, resulting in a collusion to avoid these uncomfortable emotions. It is the responsibility of the analyst not to allow this sort of collusion to occur, although in supportive psychotherapy some forms of it may be useful.

An especially central role involving the transference in both psychoanalysis and psychotherapy is presented by Gill (1982, 1984). Muslin and Gill (1978) illustrated, using Freud's famous case of Dora, how the transference must be interpreted at all stages of treatment, and that failure to do so leads to an unmanageable transference situation or premature interruption of the therapy. Gill was especially concerned with the analyst's here-and-now behavior as profoundly influencing the transference that develops, so for him transference is the result of the interaction between the patient and analyst and is therefore always present. It may be more commonly manifested by allusions to it in dreams and associations, and the analyst must continuously look for it, clarify the contribution of the analytic situation to it, interpret the patient's resistances to awareness of it, and finally translate the disguised and displaced expressions of it into direct experience and discussion. In such resolution of the transference, Gill emphasized the corrective emotional experience that is involved, since by such a procedure the analyst behaves quite differently from what the patient has come to expect and even provokes from others. The most controversial premise of Gill's view is the assumption of the centrality of the transference in *all* the patient's material, and his emphasis on the role of the analyst in determining the development and nature of the transference.

The analyst must also be very carefully aware of what is sometimes the serious danger of acting out of the transference outside the analyst's office. All reports by the patient of interactions outside the therapy, and even dreams containing such interactions must be closely examined for veiled allusions to the transference. Some analysts believe that every reported dream contains information about the state of the transference at the time. Certainly every reported dream should be examined for such information, because we regard the transference as of central importance.

THE TRANSFERENCE NEUROSIS

One of the most controversial concepts today is that of the transference neurosis. Freud's original designation of the transference neurosis was from a clinical psychoanalytic situation in which the patient developed such intense transference feelings to the analyst that everything else in his or her life became of lesser importance. The classical conception of the transference neurosis has it that the infantile feelings and conflicts of the patient become focussed almost exclusively onto the analyst. The transference neurosis could also be thought of more generally as an extremely important object relationship, the affectual nature of which is determined predominantly by the patient's projection of repressed split-off self and object representations. Other conceptions such as those of Kohut (1971) stress the role of the search for crucial missing aspects of psychic structure rather than drives and affects.

The concept of transference neurosis has run into difficulty because very often, even in a formal psychoanalysis, the classical transference neurosis simply does not appear. One always sees a great many varieties of transference phenomena, but a focal, sharply defined transference neurosis cannot invariably be expected to take place. The reasons for this failure of pure transference neurosis formation are a matter of considerable debate, but it is not always just the result of poor technique. Because of this many contemporary authorities would like to eliminate the term.

To avoid needless confusion and controversy I wish to define transference neurosis in this book as an intense transference, one that is obviously significant and important in the analytic process and will usually[1] require interpretive attention sooner or later. Important clinical features of the transference neurosis (feel free to call this "the predominant intensive transference at the time") so defined are:

- The transference neurosis revives the infantile neurosis.
- It is created out of frustrated demands that, in turn, arise out of the therapeutic situation as we structure it, following the rule of abstinence.

- The symptoms of the transference neurosis are dynamic, shifting, and changing; it is not a static concept.
- Important in the development of the transference neurosis are the mechanisms of regression and repetition.
- The transference neurosis is not identical to and does not describe in a one-to-one manner the nature of the infantile relationships that have been transferred.

There is a process of layering of subsequent meanings onto those infantile relationships and events that reflect current interests and conflicts. These layers coalesce into meaningful transference patterns.

Eventually the transference neurosis itself may become involved in a resistance to treatment. This is known as transference resistance (Gill 1982), a resistance to the resolution of the transference as manifested, for example, by refusal to see determinants in it from the past or by a complete preoccupation with the demand for gratification of transference wishes. If the analyst breaks Freud's rule of abstinence and provides massive gratification, further insight becomes impossible and a stalemate usually results, with an interminable therapy.

The management of the transference neurosis permits the undoing of repression and is in my opinion the central issue of psychoanalytic treatment. Concentration on and central focus on the process of interpretation in resolving the transference neurosis differentiates psychoanalysis from other forms of treatment, even psychoanalytically informed psychotherapy. It is important to clarify this issue a little more. According to Freud's psychoanalysis, a transference neurosis develops in an orderly and manageable fashion. This is then interpreted, and such interpretation permits an undoing of the transference neurosis, which, in turn, frees the patient from the nuclear infantile conflicts by allowing the adult ego to resolve them in new ways. It is the preoccupation with the transference neurosis that differentiates psychoanalysis from other forms of treatment; the special efficacy of psychoanalysis is believed to be in the removal of the transference neurosis through interpretation, rather than through any other of the many aspects of the treatment which may be necessary to allow the full manifestations of intense transference to appear.

Transference neurosis may also appear in psychotherapy. It is not necessary for a patient to come in four or five times a week and lie on the couch for a transference neurosis to develop. On the other hand, it is much more likely that, if the transference neurosis is going to develop, it will appear under the conditions of formal psychoanalysis. But it is very important for anyone doing psychotherapy to understand the concept of the transference neurosis and to be aware of its appearance, if it should appear in the psychotherapy. Lack of recognition of this has led to many unfortunate consequences for both patients and therapists.

The actual occurrence of a transference neurosis can be very dramatic. When all the factors I have described as powerful intense transference or transference neurosis actually present themselves in psychoanalysis, it can be a remarkable experience for both the patient and the analyst. The sharp focusing of infantile demands and powerful emotions in a totally inappropriate manner on the analyst, when the patient and the analyst are actually both aware of the irrationality of this phenomenon and have both observed it to develop out of the psychoanalytic situation, often constitutes the most crucial experience of psychoanalytic treatment.

Unfortunately, the appearance of a transference neurosis is not always a reason to be jubilant. A transference neurosis can arise in situations where the patient has a very weak ego and poor defenses. In such situations the patient cannot actually utilize the transference neurosis toward the working through of intrapsychic problems. If a profound transference neurosis seems to be developing in a psychoanalysis or psychotherapy, the analyst must be careful to ascertain the ego state of the patient and to determine, by the use of interpretation, whether the patient is actually capable of utilizing the developing transference neurosis. If the patient cannot utilize it, efforts should be made to break up the transference neurosis by decreasing the frequency of the treatment, by active interpretation and support, and so on.

It is often diagnostic of borderline patients that they develop highly negative or strongly eroticized transferences very early even in once-a-week psychotherapy. These must be resolved by early interpretation, today usually based on Kernberg's concepts of projected split-off all bad or all good self and object representations. Or, if self psychology is utilized, transferences powerfully infused with lust and aggression appearing early and suddenly in therapy are analyzed as manifestations of profound disappointment in the patient's expectations of empathy from the subjectively perceived selfobject analyst. Failure to resolve such disruptive transferences typically destroys the therapy.

I am not advocating that psychoanalysts should become afraid when transference neurosis manifestations appear, and break up the therapy because they cannot stand the strength of the emotions that are aimed at them. They must be sufficiently mature and aware of themselves that they can make a correct judgment as to whether a powerful transference neurosis appearing in the treatment is actually workable and analyzable by them or not. For example, an incorrect response to a highly eroticized transference can deadlock the treatment in an unconscious conspiracy of mutual admiration and endearment and even lead to serious boundary violations.

A transference psychosis sometimes appears. This is always a very undesirable situation that resembles the strong transference neurosis, but the patient has absolutely no insight into it and denies completely that the phenomena he or she is experiencing are transference at all. Situations such as falling desperately in love with the analyst can be understood as a transference psychosis if this refuses to yield to any kind of interpretation; the patient insists that the love is genuine and based on the marvelous qualities of the analyst, and definitely refuses to see any transference phenomena involved in it. Clinical judgment is required here to distinguish between an object-instinctual transference which has exploded without insight, and Kohut's (1971) "idealizing transference," described by him as appearing in the psycho-analysis of patients with serious narcissistic problems. The latter contains a more eerie and vague form of idealizing of the analyst which can be mistaken for a psychotic phenomenon. Interpretations are met with rage because the patient needs such a transference during the process of repair of the psyche, and experiences the analyst's attempts to break it up by interpretation as a severely disappointing failure of empathy and understanding.

Transference as Resistance

The transference often becomes a part of the patient's resistance maneuvers in a further effort to avoid undoing the forces of repression. This leads to termi-nological confusion because *all* transference can be thought of as a form of resistance to remembering. The difference is that transference as a resistance maneuver arises more specifically in certain situations in psychoanalysis that call it forth and then functions as a resistance to further psychoanalysis.

The most typical example of this situation occurs when patients wish for gratification in the transference. Quite frequently, patients develop a strong wish for some kind of gratification from the psychoanalyst at some point in the therapy; the patients may concentrate on that, refuse to cooperate with the treatment, and rage for many hours because they are not getting the gratifica-tion they want. The kind of gratification demanded can be of all varieties. Sometimes it is a very minor matter, such as raging by a woman because the analyst will not help her with her coat. In other instances it can be major, such as demanding that the analyst marry or go to bed with the patient, give the patient advice, or drugs, and so on.

The problem of how much gratification to give a patient in psychoanaly-sis is a very thorny one indeed. One general principle that can be kept in mind is: the more gratification the patient is given in the transference, the less uncovering is going to be possible, and the more difficult it is going to be to resolve the nuclear conflict. There are some situations where the transference demands become so overwhelming that the therapy cannot go on unless something is done. When this repeatedly happens, it is often an indication that the patient cannot tolerate uncovering psychotherapy, and the therapy should be shifted to a more supportive and less frequent approach. On the other hand, some analysts are so concerned about avoiding gratification of the patient that they create a cold and sterile ambiance in the treatment, which leads the patient to withdraw into an "iatrogenic narcissistic neurosis."

A different form of transference resistance is sometimes called a transference defense or "defensive transference reaction" (Greenson 1967). In this situation, just as the patient would be expected to arrive at a certain insight out of the material that is being presented, there suddenly appears instead a powerful transference reaction, most typically a negative transference.

For example, a patient who has had a dreadful and frustrating childhood, arrives at the point where he is becoming aware of his tremendous yearnings for love and affection from one of his parents. This has only come about after a long working through of many defenses and resistances against anyone meaning anything to him, against needing anyone, even against forming a therapeutic alliance itself. At the point where one might expect the patient to show the first signs of some transference yearnings for the analyst, there appears suddenly, without any previous warning, the explosive feeling that everything the analyst says is a form of hostile criticism. If it is not in his actual words, it is in his tone of voice. The patient absolutely cannot shake off the feeling that everything the analyst is saying is hostile and critical.

An investigation of this reaction brings the patient to the realization that mother was a very hostile and critical person who was constantly making the patient an object of her criticism. The working through of this maternal transference defense, which came up suddenly in the middle of a session when the patient was on the verge of experiencing some positive feelings for the analyst, enabled the patient later on to begin experiencing those yearnings and permitted the future development of deeper and more powerful transference phenomena. It allowed the patient, via the transference, to become aware of his previously repressed deep longings for his mother to have been loving and empathic toward him.

The sudden and sometimes dramatic appearance of strong transference manifestations at a sharp point in a psychoanalytic session gives rise to the possibility that the patient is using the transference to defend against feelings, memories, or emerging insight that must be denied at the time. The analyst must be vigilant and constantly aware of the appearance of transference manifestations that can show themselves either in small or subliminal ways, as well as in dramatic explosions.

Some authors (Schlessinger and Robbins 1974) define the term "defense transference" as a transference which forms to defend against awareness of a deeper, more important transference. Defense transference is the characterological defensive organization, evident at the onset of an analysis, which serves as a shield against the development of a transference neurosis, and as a major coping mechanism of the ego in the face of conflict. For example, a highly idealized transference commonly develops as a defense against the awareness of a hidden negative transference. Here, one form of transference is habitually used to defend the patient from the emergence of another more intense and upsetting transference into awareness, and so the defense transference serves the function of tension regulation (Schlessinger 1984).

Other authors (Greenson 1967) refer to character transference phenomena. These character transference phenomena can be thought of as hidden in the patient's more general behavior patterns. The term is somewhat misleading and confusing, but what distinguishes this form of transference from others is that the reaction to the analyst is part of the patient's habitual, representative, and typical responses to people at large, and the transference behavior is characteristic of the patient's relationships in general. It is this quality of the nonspecific behavior that has led to the term "character transference." The important point is that the patient may be reacting to the analyst with his or her habitual reactions to a different kind of person than the analyst actually is. This is what the analyst has to be aware of in watching for character transference phenomena. Both character transference phenomena and transference neurotic phenomena are dealt with in a similar way in the process of psychoanalysis, but the former is usually more subtle and tricky and more difficult to resolve.

ARCHAIC TRANSFERENCES

One should be aware that patients have some very confused notions of what the transference is supposed to be or not supposed to be in psychoanalysis. For example, some patients begin the treatment by asking the analyst whether they are expected to fall in love. The kind of question, "Am I supposed to fall in love with you?" hides behind it a number of anxieties and concerns that should be dealt with in a very straightforward manner. The patient is told that he or she is expected to report whatever thoughts and feelings come to mind, but there is nothing that is supposed to happen. We must be able to deal with whatever arises in the therapy in a nonanxious interpretive manner.

Much recent work has been presented in the literature on the so-called archaic transferences, stimulated by the work of Kohut (1971, 1977, 1984). Kohut described the now well-known mirror and idealizing transferences found in narcissistic personality disorders, which are not transferences in the technical sense because they do not involve instinctual wishes that cross the repression barrier. They are instead a demand for a "selfobject" in order to fill in intrapsychic defects and allow, in the treatment, a resumption of development from the preoedipal narcissistic stages. More generally, the archaic transference is marked in preoedipal disorders by an intense and overt demand for gratification, making the psychoanalyst feel almost like a prisoner and forced away from the analytic analyzing attitude. Refusal to comply is often followed by seriously disruptive rage and chaos, and certain authors feel that some gratification is necessary, but always followed by interpretation. This remains a controversial technical area. Adler (1980) points out that the hallmark of the borderline patient's transference is the rapid disintegration of the selfobject transference as soon as gratification is not forthcoming, and recommends the use of one's best judgment about how much deprivation is tolerable in such situations. Therefore the instability of the transference is an important hallmark of an archaic transference, and poses extremely difficult problems for the analyst.

Kleinian analysts (Spillus 1983) characterize this as projective identification in the transference, marked by pressure placed on the analyst to do something, which of course represents an obstruction to understanding. There is always the danger of "externalization" (Chessick 2000a) in the archaic transference, in which analysts are subtly made to feel and even to behave like the person or introject projected onto them. Thus the identification and handling of archaic transferences becomes a specialized aspect of psychoanalysis, requiring the willingness to work with very primitive and disruptive patients.

The most destructive flaws in the handling of transference reactions are from the subtle, chronic, unrecognized ones that go on for years without being detected. These flaws usually stem from two main sources: (1) countertransference reactions and (2) incorrect understanding of the patient for reasons other than countertransference, for example, due to cultural differences, and so on. I will discuss countertransference in the next chapter; Freud considered it to be a nuisance but today it is recognized to be ubiquitous and valuable for understanding of the transference. The greatest problem posed by the development of transference occurs if the analyst misses what is going on. One of the most common causes of stalemate or failure in psychotherapy is when—due to various intrapsychic reasons—psychoanalysts are unable to be aware of important manifestations of transference appearing in their patients.

WHAT IS THE ORIGIN OF TRANSFERENCE?

The most significant conflicts in life arise in early childhood and give rise to unconscious fantasies that act subsequently as persistent, guiding, motivational forces. The unconscious conflicts in the patient occurring early in life create a mental set which is characteristic for each individual, a predetermined tendency to respond to events in a characteristic way, that is, to perceive, interpret, and respond to stimuli from without or from within in keeping with the scenarios of childhood fantasy. These fantasies go through convolutions as one develops, and some later editions may even provide defensive distortions of earlier fantasies. Arlow (1985a) states, "One can observe how the symptoms of the patient's illness, how his life history and his love relations, his character structure and his artistic creations may all represent in different ways derivative manifestations of the persistent unconscious fantasy activity that governs the individual's life" (534).

At the core of every person there resides a crucial fantasy activity, interwoven with early infantile experiences to a greater or lesser degree, depending on how traumatic these experiences have been. What constitutes trauma is not simply inherent in the actual, real event, but rather the individual's response to the disorganizing, disruptive combination of impulses and fears integrated into a set of unconscious fantasies. The individual's experience is usually organized in terms of a few, leading, unconscious phantasies which dominate an individual's perception of the world and create the mental set by which she or he perceives and interprets experience. Transference is not a repetition of the patient's actual early interactions with present objects, but expresses derivatives of the patient's persistent unconscious childhood fantasies, the psychic reality of these early interactions for the patient.

The result of the pressure of these internal childhood fantasies is that there is a tendency to reenact them in all interpersonal relationships, always attempting to actualize a derivative representation of an unconscious fantasy. Without being aware of it, the individual tries to impose a preconceived situation onto a new situation, and this attempt may lead to all sorts of difficulties in living of an acute or chronic nature that bring the patient eventually into psychotherapy or psychoanalysis suffering from the untoward consequences of trying to actualize these unconscious fantasy wishes.

The analyst's behavior or style or countertransference is a stimulus to the patient's unconscious fantasy life that sets off the reaction we call transference. The analyst is given an assigned role to play in the preconceived drama and tremendous pressure is placed on him or her to act and speak in a way consistent with that unconsciously assigned role. In the ordinary analytic situation, because the analyst remains relatively neutral and does not respond to seductions or provocations, the derivatives of these fantasies and wishes stand out in bold relief and take on varied and dramatic forms which allow the analyst to demonstrate them to the patient. Difficulty occurs either when the patient's pressures are so great that the analyst is literally forced into certain behaviors and roles outside the traditional analytic situation, or when the analyst does not realize that he or she has been successfully manipulated into a predetermined role through the unconscious but nevertheless effective ministrations of the patient.

The interpretation of the transference and of extratransference situations in psychoanalysis should ultimately aim at focussing down on the central psychic core of the patient through the continuous analysis of derivatives of that core. The patient's observing ego must engage with the analyst and eventually take over the search for the crucial infantile fantasies and identify them. What counts as the patient's psychic reality are infantile conflicts, memories of traumata, and the fantasies woven around all this, that constitute a unique kind of unconscious core of the personality. In some patients the material will be almost pure fantasy and in others the most serious kind of abuse has taken place. Still, no matter how great the actual traumata, it is the combination of infantile conflicts, memories of the traumata, and the basic fantasy activity that combines all this together in a fashion specific to that individual, forming the foundation of that person's mental processes. It has a primary effect on all of the person's subsequent behaviour, self-esteem, predominant affect, experience of the world, and the capacity to relate to other people.

This view of the mental set produced by both unconscious fantasies and unconscious background practices acquired early in life casts considerable doubt on theories which emphasize the direct curative power of either empathic responses or of nontransference interpretations by the analyst. This is because until his or her assigned role has been analyzed and understood, whatever the analyst says is experienced by the patient as belonging to that assigned role or as an opportunity to manipulate or pressure the analyst into that role.

For example, when the analyst finds himself or herself taking an educating or counseling or advising role with any given patient, careful study of countertransference is necessary. This may reveal some indigenous need in the analyst to play such a role, an unnoticed pressure or manipulation from the patient to edge the analyst into a scenario, *or* a genuine empathic response to somebody with a primary deficit that needs to be corrected. Even when education is called for it may not at all be experienced as such by the patient although it is offered with the best of intentions. The core fantasies and transferences may have to be revealed and interpreted first. On the whole, I prefer in my psychoanalytic work (1996a, 2000a) to let education or corrective emotional experience take care of itself out of the natural human relationship that can form between patient and analyst, what Freud called the unobjectionable part of the positive transference, and to concentrate my therapeutic endeavors on proper listening, identification, and interpretation, with a special focus on the major transferences. This is true even in the psychoanalysis of quite disturbed patients—and I believe many of them can be successfully psychoanalysed—and avoids the temptation to exhibit one's self as an educator or to assume authority with them, that invites the usual battle over compliance, parenting, and here-and-now issues.

8

The Effect on Countertransference
of the Collapse of Civilization

> So you can understand that our knowledge
> Will be entirely dead, after the point
> At which the gate of the future will be shut.
> —Dante (*Inferno* X:106, Sisson Translation)

The late Pierre Bourdieu, French philosopher and sociologist, offered gloomy thoughts about the direction civilization is going. He bemoaned the drift of our culture away from scholarship and high culture as sources of social prestige and toward journalism and entertainment. He had nothing but denunciation of anti-foundationalists and postmodernists for their relativism and obscurantism, and he urged scholars and writers to utilize their knowledge toward helping to propose and debate the solutions on vital social and political issues. He did not think this would be possible on a TV or radio talk show, especially those (see Alterman 2002) featuring rude, vulgar, and disruptive interruptions of each other by the speakers. Bourdieu insisted that the appreciation of high culture requires a socioeconomic background permitting leisure, education, financial security, and the capacity to indulge in and enjoy the life of the mind. I have reviewed the concept of leisure as the basis of culture (also see Pieper 1952) and described the basic stance of reverence for human life that it engenders (1999e). Clearly this stance and its corollary, the physicianly vocation, has to be at the foundation of the psychoanalyst's approach to his or her patients.

But what happens when the civilization in which the psychoanalyst is immersed begins to crumble and makes the opportunity to live what Aristotle called the contemplative life, or the life of the mind, increasingly difficult and politically incorrect? We saw many examples of German intellectuals and psychoanalysts who gave in to the Nazi ambiance and, although they did not necessarily actively support the Nazi movement, by passive acquiescence they gave credibility and prestige to what was essentially a gang of murderous thugs. At some level they knew they were out of cowardice turning a blind eye to the evil surrounding them. How at the same time could those who were psychoanalysts insist that their patients look honestly and squarely at every aspect of themselves? In that situation a collusion to ignore what should have been a central issue of concern to both the patient and psychoanalyst took place, resulting in a tacitly condoned area of their lives that would not be explored. This has to have a grossly distorting effect on the psychoanalytic process as well as producing a secret depreciation of the psychoanalyst in the mind of the patient, who knows that the analyst knows better but out of fear is being dishonest. The result has to be that because the psychoanalyst allows some aspects of his or her life to be unexplored or, worse, to be denied, the patient considers himself or herself entitled to the same privilege. This is an aspect of countertransference that has not been properly explored or recognized.

COUNTERTRANSFERENCE

Countertransference can be thought of as either the analyst's transference to the patient, or the analyst's reaction to the patient's transferences, or the analyst's reaction to the whole patient. Basically there is what might be called subjective countertransference, which arises as a kind of transference to the patient from the therapist out of the therapist's unanalyzed infantile core, and an objective countertransference, which pertains to feelings and behavior realistically induced or induced through projective identification as a response to the patient's transference feelings and attitudes. The former, but at times also the latter, can give rise to what is sometimes called countertransference resistance, seriously interfering with the analyst's capacities.

Another way to divide countertransference is to distinguish "totalistic" countertransference (Kernberg 1975), which includes all the reactions the analyst has to the patient, from a more limited form of countertransference induced primarily by the patient's transference. An extreme example of totalistic countertransference is the countertransference hatred described by Maltsberger and Buie (1974), which can develop in the treatment of borderline, psychotic, and suicidal patients. Totalistic countertransferences tend to develop as a response to intense archaic transferences, although Winnicott (1958) argues that some hate is always present in latent form in all countertransference to all patients; it becomes a problem especially in the treatment of more psychotic types of patients and a great strain on the ana-

lyst of such patients. Chediak (1979), however, prefers to call these coun-
terreactions rather than countertransference.

Countertransference reactions have a very important impact on the
process of psychotherapy. The whole subject is controversial and poorly
understood, and the therapist will have to be satisfied with a variety of definitions and conflicting attempts at clarification of the situation. Arlow (1985a)
gives three typical situations that evoke or foster countertransference: (1) a
fixed identification with the patient due to a correspondence of unconscious
wishes and fantasies; (2) fantasies and wishes of the analyst evoked by the
patient's wishes and fantasies, such as the patient's wish to be rescued and the
analyst's wish to rescue; and (3) the analytic setting, which offers tempting
opportunities for the analyst to gratify narcissistic needs. Singer (1970) points
out that countertransference seems to appear "when the therapist is made anx-
ious by the patient, when he fears feelings and ideas which therapeutic investigation may arouse in him, and when his desire to avoid anxiety and its
dynamic roots force him into assuming defensive attitudes" (296). These
defensive attitudes interfere with genuine therapeutic understanding of the
patient. Dewald (1976) conceives of the psychoanalytic process as involving a
new model of interpersonal interaction. Countertransference leads to disruption when the analyst's response repeats that of the patient's parents and so
repetition rather than a new experience prevails.

In the broadest terms, countertransference is best thought of as a manifestation of the therapist's reluctance to know or learn something about himself or herself. It is a reflection of a wish to remain oblivious to certain facets
of the psyche and to allow unresolved intrapsychic conflicts to remain buried.
This powerful counterforce can move the therapist to quite hostile behavior
against patients. The hostility, which can be either overt or covert, may be
expressed in acts of omission or commission or in irrational friendliness or
irrational annoyance or anger. In fact, McLaughlin (1981) suggests dropping
the term "countertransference" entirely as it assumes that the analyst was
pushed by the patient from his or her usual neutral "wise" state. He suggests
the term "analyst's transferences," to stress the shared adventure of two
humans together. Similarly, Brenner (1985) sees no need for the term "countertransference," which for him simply is the transference of the analyst in an
analytic situation. The set of compromise formations "that being an analyst
is," involving these drives and defenses against them, allows normal analytic
functioning; when these shift due to various circumstances, analytic work is
helped or hindered.

Probably the most quoted study of countertransference is by Racker (1968),
who tried to understand the deep infantile and possibly neurotic roots of countertransference reactions in some very controversial ways utilizing Kleinian theory. Racker points out that the significance given to countertransference

depends on two misfortunes that it generates: (1) countertransference may distort or hinder the perception of unconscious processes in the patient by the therapist; and (2) countertransference may not interfere with the therapist's perception of what is going on, but it may impair the interpretive capacity of the therapist. So the manner, behavior, tone of voice, form of the interpretations, even the attitude toward the patient consciously or unconsciously may be vastly influenced by countertransference. A patient's complaint of the tone, manner, or voice of the therapist is not always a manifestation of transference to the therapist. It may instead represent the patient's perception of a countertransference problem in the therapist, for, as Arlow (1985a) reminds us, "much as we observe and study the patients, the patients do the same to us. They observe our reactions, often in order to ascertain what they can do to provoke the gratification of their infantile strivings" (172).

Racker (1968) and others have distinguished between a "countertransference structure," a "countertransference neurosis" (see Greenson 1978; Searles 1965), and a "countertransference character disturbance." Countertransference structure is a consistent and relatively permanent aggregate of feelings, fantasies, and ways of reacting that develop in the therapist as a response to the transference and the personality of the patient over a long period of psychotherapy (Tower 1956).

Countertransference character disturbance would involve certain forms of behavior and a general interpersonal approach to the patient, suggesting that the patient was experienced as someone significant in the therapist's past life who called forth this general character pattern in the therapist. It is sometimes very difficult to spot this, but it is very important and does not get nearly the attention it deserves. Many failures in psychotherapy and psychoanalysis can be traced to unconscious countertransference character disturbances.

A variety of authors (see Menninger 1958) have discussed the signals that indicate the presence of a countertransference problem. After establishing a particular therapeutic frame and routine of procedure with each patient, the analyst should carefully examine any departures from the routine because they may well be related to countertransference (Langs 1979). This includes the decision to offer ancillary psychopharmacological agents and other modalities.

Even the most mature and well-analyzed psychoanalyst is going to have important countertransference reactions to patients over a period of time. The difference between the novice and the experienced psychoanalyst is that the experienced psychoanalyst is constantly on the lookout for the countertransference and the countertransference structure, becomes aware of it when it occurs, engages in continuous self-analysis, keeps countertransference in check by not permitting the acting out of countertransference feelings, and holds it in abeyance and even utilizes it for the purpose of better understanding of the patient. In attempting to identify countertransference, therapists must apply the same standards of honest and forthright self-appraisal to themselves that they expect of their patients. Turning a blind eye to the collapse of the civilization in which the analysis is being carried out and the effect of it on both the patient and the analyst represents a violation of this basic requirement.

Kohut (1971) described the typical countertransference responses to the mirror and idealizing transference encountered in narcissistic personality disorders (and also in other preoedipal disorders or patients who have defensively regressed to such transferences). The typical countertransference to the idealizing selfobject transferences occurs though the mobilization of the therapist's archaic grandiose self, leading to an embarrassed defensive "straight-arming" of the patient by denial of the idealization in various ways. Typical countertransference reactions to mirror transferences are boredom, lack of involvement with the patient, inattention, annoyance, sarcasm, a tendency to lecture the patient out of counterexhibitionism, or an attempt to gain control of the therapy by exhortation, persuasion, and so on.

Utilizing self psychology, Gunther (1976) explains countertransference phenomena as aimed at restoring narcissistic equilibrium in the therapist, which is endangered especially in preoedipal cases by archaic demands of the patient. This valuable concept can help explain countertransference fantasies and unethical behavior on the part of narcissistically depleted therapists and therapists with narcissistic personality disorders. In my supervisory experience, narcissistic disequilibrium problems are the most common generators of disruptive countertransference, although it is not possible to judge from supervision whether these problems defend against deeper unresolved infantile sexual conflicts.

Wolf (1985) stresses the regression of both the patient and the analyst in psychoanalytic treatment, and the defenses against this regression. This can lead to what self psychologists call self-state anxiety in the analyst. But it can also have favorable consequences, including stronger motivation to remain empathically in tune with the patient and some idealization of the patient. The latter is experienced by the patient as a confirmation of his or her unrealized potential and as a stimulus to live up to it. Thus countertransference is not necessarily pathological and can be a positive force in the treatment.

The interaction of the transference of the patient and the countertransference structure of the analyst is probably one of the basic and most important factors in healing through psychoanalytic psychotherapy. A parallel struggle goes on throughout the process of psychoanalysis in both patient and psychoanalyst. In the patient there is a struggle between the forces of resistance versus the innate biological and psychological forces toward health and towards mastering neurotic conflicts. In the analyst there is a struggle arising from the stimulus of the personality and transferences of the patient. This struggle occurs between the desire to understand and interpret the transferences properly and the tendency to overlook, misunderstand, and misinterpret the transferences out of countertransference problems. The patient must fight to overcome the forces of resistance. The analyst must struggle within to understand and master the forces of the countertransference structure, which always interfere with correct understanding of and interpretations to the patient.

Unanalyzed negative countertransference experiences over a prolonged period can produce what Wile (1972) calls "therapist discouragement," an irrational pessimism regarding one's therapeutic work and personal life. This leads to premature termination of therapy cases, even the abandonment of the profession itself, the susceptibility to new fads and shortcut active techniques, or an irrational overoptimism and overconfidence in one's powers of healing. Perhaps worst of all: "Deprived of his sense of purpose and value in what he is doing, the therapist may turn to his patient for compensatory reassurance and affirmation" (Wile 1972, 52). Similarly, I already delineated the factors leading to "burnout" in the psychoanalyst in chapter 5.

But what kind of countertransference occurs when the psychoanalyst is working in a collapsing social framework? The contemporary situation is as Steiner (1971) describes it: "The widescale reversion to torture and mass murder, the ubiquitous use of hunger and imprisonment as political means mark not only a crisis of culture but, quite conceivably, an abandonment of the rational order of man" (48). Nietzsche was the prophet who most vividly forecast this disintegration in the twentieth century. About two years ago I sent for a series of tapes purporting to be a review of the philosophy of Nietzsche. These tapes were of lectures by a Texas university professor who apparently was addressing a college audience. He peppered his discussion of Nietzsche with innumerable references to popular songs, current movies, singing stars, movie actors and actresses, and sports allusions. There were so many of these that I could not understand or had never heard of, that I was unable to utilize the lectures at all, especially because the professor thought it necessary to include a number of jokes which I did not think were very funny. Perhaps he thought all this would appeal to the adolescent mentality of his students. He did not realize he was illustrating the very deterioration Nietzsche predicted.

OUR CONTEMPORARY CULTURE

In January 2002, one of the greatest financial scandals in American history was exposed, involving a whole host of politicians and executives of one of the biggest corporations in the United States, Enron. The matter was immensely more disturbing because Arthur Anderson LLP, the professional accounting firm for Enron, was allegedly in collusion with Enron executives, and other high ranking executives in the business world. The end result was that the high executives of the company came away with billions of dollars while the many people who worked for this enormous company lost their retirement savings. *The Wall Street Journal*, certainly no left wing publication, carried an editorial about it by Bartley on Monday, January 21, 2002. He wrote:

> What is particularly disturbing about Enron, though, is that failures run far beyond individual executives. Directors suspending their ethical guidelines to allow self-dealing partnerships. Accountants and lawyers studiously looking the other way, even to the point of personal jeopardy. Wall Street analysts failing in their principal duty of correctly evaluating share prices. (A13)

Bartley intelligently points out that the failure of this entire system is one of the "societal collapse of standards and morality over the last three decades or so." He complains that we seem incapable of judging the behavior of prominent entertainers, sports figures, or even presidents: "We have a legal profession that tolerates and even promotes abuse of the legal system and class actions suits . . . enriching lawyers while not even trying to give a cent to supposedly injured plaintiffs" (A13).

What Bartley does not emphasize is the insatiable greed of so many of the rich and how it is ruthlessly gratified in a situation where our civilization has reached what is loosely called an Alexandrian phase. Such a phase, in so-called advanced civilizations, is usually associated with flexible morals, perfunctory religion, populist standards, cosmopolitan tastes, exotic cults, and the rapid turnover of high and low fads—in short, a falling away from the strictness of traditional rules, embodied in character and enforced from within.

This insatiable greed has produced an explosive situation in our time. For example, an insightful study of the impact of the ever widening gap between the world's rich and the poor in our current world has been by Lewis (2002) based on his many years of investigating the disastrous situation in the Middle East. This study was carried out before the September 11 attack on the United States, an attack made possible by the enrichment of the Saudi's, including the family of Osama bin Ladin, by United States demand for Saudi oil. The disintegrating impact of the rapidly advancing materialistic civilization of the west on the culture of Islam is a good example of what is not empathically understood by the executives of international corporations, whose overt purpose is to maximize profits. The result of all this is a distortion of human values and a huge discrepancy between the few rich and the many poor; it represents an unsatisfactory ending point for history and the system will undoubtedly be replaced by something else, just as the Roman Empire eventually fell of its own corruption and weight to the violent barbarian invasions at the time, leading to the end of civilization (Ward-Perkins 2005). What that something else will be, we do not know; Marxism in practice is now largely discredited. But who can tell what ideas will be generated in the future?

We must practice psychoanalysis in the ambiance of our era, an era of science, materialism, greed, and corruption which is infesting and impacting the entire natural lived-world at this point. One can even argue that the senseless random bombings and killings of civilians all over the world represents a disintegration of the postmedieval faith in both the religious humanism of Erasmus and the great optimistic hopes of the Enlightenment for humans to improve their lot by the use of reason, leaving us all adrift.

What Went Wrong?

Lewis (2002), in his controversial book *What Went Wrong?* does an interesting job of describing how the Moslem civilization has refused to participate in this disintegration of our culture, a refusal of both westernization and modernization. Lewis does not really explain why this refusal has occurred, except to point out that the Moslem states are all theocracies (but then so is Israel) whereas the democratic spirit in the West has enabled us to develop modern science even when it disproves the Bible and renders fundamentalist assumptions patently ridiculous. The lack of emancipation of women, states Lewis, is the cardinal example of the Moslem refusal of westernization and also deprives their people of the contribution to the sciences and the arts of half of their population. The Moslem world has persisted in this and has also attempted to reject Western music and art. He does not go into the causes of this self-defeating Moslem intransigence, although he demonstrates it very well by pointing out how, by way of contrast, all of Asia has now joined the globalization of scientific progress. He does not discuss the economic reasons for this retardation of progress in the Moslem world, the support by global capitalists of the dictators in the oil rich countries in return for being allowed to tap and exploit their oil reserves. Although he points out how most Moslem countries are ruled by tyrants, he does not sufficiently emphasize the viciousness of these tyrannies and how those in the ruling class benefit from and encourage the stultifying fundamentalism of the impoverished and ignorant peasants. I agree with his pessimism about the future as far as any chance for bringing these Moslems into the modern world is concerned—not because they are stupid, for at one time they led the entire world in scientific and intellectual progress—but because of the alliance between the international oil corporations and the legislatures of the Western world which are financially beholden to them, with petty tyrants such as the rulers of Saudi Arabia—a country that seems to generate the most vicious terrorists. Lewis concludes rather weakly that the Moslem countries will have to make a choice about whether they wish to cross the apparently unbridgeable gulf between their countries and the West, choosing whether to remain mired in the Middle Ages or to become a modern Westernized people.

On the other hand, one can imagine a Moslem scholar writing a mirror image book with the same title, "What Went Wrong?" In it he would ask why, along with the success of capitalism, material wealth undreamed of in history, and incredible technological accomplishments in the West came arrogance, oppression, corruption, pornography, loose sexual morality, rising street crime, and the leisured pursuit of trivia, all celebrated by what Heidegger (1962) called "the repetitious prattling on" of the media. The destructive effects of the media have been documented by Gitlin (2002), who calls attention to our current ambiance of being surrounded by constant hucksterism, "spin" and hyped nonsense. Even our homes are no longer private; we are invaded by obnoxious telephone solicitors.

Louis Menand, author of the currently popular *The Metaphysical Club* (see Chessick 2001d), recently reviewed a book titled *A Company of Readers*. The latter consists of a collection of forty-five essays written by the editors of the now defunct Readers Subscription Book Club, which began in 1951 and closed in 1963. In that excellent review he discusses Greenberg's famous critical essay, in the 1939 issue of *Partisan Review*, that differentiates between avant-garde and kitsch art and culture. To some extent this was a reaction to Adorno's notorious conception of the "culture industry," establishing the dogmatic Marxist notion of the rupture between high culture and low culture as an absolute difference between them. Adorno used the term "low culture" to avoid the usual term "mass culture" because he was afraid this latter term would suggest art that is rising from the people. Adorno and Horkheimer, of the Frankfort School, were Marxists who believed that low culture such as Hollywood movies saturated with violence and lust, detective stories featuring gruesome murders, inane radio and television shows, astrology columns, popular music, and so on were imposed on the masses by businessmen for the purpose of convincing people that life under capitalism was natural and good. They contend this is why low culture art is purely representational, as in, for example, the Norman Rockwell illustrations showing the capitalist and bourgeois world as the only world of any value. They also made the typical Marxist complaint that low culture is for the purpose of narcotizing the proletariat.

It is not so simple as that. Greenberg's "kitsch" is the same as Adorno's "low culture," although he elaborated it into another division between high-class kitsch for the luxury trade which waters down avant-garde art and peddles it as a commodity, and low-grade kitsch like the audiovisual garbage that infests almost all the radio and TV stations and pollutes the air waves. By the 1960s, it became an assumption that being an intellectual meant despising popular culture. Somewhat to the dismay of the intellectuals, however, it was subsequently discovered that Europeans and Asians were not any more interested in high culture than Americans and they overwhelmingly preferred American kitsch! So, as Greenberg pointed out, kitsch has gone on a triumphant tour of the world.

Dwight Macdonald (1962) created quite a stir as a follower of Greenberg. In a series of essays he introduced the concepts of "masscult" and "midcult" in order to point out that, although masscult was as Adorno had said, there was also a midcult or middle-brow infection of high culture, which Macdonald describes as "tepid ooze." This tepid ooze is kind of a debasement of high culture, bringing it down to a level where the readers or audience can pretend they are enjoying true art without putting in any great effort. I believe he would have labeled the Readers Subscription essays mentioned above as an example of midcult. Certainly Macdonald's conclusion that one should never underestimate the ignorance and vulgarity of publishers, movie producers, network executives, and other architects of masscult, has been borne out increasingly in the current day.

This third aspect of our current culture, Macdonald's "midcult" has been delineated by a number of authors. For example White (2002) suggests a third force, called the "Middle Mind" which asserts its right to speak for high culture and at the same time is indifferent to the traditionalist and radical right as well as to the academic and socialist left. The Middle Mind, says White, is liberal but "most importantly, the Middle Mind imagines that it honors the highest culture, and that it lives through the arts. . . . The Middle Mind's take on culture is both well-intended and deeply deluded" (15). What he is trying to say is that a substantial group of individuals exist in our culture who are not fundamentalist or crazy but who water down the depths of the arts and music and literature into a culture of mediocrity. This mediocrity actually replaces real intelligence and "One of the most common gambits of the Middle Mind is the claim to provide high culture while really providing something a good deal less" (18). The Middle Mind's motto, says White, could be "Promise him culture but give him TV." Thus we have, for example, TV or film "adaptations" of famous classic novels, and so forth. Steiner (1971) describes this as the undermining in all the divisions that characterize civilization, between the upper and lower strata of society, between Western civilization and the other civilizations of the world, between the learned and the untutored, between the sexes, and between the dependency of youth and the authority of old age. And there is no going back!

EFFECT ON THE PRACTICE OF PSYCHOANALYSIS
AND THE APPRECIATION OF THE ARTS

Returning to the beginning of this chapter brings me once more to the major work of Bordieu (1984), who manages to write convincingly about how cultural needs and practices are a function of home upbringing, education, and financial freedom. The social hierarchy of the arts, in Bordieu's view, is a function of the social hierarchy of consumers. Clearly a work of art has meaning and interest only for those who possess the cultural competence in which it is encoded. So in that sense art and culture function to legitimate social differences. Remarkably, Bordieu tries to show the correlation between taste in the arts and taste in dining habits, which is rather amusing and interesting, and functions very well as a metaphor for his point of view. Here he takes advantage of the obvious dual meaning of the word "taste."

Bordieu contrasts his view with what he labels Kant's "charismatic ideology." In proposing what he calls an "anti-Kantian aesthetic," he argues that art has no intention and standards in the dogmatic sense that Kant set forth. Instead, Bordieu claims the appreciation of art is a function of one's disposition, which in turn depends on one's material conditions, economic power, and accumulated cultural capital as well as one's competence and education. A person cannot enjoy the arts and really be immersed in culture unless he or she is capable of the bracketing of ordinary urgencies, of a certain distancing, and of contemplation as an end in itself. The parallel to the position of the psychoanalyst is important here; psychoanalysts also need a certain capacity to bracket personal concerns and interests as they listen to their patients. The ability to distance one's self while not avoiding an intimate relationship with the patient—what Sullivan called participant observation—is clearly necessary.

Similar to White's Middle Mind is what Bordieu labels "Middle-brow culture"—culture without effort. As part of this middle-brow culture he cites those psychoanalysts and the attendant core of so-called "mental health professionals" who in the newspapers, on TV, and on the radio as well as in the clinical situation offer answers to all problems and also give innumerable rationalizations for the deteriorating ethic of our society, an ethic which functions to excuse and orient the perfect consumer towards more and more pleasure and consumption. Bordieu points out how the style of life that a person lives is inversely proportional to the material constraints and the urgent life problems that person has, such as illness, et cetera. He also alludes to Adorno's concept of the culture industry and, as an example of the deteriorating ambiance of our Western culture, refers to the typical couch potato sports fan, a passive onlooker rather than a participant. So, argues Bordieu, there is no Kantian "pure taste" and the view of Schopenhauer, which was close to Kant's view on this, is wrong. Bordieu claims that this charismatic ideology is simply a rationalization of the ethos of the dominant class in bourgeois society.

It is the materialistic deterioration of our cosmopolitan and civilized ethos and the infestation of the arts and music by an increasingly Middle-brow or Middle Mind orientation that will have an important impact on the capacity of the psychoanalyst to be creative, to bracket his or her personal interests, to remain equidistant between the id, ego, and superego as Anna Freud recommended, and at the same time to intensely participate rather than passively observe.

Coming from another quarter has been a different sort of assault on Western civilization. The importance of this assault is somewhat debatable. Windschuttle, a right-wing critic (2002) writes:

> Until thirty years ago, when Western intellectuals reflected on the long term achievements of their culture, they explained it in terms of its own evolution: the inheritance of ancient Greece, Rome, and Christianity, tempered by the Renaissance, the Reformation, the Enlightenment, and the scientific and industrial revolutions. (4)

Windschuttle claims this has changed and in place of a universal admiration of Western culture, there is "the relativism of multi-culturalism, a concept that regards the West not as the pinnacle of human achievement to date, but as simply one of many equally valid cultural systems" (5). He lumps postmodernism, poststructuralism, and postcolonialism under the rubric of multiculturalism also and considers it all basically as an entire negation of Western culture and values. The insistence that Western literature and art endorse imperialism, are antifeminist and politically contaminated, has become very popular in academia according to Windschuttle.

Citing Alan Bloom's (1987) famous work *The Closing of the American Mind*, Windschuttle stresses the relativism of this new approach:

> This notion of cultural relativism entailed a radical re-thinking of Western intellectual life. In aesthetic criticism, it meant traditional standards had to be jettisoned. Italian opera could no longer be regarded as superior to Chinese opera. The theatre of Shakespeare was not better than that of Kabuki, only different
>
> . . . Rather than principles that were eternal or self-evident, cultural relativists said these values were bound by their own time and space. They were simply the ethnocentric products of the eighteenth century European Enlightenment. (13)

This attitude inevitably leads to a moral nihilism and to situations like that produced by the chief executive officers of Enron.

CIVILIZATION DISTINGUISHED FROM CULTURE

It is necessary now to make a distinction between "culture" and "civilization" for our purposes here. We may regard "culture" as an anthropological term that describes the body of artifacts and ideas, habits, and traditions, that delineate a given group of people. "Civilization" on the other hand, might be thought of as that way of life which was exemplified in the European Enlightenment, is based on reason, is open to new ideas, and is focused in its educational aspects on what Matthew Arnold (1882), in his work *Culture and Anarchy* called becoming acquainted with the best that has been thought and said in the world. Or, as I have put it in discussing the work of the great educator Robert Hutchins (1999b), a civilized education allows one to be at least a part of an audience for, if not a participant in, the great conversation of mankind with its Hebraic and Greek roots in the Bible and poetry of Homer respectively. In this way one becomes a civilized person, a citizen of the world, and respects human life and the planet on which we dwell.

All this is immediately subject to the complaint of elitism because the concept of "civilization" implies that there is indeed a hierarchy of human societies, which may be classed in terms of the importance of the role of reason and the intellectual life as well as the importance of human rights and focus on the freedom and dignity of the individual. Accepting this form of elitism, which is of course a pejorative term, it is important to understand that four hundred years ago scholars enjoyed much higher esteem than they do today. Thomas (2001) writes, "Monarchs competed for their services and their work was assumed to be of crucial importance to everyone . . . they were custodians of traditional wisdom, persons to whom rulers turned at times of crisis, essential authorities on how one should live. Most societies have such sages, and the more complex their traditions, the more intellectually demanding is the sage's role" (12). In those days scholarship had a political, religious, and social utility and so it was supported. By way of contrast, most modern academic scholars are not public intellectuals, they are not supported because of their utility to the state or to any group or organization. Often they write in a complex jargon that is only understandable by other members of their subsection of their own disciplinary community.

Scholars were highly competitive; for example, John Milton believed that a desire for honor, repute, and immortal fame was the driving force in the breast of every true scholar. But people who follow the life of learning have done so for other than narcissistic reasons; there are intrinsic attractions to it. In traditional times, it was accepted that the desire for knowledge was a natural appetite and, as Aristotle pointed out, the pursuit of knowledge was the highest form of human activity. One of the important bulwarks against the moral nihilism described in the above paragraphs can be the life of learning, sustained mental endeavor based on memory, imagination, science, and accurate observations concentrated through a prolonged period whether it be on the natural world or on literature and the arts. The practice of psychoanalysis can be a prime example of this kind of life of learning. In his British Academy lecture, Thomas concludes that the life of learning has an exemplary morality to offer:

Where else, save in other forms of academic inquiry, can we find the same scrupulous concern for truth, the same requirement that all propositions which are not self-evidently true should be documented, the same conviction that getting things right is more important than a quick fix, the same acceptance of the complexity of things and the same refusal to contemplate any dumbing down?. (13)

These jeremiads about the destruction of civilized high culture neglect the fact there are still isolated instances of civilized high culture available and in many ways continue to be respected. Take, for example, the contemporary novels of Anita Brookner. As far as I am concerned, such novels give us as much information about the psychology of humans as the publications of psychoanalysts. For instance, in *Look At Me*, Brookner (1983) tells us about people who write:

I felt a revulsion against the long isolation that writing imposes, the claustration, the sense of exclusion; I experienced a thrill of distaste for the alternative life that writing is supposed to represent. It was then that I saw the business of writing for what it truly was and is to me. It is your penance for not being lucky. It is an attempt to reach others and to make them love you. It is your instinctive protest, when you find you have no voice at the world's tribunals, and that no one will speak for you. I would give my entire output of words, past, present, and to come, in exchange for easier access to the world, for permission to state 'I hurt' or 'I hate' or 'I want.' Or, indeed, 'Look at me.' (84)

PSYCHOANALYSIS AT A TIME
OF COLLAPSING CIVILIZATION

By this time the mental health professional reader may be asking, Why is all this included in what purports to be a book on the future of psychoanalysis and in a chapter focused on countertransference? The answer is contained in the newly acquired insight Heidegger (1962) has given us: Our understanding grows or decays according to the kind of lives we are leading and the kind of civilized or uncivilized situation in the culture we inhabit. All questioning in or out of the psychoanalytic process carries certain presuppositions which govern the inquiry and predetermine to a certain extent what can be discovered. Indeed, we offer the answer in the light of what we already know. Or, as Moran (2000) tells us in his discussion of the hermeneutics of Hans-Georg Gadamer:

Understanding takes place within the finite boundaries of essentially limited and historically conditioned human living, as both Hegel and Marx knew well, and as Heidegger concretely described in *Being and Time*. Understanding only takes place in the context of an existing tradition. In this sense, we already presuppose a huge amount in every act of understanding—we take on trust our own presumptions or prejudices. (251)

As I have discussed at length in chapter 4, phenomenologists argue that Galileo's discovery was one of the starting points of the loss of faith in the lived world. We know that modern science depends on mathematics and this overrules even the direct experience of nature itself, the "lived world," as Husserl (1970) called it. Through the use of mathematics humans can achieve a universal standpoint taking them beyond the lived world. The attempt to deal with this loss of faith in the lived world is through dominating the world by the use of science and the resultant distancing from human intimacy. This is another way to describe Lasch's (1978) *Culture of Narcissism*, although Lasch, influenced by Kohut, tends to blame it more on the change in child raising situations. But many phenomenologists and philosophers such as Husserl, Heidegger, and Gadamer have been concerned with the effect of the modern natural science outlook on human being-in-the-world, a very important contribution of phenomenology. This concern goes all the way back to Plato, which is why, as Whitehead said, we regard all philosophy as a series of footnotes to Plato. In the *Philebus*, Plato condemns the so-called naturalists, empiricists, *oi physikoi* in his Greek, who concern themselves only with "what has become, is becoming, and will become" and totally ignore "what always is" (59a–b).

Granting this, it follows that as civilization becomes more and more infested with kitsch, low culture, and even midcult, there are going to be effects on the psychoanalyst's capacity for understanding and forming conceptions of his or her patients. That is to say, countertransference in all its forms and how it is experienced by the psychoanalyst, is intricately and inextricably bound up with the particular cultural milieu and the civilization into which the psychoanalyst finds himself or herself thrown, to employ here Heidegger's (1962) conception of the facticity of *Dasein*. As civilization disintegrates, those who attempt to hold out and retain some aspects of the scholarly or humanistic approach to life as described above are going to have increasing difficulty in understanding the allusions and preoccupations of their patients.

If a patient dreams of me as Richard Nixon, it is imperative that I be aware of what is going on or has gone on in Richard Nixon's behavior and subsequently formed his image and impact on society in order to understand the transference and countertransferential aspects of such a dream. Now surely most psychoanalysts are aware of Richard Nixon, but what if a patient dreams of you as a rock star and you are totally unacquainted with rock music? Or a movie actress that you have never heard of even though she is temporarily very much at the center of adolescent popular culture? This is not simply a function of the aging of the psychoanalyst and of the different interests of the younger generation. In fact, one of the most interesting aspects of current popular culture is that the old and the young seem to have the same tastes; today the old emulate the tastes of the young, a kind of reversal of what has gone before in the Western world and is still extant in other contemporary civilizations. Lack of interest and knowledge about popular culture puts the psychoanalyst in a difficult bind; if he or she is attempting to live a civilized life, often there will be an ignorance about masscult, kitsch, and low culture. Complaining about this will get the psychoanalyst labeled as elitist. On the other hand, if the psychoanalyst immerses himself or herself in those uncivilized forms of culture, which are becoming more and more pervasive every day, there will be little time to study the poetry of Homer or Dante and many other great authors and artists as well as the great philosophers, whose works are all brimming with profound and important insights into human psychology and behavior. Shakespeare, for example, may be regarded as the greatest psychologist who ever lived, greater even than Freud. The eminent literary critic Harold Bloom (1998) actually credits Shakespeare with the "invention of the human," characters with highly indivudal and realistic personalities that change and develop over time.[1]

EFFECT ON THE FUTURE OF PSYCHOANALYSIS

And what about the moral implications of this? If the above discussion is correct, the increasing immersion in low culture is accompanied by an increasing relativism and moral nihilism. An example of this is the contemporary subservience of the U.S. psychiatric profession to the wealthy and powerful international pharmaceutical industry. More heinous examples can be found in various instances of exploitation of patients. It is very difficult to educate the young not to cheat when the leaders of our society and our politicians are continuously embracing the kind of individuals that ran Enron Corporation, WorldCom, Arthur Anderson, and a whole host of others since that time.

Is it just that "We *Feinschmeckers*[2] have to live with vulgarity in popular culture, the sight of overweight middle-aged men wearing shorts and baseball caps, weak coffee and the blare of the television set in every airport waiting lounge" (Crain 2002), or is something more disastrous afoot? In *The Dehumanization of Art*, Jose Ortega y Gasset (1925) described the grave dissociation of the past and present in modern life, the loss of the traditional spirit, and the predominant fading of the sense that the great thinkers of the past can have anything to say to us. Hence "the great conversation" I mentioned above becomes irrelevant and not worthy of attention any more. Winterer (2001) reports, how in 1994, only six hundred American college students received a bachelor's degree in classics, out of over a million degrees awarded. Ancient art and literature have lost their central place in the larger civic culture where they once were. Who studies Latin and Greek anymore, even in the universities? There the huge financial grants go first of all to the athletic department and second to the sciences, which are now charged with keeping us one step ahead of the military discoveries of the sciences in other countries rather than the disinterested pursuit of truth. The humanities, including psychoanalysis, have become marginalized and unsupported and unappreciated.

Obviously this is going to have a major effect on the practice of psychoanalysis and its future. For example, take the recent attempt, which I have objected to repeatedly in previous publications and in this book, of converting psychoanalysis into "neuropsychoanalysis," thus making it more acceptable to the science departments and those who govern managed care payments. There is a huge danger here of losing the phenomenologic, the hermeneutic, the creative, and the artistic aspects of psychoanalysis, aspects which, for example, as any lover of Shakespeare knows, offer boundless opportunities to understand humans. The pressure of our current cultural ambiance on the practicing psychoanalyst is relentless and goes to the heart of the economic well-being of himself or herself as well as the analyst's family.

In the view of Friedman (2001), the relationship between the patient and the analyst is the centerpiece of the therapeutic action of psychoanalysis. This is still a very debatable point. Friedman argues that the analyst needs to fulfill the relationship need of the patient and provide hope. He claims that if the analyst is not sincere in the relationship to the patient, it is experienced by the patient as a narcissistic wound. Whether *so much* emphasis on this aspect of the treatment takes it out of the realm of psychoanalysis or not is one of those current unsettled issues for argument. There is no question, however, that the unresponsive psychoanalyst will lead the process into a treatment that involves mutual frustration and hatred. Friedman advocates the well-known and controversial claims of Renik, who insists that the analyst must disclose his world view to the patient and that both parties must be relaxed in order for successful treatment to move forward. In my opinion this does not require actually lecturing the patient on one's point of view or *Weltanschauung*, because over the years of frequent sessions the patient gathers a pretty accurate idea of what the analyst is really like regardless of what he or she says he or she is like, and what his or her value system is anyway. The concentration on the relationship as central to the treatment is what marks out the views of Renick and Friedman from those of Freud's psychoanalysis. Friedman writes:

The erosion of the hegemony of the classical psychoanalytic technical triad of anonymity, abstinence, and neutrality has proceeded
slowly and erratically. It is worth emphasizing a confluence of influences coming from contributors of differing backgrounds but leading
in an inexorable fashion to a change of technique in the practice of
psychoanalysis. To have a successful practice of psychoanalysis in the
contemporary world, psychoanalysts have had to be adaptive according to their circumstances. (649)

Here is where the issues of countertransference and of the deterioration
of civilization obviously intersect. The world view or value system of the psychoanalyst is affected by the cultural milieu in which he or she lives and the
educational background that culture has to offer, just as the capacity to appreciate the arts is similarly affected, as discussed above. Whether the analyst's
personality is the main factor in moving the patient in the direction of health
and renewed vigor or just an important ancillary factor, most psychoanalysts
today would agree that the analyst's personality and value system has at least
some significant effect on the treatment. Friedman correctly points out this
does not require abandonment of conflict theory and its corollary of maintaining that drive derivatives are essential determinants of psychological
states. Friedman claims, and I entirely agree, that the "analyst's belief in the
concept of unconscious drive derivatives from the infantile period has become
the litmus test for conservative analysts" (654), and he concludes:

If the patient is viewed as the author of his own suffering because of
his own unconscious wishes and the resultant unconscious guilt, then
those who advocate a minimalist analyst as essential for the emergence of a regressive transference neurosis will feel justified in con-
demning those relational analysts who do form a meaningful relational presence and influence in their patients' lives as not behaving
as "real" analysts. (657)

Here Friedman seems to imply that you cannot both adhere to the concept of
drive derivatives and infantile experiences as being primarily etiological in
mental illness and at the same time intensively relate in a "real" fashion to
one's patient. I disagree with this point of view, and one can simply read the
case histories of Sigmund Freud to see how Freud combined both of these
aspects of psychoanalytic practice in his own work with consummate skill.

The analyst must be able to sustain feelings of countertransference in
order to subordinate them to the analytic task. Today, it is generally agreed
that countertransference is an instrument of research into the patient's unconscious, although a number of unanswered questions remain. It is difficult to

differentiate those components of the patient's material that are the result of the analyst's unconscious countertransference and those which are the patient's genuine transference as part of the regressive process in the treatment. There has been a lot of discussion of the therapeutic function of the analyst as a "container" of the patient's projections but not much discussion of the therapeutic function of the patient as a "container" of the analyst's unconscious countertransference projections!

As explained in chapter 1, Whittaker and Malone (1953) insist it is vital for successful therapy that the therapist bring his or her patient vectors along with his or her therapist vectors into the treatment. They call this a total participation with the patient. In this manner, the analyst always expands the frontiers of his or her own emotional growth during the therapy. If he or she refuses to participate totally in this fashion, it is felt by the patient as a severe rejection . . . what today we would call a narcissistic wound. Of course Whittaker and Malone contrast the gross pathological patient vectors of the immature therapist with the minimal or sliver type of residual patient vectors in the mature therapist, and so a thorough training psychoanalysis becomes mandatory for anyone who wishes to do uncovering psychotherapy or psychoanalysis without harming their patients.

Another aspect of countertransference that does not receive sufficient attention is mentioned by Issacharoff (1993), who suggests we consider the important influence of an inordinate amount of greed which may be provoked in the analyst by the intensified deprivation he or she has to suffer in the relationship:

> The pursuit of knowledge, when severely thwarted and impatient of being confined, arouses powerful and insatiate longings in the analyst. . . . Arousal of greed in the analyst occurs as a result of the patient's withholding of whatever is "valuable" for the analysis. And the stronger the greed that has to be suppressed, the smaller the capacity to bear frustration and to maintain an empathic link with the patient. (40)

What Issacharoff does *not* discuss is the impact of a culture in which, due to the deterioration of civilized life, greed becomes an increasingly powerful and acceptable motivation for behavior, thus loosening the restraints and inhibitions crucial in the value system of an analyst who is immersed in this ambiance of universal greed. The arousal of greed and its frustration can, for example, either lead to a secret envy, anger, and hatred of the patient or to a reaction-formation characterized by feeling much love for the patient. These are very common problems in the practice of psychoanalysis in our culture today, as any supervisor knows, and lie behind many difficulties in the psychoanalytic process, including even stalemate or abrupt termination of the treatment by either patient or analyst. Of course we hope the analyst will neutralize these intense countertransference feelings before communicating them, although some authors even advocate direct spontaneous affectual communication of feelings like hatred and love to the patient. I believe this, if it is engaged in at all, should take place only after careful self-analysis and only on selected occasions with selected patients, as it offers opportunities for sliding into massive and destructive acting-out behavior by both patient and analyst.

Boyer (1993) recognizes the vast literature pertaining to the influence of cultural background, "determined by the patient's socioeconomic, religious, or other subgroup of Western culture" (364) on the patient and on the psychoanalytic process. But he does not bring up the importance of the *analyst's* cultural and educational background in determining the analyst's capacity to deal appropriately with and understand the patient. It is not simply a matter of studying the patient from a different culture by trying to learn about that patient's cultural background, it also requires the analyst's awareness of the influence not only of the analyst's cultural surround but also of the deterioration of that surround on his or her own analytic analyzing instrument.

In this chapter I have tried to demonstrate an aspect of countertransference that has not been thoroughly discussed in the literature, namely the effect on the analyst's countertransference of the deterioration in the civilized ambiance of the culture in which he or she is immersed. This deterioration of civilization in our current Western culture has been portrayed by a number of sociological thinkers and philosophers. Changes in the value system of the analyst and his or her turning a blind eye to the injustices and barbarism that surround the analyst affect the analyst's capacity to immerse in the creative process of psychoanalysis as well as to appreciate and understand the material from the patient. Interestingly, this situation is parallel to the problems involved in the appreciation of the arts. I have tried to emphasize the importance of the collapse of our civilization in the midst of which the analyst must carry on a psychoanalytic practice, and its effect on the treatment process. If the analyst is to be a real person to the patient—and if not, it is surely narcissistically wounding to the patient—the impact of the dumbing down and deterioration of the educational, cultural, and home upbringing milieu of the new generation of psychoanalysts will be profound in influencing the future practice of psychoanalysis.

9

The Contemporary Failure of Nerve and the Crisis of Psychoanalysis

> It is especially the case in psychiatry that the continuous encounter between the thinking of the natural scientist and that of the philosopher is very productive and exciting.
>
> —Martin Heidegger (*Zollikon Seminars*)

Everyone agrees that the field of psychoanalysis is undergoing widespread dispersion and dilution these days, with many conflicting schools of thought and many new opinions. In order to maintain our sense of identity as psychoanalysts, we need to have a clear notion of what we regard to be psychoanalysis and what it stands for. As a contribution to the resolution of this critical problem and to address the issue of what the American Academy of Psychoanalysis and Dynamic Psychiatry (the organization to which I loyally belong), represents, and also to warn of the dangers to our professional future, I will first discuss the decline and closing of the most famous Academy of all time, that of Plato, and review historically how and why Plato's academy disintegrated. Historians agree this disintegration represented a failure of nerve in the thinkers of the time as a consequence of their efforts to fit into the prevailing Christian cultural milieu. Christianity as a secular power was increasingly replacing that of classical Greece and its derivative, the Roman Empire. The goal of Plato's academy members shifted from the disinterested pursuit of truth to one of accommodation to the new prevailing powers. I suggest that a similar failure of nerve is taking place today. As Foucault (1973a, 1973b) pointed out, the nature and structure of the human sciences or "disciplines" in a given era are generated by the prevailing political and economic powers of that particular era.

157

I will go on to describe once more what I think is fundamental to the practice and theory of psychoanalysis and present a clinical example of a typical type of patient that we are dealing with today. Although such patients seem to stand sharply in contrast to the traditional hysterical patients of Freud, they still can be understood and treated using his methodology. In fact an argument could be made that some of Freud's patients showed evidence of being what today would be diagnosed as a borderline personality disorder.

I will follow this by a discussion of the mind-brain problem in the philosophy of science, which indicates there is an unjustified optimism in the current trend towards "neuropsychoanalysis" and in its basic assumption, a mereological fallacy, that if we know all about the workings of the brain it will completely explain the workings of the mind. Actually, there are many philosophers who disagree with this assumption and point out that even if we knew everything about the workings of the brain, it would not eliminate our need for a science of mind, the best of which is the practice and theory of Freud's psychoanalysis.

Because we are in the era of the popularity and reputed progress of brain studies, there is a tendency to forget that psychoanalysis, as pointed out in chapter 1, is a unique discipline combining natural science observations of the transference with hermeneutics and energetics (Ricoeur 1970). Being unique, it is not replaceable or reducible to any knowledge of a materialistic substrate. I will conclude by outlining what I believe should be our basic ideals as psychoanalysts, the glue that should hold the profession together. I hope to convince the reader that the founder of our discipline, Sigmund Freud, offered a towering edifice that still in its basics can form the foundation of modern psychoanalytic theory and practice, even though I agree with the current tendency to de-idealize Freud, the person.

CLASSICAL GREEK THOUGHT

For Pythagoras, in about 550 BC mathematics was the key to the order and the beauty of the universe. The intellectual satisfaction of mathematics leads us, as Plato subsequently said, to the realm of the perfect; it is, he thought, a way of truth, a way to recognize the real objects of the world, a way to approach the Form of the Good. Similarly, Aristotle believed that a life of *theoria*, pure inquiry, was the best life.

Everything from that time on went down hill. For example, the sophist Antiphon said that the whole of life is wonderfully open to complaint; it has nothing remarkable, great, or noble, but all is petty, feeble, brief, and mingled with sorrows. But Plato believed that reason was for the purpose of enabling humans to live for something, to identify and set up appropriate goals and then focus one's life on achieving them. However, even Epicurus and Lucretius already recognized that few humans are not slaves to lust and aggression, and with the decline of Greek civilization began a basic controversy that exists to the present day. As Gottlieb (2000) describes it in a recent historical study:

> The Epicureans said that the world is the unplanned product of haphazard forces; the Stoics said it is rationally organized down to the last detail. The Epicureans said that the universe does not operate with any purposes in mind and that the gods are permanently on holiday; the Stoics retorted that a beneficent god, or providence, is thoroughly in charge and always on the job. The Epicureans said that the course of nature is not wholly determined in advance—there are, for instance, random swerves of atoms; the Stoics said that everything unfolds according to fate in an inexorable chain of cause and effect. . . . The Epicureans held that each person is completely free in his actions; the Stoics denied this, because of their belief in fate. . . . (311)

The first academy known to history, and devoted to the examination of humanistic issues, was opened by Plato after the death of Socrates. Over the entrance was the admonition that one must learn mathematics before entering. This academy lasted about nine hundred years in one form or another. It was founded in about 387 BC when Plato was forty, on a property about a mile outside the walls of Athens and near a grove sacred to a hero named Academus. The first academy was like a college or a group of self-supporting intellectuals teaching an enormous range of subjects. Members of this academy were required by Plato to have certain natural gifts for the pursuit of learning: a willingness to work very hard, and to adopt a well-ordered scheme of living. Plato hoped the love of knowledge in its purest form would be the basic motivating force of those who were admitted to his academy.

THE DISINTEGRATION OF THE ACADEMY

It is very interesting to study the subsequent development of the academy after Plato's death. It broke up into groups of quarreling factions in which, for example, some leaders developed and rigidly followed what they took to be Plato's dogma and doctrines, while other groups adopted a more tentative questioning and somewhat more sceptical approach in the attempt to acquire knowledge. For example, a philosopher named Arcesilaus (c. 315–240 BC) became the leader of a major faction in Plato's Academy and brought scepticism to the point where all sorts of theories were subjected to dismantling. Arguments between the factions finally led to a fragmentation of the membership and the establishment of new schools, institutes, and academies such as the Pyrrhonist revival and many others.

Aristotle, Plato's most famous pupil, split off and developed a philosophy that only remotely resembled that of his master Plato. When Plato died, his nephew Speusippus inherited the leadership of the academy. Aristotle, resentful he was not appointed leader, went with a few students to Atarneus, a small city on the west coast of Asia Minor governed by a friend who had been a student at the academy. On land this friend gave him, near the site of ancient Troy, he established his own "institute." . . . Does this sound familiar? A few years later, his friend was assassinated and Aristotle had to leave. He then spent three years on Lesbos at the home of another friend from the academy, where he collected data for his biological studies, and meticulously reviewed the entire philosophical system he had learned from Plato. By the end of that time he had completely criticized and revised Plato's doctrine.

He then was called as tutor to King Philip of Macedon's thirteen-year-old son, Alexander. When Philip was assassinated, Alexander became king and went off to conquer the world; Aristotle moved back to Athens, where to rival the Academy he founded his own "institute" at the Lyceum, a public garden dedicated to Apollo. He strolled there every morning on a covered walk (*peripatos*) accompanied by his students while he lectured on many subjects; hence his institute became known as the peripatetic school. It soon came to seriously compete with the academy and lasted for about eight hundred years. Aristotle himself only taught there for twelve years, because when Alexander died it was dangerous for him to remain in Athens so he moved to Chalcis, where he died at the age of sixty-two. His successor in the Lyceum was Theophrastus, who then edited his lecture notes, rough drafts, and notes of his students. The material was stored in a damp basement and discovered by accident many years later; it was brought to Rome in 86 BC in chaotic and disorganized condition.

The first two centuries after Aristotle's death were marked by a spirit of competition among the proponents of rival philosophies between and within various academies or "institutes." Others attempted to reconcile them and still others simply dogmatically promulgated the doctrines of earlier idealized thinkers. The debates degenerated and took on an increasing mystical tone because there were no ways of convincingly demonstrating who was right and who was wrong. The importance of clinical or empirical studies was not even recognized as a legitimate method to settle humanistic disputes. The final stage of Plato's Academy was represented by thinkers such as Proclus (AD

410–485), who was head of the Plotinian philosophical school in Athens, which represented the remnant of Plato's Academy and whose work contained mystical combinations of appeals to the pagan gods and obscure abstractions, a kind of degenerate version of the philosophy of that great Neoplatonist, Plotinus.

By this time, Christianity was ascendant in the classical world and the aims of the academy had shifted from the pursuit of knowledge for its own sake to attempts to reconcile classical philosophy with the increasingly influential Christian theology, to fit in, so to speak, with the prevailing cultural ambiance. The Christian emperor Justinian found a quick way to put an end to all this obscure philosophical squabbling by simply closing down all the philosophical schools in Athens and attempting to ban all non-Christian philosophy throughout the Roman Empire.

To close the academy was not difficult by this time because the days of open-minded inquiry had faded away long ago and been replaced by the mystical and religious strains in Greek thought. As Gottlieb states:

> The rationalistic spirit shared by Thales, Anaxagoras, Democritus and Epicurus; the radical questioning shared by Socrates, the Sophists and the Sceptics; Plato's love of logical argument; Aristotle's wide-ranging intellectual curiosity—all of these qualities were dying, or at least mutating. (346)

So the closure of all the Athenian institutes and academies in 529 AD was not in itself a momentous event, but forms an historical milestone from which time philosophy became the handmaiden of Christian theology for about a thousand years until, perhaps, the emergence of a new genius named Descartes was made possible by the changing cultural ambiance.

I think it is fair to label this story of the progressive degeneration of the academies and institutes and schools of thought as a loss of nerve among the intellectual lights of classical antiquity. Hegel (1830) in his *Lectures on the Philosophy of World History* pointed out that all the contributory factors that led to the eventual decline of the Greek world can be ultimately condensed into a single one: the emerging principle of corruption. In a world caught up in a decline like this there are only three possibilities left for autonomous individuality, points out Althaus (2000) in his study of Hegel: "to despair, to seek refuge in philosophy, or to die fighting" (180). Indeed, with the death of Alexander, Hegel believed, the moment when Greece was a significant power departed from the stage of world history and the role of a world-historical people now passed to the military and barbaric Roman empire, rendering the world spiritless and heartless in comparison with the Greek world that had preceded it.

A New Failure of Nerve

The parallels to the current cultural situation and our current situation in psychoanalysis are obvious. For example, one may ask which concept of *Bildung* should we follow, both of which were extant during the time of Hegel. The first conception, developed by philosophers such as Fichte, views *Bildung* as a spontaneous, natural instinct towards self-development. The opposing concept, presented by Hegel, refers it to a process of development whereby the merely natural individual is transcended, raised to the level of spirit as a member of a moral community, or as a citizen of an ethical state. In today's world the first concept of *Bildung* is what we use in explicating the goals of psychoanalysis and we are inclined to think that the second concept represents a value system that should not be imposed upon the patient. It is important to point out that this decision to reject the second concept represents an underlying philosophical premise about the nature of humans. For example, Marx argued contrary to this premise. He claimed that humans are predominantly species-beings, borrowing Hegel's notion of *Bildung*, and insisted that given the proper conditions humans naturally would develop to where they would be concerned with each other's welfare. This clashes directly with the spirit prevalent today, so-called rugged individualism, the spirit of "me-first."

Körner (2002) also stresses the importance of "*Bildung*." He explains,

> The main characteristics of '*Bildung*'—as opposed to professional training—are that the objectives remain undefined and there is no attempt to achieve defined and operationalisable professional qualifications. The relationship between teacher and pupil is characterised by authority and trust. A psychoanalytic education by means of a 'liberal education' is based upon the assumption that the student should be motivated and supported in achieving competence through a passionate study of the world of psychic reality. (1395)

The Germans used the word *Bildung*, to contrast with the word "*Erziehung*," which designates a vocational education. *Bildung*, is concerned with the acquisition of cultural qualities, both intellectual and ethical, together with the development of the individual into a responsible human being (1397). *Erziehung*, on the other hand, is concerned with the acquisition of knowledge and professional skills.

Körner describes the transition in the healing professions, including physicians and teachers, from a value-oriented approach to a goal-oriented approach. He describes this as the transformation of a profession from a classic to a modern form. In this transformation we move from a situation in which society relied on internalized quality control of its professionals: "It was expected that their behaviour—after a thorough professional training, which always also included aspects of a broad liberal education—would be governed by high ideals" (1399), to a demand for external assessment of both the quality and the effectiveness of professional performance demanded by contemporary society, insurance companies, political bodies, and so on. Körner points out how, although there is good reason for psychoanalysts to resist this transformation, if they do so they "risk becoming marginalized within a modernising society, by being considered to be behind the times and under suspicion of trying to protect their levels of performance from public scrutiny" (1399).

I would like to suggest that a new failure of nerve is taking place today in our intellectual ambiance of so-called postmodernism, and it is reflected in the field of psychoanalysis. We tend to forget that, as Abend (2001) tells us,

> The analyst's task is to strive to have and sustain an analytic attitude towards patients, and to maintain as much self awareness about his or her variations from this model—temptations to add something more or to take something away from it—as possible. . . . I do not agree at all with those who suggest that attempting to adhere to this formula turns the analyst into an uncaring, unempathic surgeon of the psyche, indifferent to outcome or suffering, or unengaged with the patient's life. On the contrary, I think it holds the promise of maximizing the patient's prospects for defining and finding his or her own best potential. (13)

The whole drift and fashion in psychoanalysis today, in the direction of intersubjectivity and interpersonalism and even promoting the analyst's self-disclosure, represents a development in psychoanalysis similar to the changes that occurred in Plato's Academy. We tend to forget about Freud's admonitions and hopefulness that scientific objectivity is at least relatively possible in psychoanalysis. Bergmann (2001), in discussing Freud's structural theory, explains:

> Within this structural point of view, the aim of psychoanalysis became the strengthening of the ego against the other two institutions, and also helping the ego free itself from the power of some of its own defense mechanisms, acquired during childhood which can cripple the ego's freedom of movement. The aim of psychoanalysis became the achievement of a more favorable kind of intrapsychic compromise formation. (20)

The retreat from such lofty aims to a study of the here-and-now interpersonal interactions in the analytic consulting room represents evidence of a loss of nerve among psychoanalysts. This loss is a function of the depressive ambiance that permeates our field because it is being crushed and stamped out by the insurance companies and their refusal to pay for treatment. It is hard to maintain our original ideals in a world that is morally disintegrating around us, posing the same problem that was unsuccessfully faced by the members of Plato's Academy who attempted to live the life of *theoria* while the classical Greek culture disintegrated and eventually fell to the rule of the Roman military state.

There are still three phases in every psychoanalysis. In the first phase everything must be done to start the analytic process, which means understanding the conflicts and defenses within the patient that oppose this process as well as the patient's unconscious need to destroy the analysis. Once the patient is actually immersed in the analytic process, the analysis of transference and transference resistance becomes the center of the procedure. As Bergmann (2001) correctly and most incisively points out, "The analyst can help by continuously emphasizing free association, and not deflecting the hour away from its inherent course" (31). This requires an analytic focus on everything rather than an intrusion by the analyst in some deliberate fashion on the process of free association, a requirement that is very difficult to meet, taxing the analyst's patience, creativity, training, and personal psychoanalysis. The final phase is that of termination, and in my opinion that is still a very debatable phase of analysis and is handled differently by different analysts.

I turn now to a clinical example of a patient in psychoanalytic treatment who is typical and presents the kind of problems psychoanalysts face today. The purpose of this example is to demonstrate briefly how the preconceptions and internalized object relations of patients profoundly affect the entire "here-and-now" interaction between the analyst and patient. In the current rush to relational or constructivist psychoanalysis, this extremely important discovery of Freud has tended to become relegated to the background, whereas in my opinion it belongs in the foreground. Freud's profound delineation of how the earliest years of life affect and determine to a great extent the patient's experiences later in life or, more precisely, determine the way the given patient experiences his or her experiences is powerful evidence that Freud's basic conceptions of psychoanalysis are just as valid today as they were in his time, It would be a great mistake for psychoanalysts to lose sight of this fact. The kinds of patients we see today are not the kinds of patients for the most part that provided the cases upon which Freud built his theories, but the principles of the practice and theory of psychoanalysis should remain the same.

CLINICAL EXAMPLE

Ms. I. is very cooperative with her psychoanalytic treatment with the exception that she has from the beginning absolutely refused to use the couch.

There are many, many "good hours" in which the patient seems to be free associating and responding appropriately to interpretations, but every once in a while without warning she subjects me to a severe tongue-lashing, accusing me of totally unempathic intrusion by my interpretations. Of course self psychologists would explain this on the basis of the patient's perceived lack of my empathy with her need for a mirroring selfobject, and her consequent narcissistic rage. After much self-scrutiny, listening carefully to her free associations, and the realization that there was a pattern to these attacks, which took place from time to time apparently regardless of what I said or did, it occurred to me that the underlying motivating force producing these sporadic and unexpected tongue-lashings was not narcissistic rage but fear.

The patient had been hurt and disappointed a lot, especially by those who claimed to care about her, such as her parents, her husband, and others. In life, as a function of the repetition compulsion, she "learned" that the closer and more trusting she was of any person she became involved with, the more painful it was when they eventually empathically failed and disappointed her. These repetitive experiences generate two typical pathological or maladaptive character traits. The first is to attack others and drive them away before they get close enough to hurt one, a sort of preemptive strike. The second is to systematically interpret what other people do as unempathic and irritating rather than as representing attempts, although sometimes misguided, to be helpful, and so to get angry and drive the other person away. In many instances as an adult the patient actually was right to do this and avoided disappointment in doing so. But the patient could not discriminate between those who genuinely liked her, such as some of her coworkers whom she drove away by these tongue-lashings, as well as those who genuinely loved her, whom she drove away in the same manner, from those who are uncaring and exploitive. Because of this inability to discriminate, the patient drove everybody away as soon as she was tempted to trust them, in order not to take a chance at being badly hurt if she is vulnerable.

The patient simply could not believe someone could really love her and want to face life together with her. Declarations of love from a suitor or even manifestations of professional or friendly caring for this patient from a therapist would be experienced by her as just a threat. If the patient allowed herself to believe that such motivations from another person were genuine she would become vulnerable to the actualization of her prediction of always being eventually badly treated. Another way to put this is to emphasize the patient's fear of intimacy, both physical and emotional, something psychoanalysts these days see a lot of in their analysands and which is very difficult to overcome. Ms. I. also displayed this fear by refusing to use the couch, which immediately puts a person, as it is deliberately designed to do, in a position that promotes regression, one that entails the temptation for developing dependency and vulnerability. Of course this refusal had multiple determinants which needed to be eventually explored.

These are the typical patients we are dealing with today, people who are afraid of intimacy and who have been raised in the culture of narcissism (Lasch 1978). The first psychoanalyst to focus sharply on this problem in our contemporary era was Harry Stack Sullivan (1947; 1953), and much of the work of Freida Fromm-Reichmann (1950; 1959) at Chestnut Lodge was based on her understanding of the profound nature of such fear. But none of this profound fear of intimacy, given a well-analysed psychoanalyst, is primarily the product of the here-and-now interaction, nor is it caused by faulty neurobiological circuits. It arises from a combination of profound early childhood disappointments, the fantasies, projections, and reintrojections that these entail, and then the compulsion to repeat and reenact or actualize the fantasies in adult everyday life, which generates a series of new disappointments.

With this all too brief discussion of postmodernism and constructivism, that I (1994, 1995a,1996b, 2000a) have examined in detail elsewhere, I turn now to the current fashion, that of attempting to reduce mental functioning to brain functioning, based on the assumption that since this reducibility is possible then everything we know about mental functioning can be restated in neurobiological terms. If this is true it allows us to alter the neurobiology by the use of drugs and to ignore the language of psychoanalysis entirely. The problem is that, in the opinion of many powerful minds in the philosophy of science, it is not true. The following discussion tends to be a bit technical, but in my opinion it is an obligation of anyone who enthusiastically attempts to develop a "neuropsychoanalysis" to become familiar with the philosophical and logical pitfalls involved in the basic assumptions of applying neurobiology to mental functioning.

THE MIND-BRAIN PROBLEM
IN THE PHILOSOPHY OF SCIENCE

There is an important neo-Hegelian theme that implies, for example, that a thirteenth-century monk lived in another world than we do, the world of Dante as described in chapter 6. The monk would perceive everything as created by God; we perceive everything as possible raw material for production and consumption. But how can we decide between claims of philosophers about what should be the fundamental stance of any given age, when they clash with each other? By what methodology can we decide who is right? This has extremely important implications for morality and leads to the destruction of morality if we follow the current world picture that perceives everything as possible raw materials for production and consumption. All events within the framework of the modern fundamental stance become morally equal. So, for example, Heidegger equated mechanized agriculture with the death camps of the Holocaust, without even a glimmer of understanding of the moral difference between them and of the unbelievable and unspeakable horror which is intrinsic to the latter. Our contemporary stance, in Heidegger's thinking, is the will to power, essentially a license for Nazi brutality, rampant global capitalism, and so-called ethnic cleansing.

A similar excrescence of our current fundamental stance is the view in philosophy that any question that cannot be answered scientifically is not a real question. This leads to eliminative materialism, discussed below, as a proposed solution of the mind-brain problem. There is today a facile relativism in academia (Boudon 2005); anyone who thinks that questions have right and wrong answers is now thought by academicians to be an epistemological cave man (Nagel 1995).

Connecting what we know about the brain with what we think we know about the mind requires us to move beyond the confines of neuroanatomy and neurophysiology into the murky regions of philosophy of the mind. The third person perspective cannot convey the private nature of consciousness, the first person aspects of human life, what it is like to be conscious. So certain aspects of conscious experience are beyond the limits of science. Dennett (1991) and Ryle (1949) on the other hand question the idea that we have some privileged knowledge of ourselves that resists scientific inquiry. They object to the "Cartesian theater," a notion that each of us sits and watches our experiences pass in front of us and that the subjective "I" is clear and distinct, our own existence as a thinking thing. Dennett, for example, argues that there is no central "I" but many neurophysiological processes that think for themselves.

Dennett (1991) and certain other students of the mind-brain problem manifest a casual optimism, based on the early work of Gilbert Ryle (1949), that the mind-brain problem can be cleared up empirically; the usual solution of this approach is to simply eliminate the mind. Searle (1994) has attempted to rediscover the mind on the basis of the fact that consciousness is ontologically subjective even though it is a physical property of the brain in spite of its subjectivity. It is irreducible, he claims, arguing in contrast to proponents of eliminative materialism like Rorty and the Churchlands (1984). For the latter, mental states do not exist, they are postulates of a primitive theory of folk psychology. So all materialist theories end up denying the reality of mind by identifying it completely with something else. Or, as Chomsky (2000) suggests, by simply ignoring mental states as a legitimate subject for scientific study.

Searle (1997), on the other hand, advocates what he calls biological naturalism, a view in which consciousness is seen as a higher level emergent property (see Laughlin 2005) of the brain even though it is based on the physical, just as liquid, solid, or gaseous states are properties of systems of molecules. The crucial technical point is that physical states are ontologically objective and can be studied empirically, but consciousness is ontologically subjective. Both the distinguished philosophers Nagel and Searle agree that the solution to the mind-brain problem is nowhere in sight. In fact, Searle (1994) argues that it is a mistake to think that all that exists is comprehensible to our brains. Similarly, McGinn (1991), in his book *The Problem of Consciousness*, says that we are constitutionally incapable of understanding the mind-brain problem.

Voorhees (2000) also insists that consciousness has an a priori ontological existence. He agrees with Searle that Dennett's view eliminates the very thing—first person conscious experience, that is, subjective consciousness—that was to be explained! Dennett, a distinguished proponent of eliminative materialism, dodges the issues of the overall unity of consciousness recognized even by Kant (1781), and of how various sensory aspects of a perceptual object are parsed by the brain and so combined into a unified percept. This is called the "binding problem." Even more significant, the "hard problem" (Chalmers 1996) is the one which the artificial intelligence or functional and the eliminative materialist approaches restricted to third person empirical methods cannot answer: how does neuronal activity lead to first person experiences such as envy, love, and so on. Thus Voorhees, like Searle, concludes that consciousness is irreducible and ontologically primitive, an a priori given.

Searle (1994) marshals powerful arguments against the "functional" point of view, the idea that the mind is some sort of a computer. This view is the natural outgrowth of so-called token-token identity theory, a more sophisticated form of eliminative materialism than Ryle's (1949) behaviorism. He also emphasizes how both the philosophical rejection of realism and the denial of ontological subjectivity leads to attacks on rationality, on truth, and on intelligence. He argues, and I agree, that external realism and ontological subjectivity must be defended as basic presuppositions in all philosophical thinking about the mind-brain problem.

Searle (Fotion 2000) maintains that consciousness and its subjectivity are emergent features of what happens on a microbiological level but these features can not be predicted in advance from the knowledge of microbiological levels. So consciousness for Searle is a natural phenomenon and the mind has causal powers, but he is not a dualist and does not, like Descartes, regard the mind as a separate substance. The materialist theories mentioned above are reached by ignoring the intentionality, the ontological subjectivity, and the aspectual feature of the mind, which can not be empirically characterized in behavioral or neurobiological predicates:

> Causal reduction does not automatically give us ontological reduction. The mind still has its own features which, in fact, it is the duty of the

scientist to describe and explain. It is much the same as it is in physics when some causal reduction is given of a material such as glass. The structure of glass can be accounted for in terms of crystal formation and crystal formation accounted for in terms of molecules and so on. But glass itself can be still studied. . . . Reduced causally or not, glass is still glass. In the same vein, the mind is still the mind reduced physically or not. Its basic features of intrinsic Intentionality [sic], consciousness, subjectivity and causality are not to be denied. (Fotion, 243)

So Searle claims that the sterility of academic psychology and the bankruptcy of contemporary philosophy on the mind-brain problem is due to the failure to see that the ontology of the mental is irreducibly a subjective first person ontology. It follows that consciousness is an irreducible feature of physical reality, a causally emergent property of the behavior of neurons.

Kim's (1982) interesting concept of "psychophysiological supervenience" is acceptable here in the sense that mental states are supervenient on neurophysiological states. This is a causal supervenience, enabling mental states in turn to affect the body, and is not simply to be thought of as epiphenomenalism. The most sophisticated state of consciousness is self-consciousness, probably existing only in humans and possibly some of the higher animals.

Searle disagrees with Freud about how to conceptualize the unconscious. He argues that what we call the unconscious is primarily neurophysiological with the potential of emerging into consciousness as part of the "qualia" of consciousness, our experience of the qualitative feel of our mental states. But the unconscious according to Searle is ontologically objective because it is neurobiological and is not composed of fantasies and cognitive aspects except as potential possibilities. Searle postulates what he calls the connection principle, which states by definition that all unconscious intentional states are in principle accessible to consciousness. This means there is a division between unconscious states, into those that are accessible to consciousness and are what we mean in our everyday usage of the concept of the unconscious, and those which are not and are simply built in to our neurophysiology, such as Chomsky's (1972) postulated innate syntactical capacities. There is also an aspectual shape to our unconscious intentional states but, argues Searle, unconscious mental states when they are unconscious are purely neurophysiological phenomena. So the ontology of the unconscious consists in objective features of the brain potentially capable of causing subjective conscious thoughts. He says Freud's view that unconscious phenomena are mental even when unconscious leads to considerable philosophical confusion and is unnecessary. Searle concludes his work on the mind-brain problem by asking us to remember we must also rediscover the social character of the mind, a topic central to his (1998) later investigations.

On the whole I think Searle has the right approach and the most compelling arguments about the mind-brain problem. His disagreement with Freud is mainly semantic, in that Freud writes of unconscious mental processes as if they were already mental, that is, had already emerged from the neurobiological, in order to best explicate his theories and remain with the language of psychoanalysis. If we technically argue that they are only potentially mental they have the same influence and the same intentionality and aspectual characteristics that Searle talks about. So this is a technical philosophical or semantic issue, not a fundamental difference. Freud is using an "as-if" approach here to simplify and dramatize his descriptions of patients and their vicissitudes.

Chisolm (1957), representing the Cartesian dualist theory, insists that mental life can not be explained by science. This is almost a religious point of view, in marked contrast to those at the other extreme who would eliminate the talk of the mental entirely, for example the Churchlands (1984), who insist that neuroscience will soon replace all talk about the mind. Fodor (1975) proposes to study mental entities as objects, the approach of so-called cognitive science, a view leading to attempts to develop artificial intelligence (AI) using computers. Whether it is even possible to use computers to construct a "mind" that will pass the Turing test (1950) is a matter of intense current philosophical dispute, as even such a mind, if it could be constructed, leaves out the qualia of consciousness. We all talk incessantly about beliefs and desires in our everyday life and so Symons (2002) concludes that even if we knew *everything* about the anatomy and biochemical processes of the brain and the central nervous system we would not necessarily know *anything* about the mind.

THE ERA OF BRAIN STUDIES

Because of the intense pressure from insurance companies to avoid paying for psychoanalysis there has been an increasing tendency in our field to emphasize the importance of neurophysiology, neuroanatomy, genetics, and various other aspects of the organic study of the brain. This of course is a salutary development as far as the science of psychoanalysis is concerned. Certainly well-established contemporary neurobiological findings derived from standard empirical scientific experiments should and would cause psychoanalysts to be sure that our basic premises are consistent with them. But at this point there are relatively few generally accepted and replicated experimental demonstrations of brain function that are definitively inconsistent with the basic principles of psychoanalysis. Probably the most well-known of these is the discovery that the brain seeks stimuli rather than a state of total rest, the latter being an incorrect assumption Freud made from the neurobiology of his time. Just as Freud attempted to found psychoanalysis on what were thought to be sound principles of neurophysiologic functioning, we of course must do the same today.

However, it does not follow that we have the right to assume that with a complete knowledge of brain physiology and genetics we will automatically have a complete knowledge of mental processes. There are a substantial number of philosophers of science today who believe that in principle the so-called "hard" problem of the mind-brain enigma is insoluble. This "hard" problem is essentially the same as that which baffled Freud and caused him to abandon his "Project for a Scientific Psychology" (1895). It is the question of how one makes the mysterious leap from neurophysiological functioning to the individual subjective personal conscious experiences, the "qualia" of consciousness itself. In our enthusiasm to convince the insurance companies that we are a legitimate science, we should not lose sight of the fact that it may never be possible to base psychoanalysis completely on a knowledge of neurophysiological functioning, and so a humanistic language such as that invented by Freud when he gave up the "Project for a Scientific Psychology" will always be necessary. To put it formally, the qualia of consciousness are irreducibly ontologically subjective (Searle 1994).

Although the fundamental premises of psychoanalysis need to be of course consistent with what is currently known with certainty about brain functioning, we always need to have a basic orientation and a psychoanalytic language and identity of our own. It is the gradual loss of this identity that is generating a demoralization in the field of psychoanalysis, a loss which has been precipitated by the demands of insurance companies for empirical proof of the validity of the psychoanalytic process. It has become obvious that such proofs in the humanistic sciences can not be established with the same kind of certainty that one finds in the natural sciences and that we must be content with accumulating observational data provided by well-analyzed psychoanalysts. A vicious circle is involved here, since if it becomes impossible for patients to afford psychoanalysis then we are in a situation where less and less reliable data can be gathered out of the psychoanalytic process from the treatment of many patients.

That such a gathering is fruitful is evident from studying the history of psychoanalysis beginning from the early days of Freud's Wednesday evening society as it has evolved over the last hundred years in a direction that is clearly less idiosyncratic and much more efficacious. The emphasis on neurobiology, which has rhetorical value for obtaining third party payment, should not cause us to think of ourselves as neurologists or empirical scientists or "neuropsychoanalysts." It is because we are a unique discipline that we should proudly hold to a focal identity. Our sense of professional integrity demands this in spite of the fact that insurance companies exploit uninformed public opinion on this matter.

The problem of consciousness is the crucial stumbling block in the attempt to reduce mental functioning to brain functioning; it is indeed the "hard problem" of the mind-brain dilemma, representing what today is still a "mysterious leap." In the current rush to get on board the neurobiological express that is so much more acceptable to our current fast-fast-fast relief culture, we tend to lose sight of the fact that Freud's psychoanalysis developed a language and a methodology that allowed the investigation of mental functioning without the necessity to know everything there is to know about brain functioning. Yes, those well established aspects of brain functioning that contradict Freud's theories require a revision of the psychoanalytic theories, but it seems to me imperative that we not lose our sense of identity as psychoanalysts, clinicians, who work on the basic principles developed by Freud, in our currently fashionable embrace of the language of neurophysiology. We need to preserve that unique language of Freud and that unique discipline that he invented, and to preserve it with pride as a legitimate and separate method of scientific investigation. It is not simply an offshoot of neurophysiology soon to be discarded, it is not simply a relativistic interchange between a unique analyst and a unique patient in the here-and-now, but rather it rests on a solid foundation of accumulated information over the past hundred years and a methodology invented by Freud that has proven to be of lasting value and yielded many fruitful results and new insights into the human psyche in all areas of the human sciences.

THE CURRENT SITUATION OF PSYCHOANALYSIS

The entire field of psychoanalysis is in crisis in our increasingly barbarous, violent, and declining culture. We are facing a similar situation today that was faced by Plato's Academy during the decline of the Greek culture. If we do not clearly articulate and maintain our basic ideals, which still are best expressed in the work of Sigmund Freud, we, as it happened to the ancient Greeks, are liable to progressively degenerate into groups of squabbling physicians accompanied by a cacophony of tediously disputatious psychologists and social workers. The entire field of psychoanalysis will become marginalized in our culture and regarded as just another mystical cult without any empirical or scientific grounding and without any basic orientation. No emperor will be required to shut these schools down; they will just die by attrition and neglect, much to the joy of insurance company executives.

What are we expecting to be given by what Freud called "our science"? The centerpiece of Freud's psychoanalysis is the discovery that in the first few years of childhood, in combination with our genetic endowment, we lay down certain patterns of behavior and certain core archaic fantasies that govern the rest of our lives. These patterns and fantasies are based on combinations of experiences and our infantile interpretations of these experiences which taken together constitute a threat to the ego or to the integrity of the self. So patterns of behavior and core archaic fantasies are formed that are the result of compromise formations that allow the ego and the self to remain intact. They determine how the person experiences all object relations in life and patterns of behavior that repeat themselves endlessly, the personality characteristics of the individual, and the perpetual striving to repeatedly actualize some derivative of the archaic fantasies and desires. The gratification in this actualization immerses our life in a continuous pressure to achieve it that Freud correctly called the program of the pleasure principle. The pursuit of the pain that is also involved he considered beyond the pleasure principle, one of the evidences for a so-called death instinct as he conceived of it in his final instinct theory.

How do we uncover and hopefully correct patterns and strivings which in our patients are so maladaptive and cause them so much suffering? That method is the method of free association in a situation where there is relative neutrality, objectivity, and abstinence. The analyst observes the transference, which is the closest to natural science phenomena that he or she has available for study. Listening from at least five channels, the analyst allows his or her own mind to wander in free floating attention, picking up subjective conscious associations to the patient's material. After considerable careful and patient listening on all the channels that the analyst is trained to work with, the analyst gains a sense of conviction about the material and is able to interpret it to the patient. One then observes the patient for behavior, dreams, and further associations, in an attempt to validate or invalidate analytic interpretations, which must be thought of as hypotheses. It is very much the same as in any other scientific procedure where hypotheses are tested and accepted, rejected, or modified as the case requires. For example, if an interpretation is followed by boring flat material and causes no change in the patient and nothing new appears in free associations, dreams, or fantasies, it is either wrong or ill-timed or inappropriate.

So the most essential insights of psychoanalysis derive directly from the inference of the patient's unconscious mental life as it exposes itself through free association and resonates, as Freud (1912a) proposed, with the analyst's evenly suspended attention. Balter (1999) puts it very well:

The unique and characteristic insights of psychoanalysis include: the predominantly infantile and instinctual nature of unconscious mental life; the omnipresent influence of unconscious mental life on conscious mental life; transference, analytic and extra-analytic; the meaning of dreams and slips; infantile sexuality and psychosexual development, including the Oedipus complex; the genesis of neurotic symptoms and perversions in the Oedipus complex; the oedipal origin of a universal unconscious moral agency (the superego); the existence of narcissistic object relations. . . . They can best be validated and confirmed through the unique psychoanalytic method of inferring unconscious mental processes—free association and evenly suspended attention—the very method that fostered their genesis in the first place. (110)

I have first reviewed a situation of the failure of nerve which occurred in the history of classical Greece that is similar to the situation within psychoanalysis today. Plato's famous academy underwent progressive deterioration, disintegration, and fragmentation, until it ended up merely the handmaiden of another discipline, Christian theology, for a thousand years. So I propose that the identity crisis in psychoanalysis today has to do with our failure of nerve in the teeth of the abusive behavior of insurance companies regarding the payment for psychoanalysis and the current cultural ambiance demanding fast-fast-fast relief, as well as the domination of contemporary psychiatry by the pharmaceutical corporations. I hope for a return to Freud's basic principles as a focus for our identity. Of course we cannot ignore new discoveries in neurobiology if they are well established, or what we learn from the study of enactments in the here-and-now of the analytic procedure. Certainly the findings of Freud that are contradicted by firmly accepted empirical findings in neurobiology and other disciplines call for revision of some of his ideas, as do his mistaken views on the psychology of women and on certain other topics such as art, religion, and evolutionary biology. But this should not be permitted to blur our continuing focus on the fundamental principles of the clinical practice of psychoanalysis as Freud developed them over his lifetime.

In this book, I have reviewed those fundamental principles and proposed that we employ them as the basis for our identity as psychoanalysts and psychoanalytic psychiatrists. It represents a failure of nerve to drift this way and that with current fads and with the continuously deteriorating ambiance of our culture as the world slides into materialistic chaos. Franz Alexander said years ago (quoted in chapter 1) that psychoanalytic psychotherapy is one of the last remnants of the humanistic ideal, focussing on the individual unique person and his or her transcendent possibilities as well as maladaptive pathology. This can only be clarified if we have a sharp focus on what we basically mean by "psychoanalysis."

As Saul Bellow puts it (Atlas 2000) in discussing the disappointing current situation for the arts and the humanistic disciplines, the intelligent public is waiting to hear from these disciplines what it cannot hear from pure science:

Out of the struggle at the center has come an immense, painful longing for a broader, more flexible, fuller, more coherent, more comprehensive account of what we human beings are, who we are, and what
this life is for . . . the individual struggles with dehumanization for
the possession of his soul. (462)

Bellow points out, in talking about writers, and in a discussion equally applicable to psychoanalysts, that if we do not "come again into the center it will not
be because the center is preempted. It is not. [We] are free to enter if [we] so
wish" (462).

10

Psychoanalysis at the End of the *Third* Millennium

A Fantasy

It was then that I began my Thirty Years War against the professors, the routine years and the deaf—

—Hector Berlioz (1885)

I

Having come to the end of the third millennium, it is appropriate on this memorable day of our annual June meeting in 3000 AD, the year opening the thirty-first century, to review what has happened to psychoanalysis.[1] In order to do that, I have to first digress and summarize some historical trends that might be useful in explaining the vicissitudes of our recently reborn discipline. The outstanding thinkers in the first half of the twentieth century (1900–1950) when psychoanalysis came into significant prominence, devoted their intellectual and artistic efforts to seeing behind manifest conscious and dream and artistic phenomena, an interest which died out in the second half of that century, the so-called "era of the brain." Intellectuals in the first half of the twentieth century, stimulated by those pioneer thinkers living at the end of the nineteenth century, attempted to explore and unmask the roots of consciousness. They were led by Freud, Nietzsche, and other psychologists and philosophers who demolished the myth that consciousness was all there was to human mentation, or by artists like Joyce, who attempted to portray the phenomenology of the stream of consciousness, or by such variegated thinkers as Marx or Proust, who attempted to recapture and understand the formative elements of consciousness.

For Foucault (1973a, 1973b), who wrote presciently later in the century, the human sciences are always unstable, derived, epistemologically complex, precarious, and full of disagreement. This is due to the double nature of man. Human sciences are dubious and can never be "normal" like natural sciences. There will never be agreement on a single paradigm in the human sciences as there is in the natural sciences. He said that the psychiatrist as embodied investigator, as well as the objects he or she studies, have both been produced by micropower practices inherent in their culture, its manipulations and interactions. Background power practices produce the investigator, with his or her values and interests, who studies the human. Therefore, knowledge in the human sciences depends on discursive practices or "epistemes" (Foucault 1973b), or on nondiscursive practices, or on the distribution of micropower in any given culture at the time. No context-free, value-free, objective human sciences like the natural sciences were believed to be possible. The human sciences must take account of the human activities that make possible their own disciplines. If an unchallenged "normal" human science develops, it only means that an orthodoxy has been temporarily established (see Dreyfus and Rabinow 1983, 162–167).

Both psychoanalysis and serious literature for the most part began to die out at the end of the twentieth century and they disappeared by the early part of the third millennium, due to the exclusive preoccupation of the populace with accumulating money and acquiring a never ending collection of material things, even to the point where the owner became the slave of his or her myriad electronic and mechanical gadgets. This left no time for genuine leisure, which we know is the basis of culture (Pieper 1952; Chessick 1999e) and creativity. The creative individual is a more sensitive and a more flexible thinker than the average person and is capable of using thought processes and blending modes of thought in unusual and exciting ways, but by the end of the twentieth century and well into the twenty-first and twenty-second centuries the number of readers, people who read serious books carefully and consistently, dwindled almost to the vanishing point. The same was true of the audiences for classical music. Major orchestras went bankrupt. Authors like Philip Roth complained that the literary era had come to an end everywhere in the electronic progression from the movie screen to the television screen to the computer screen. He is reported to have said:

> There's only so much time, so much room, and there are only so many habits of mind that can determine how people use the free time they have. Literature takes a habit of mind that has disappeared. It requires silence, some form of isolation, and sustained concentration in the presence of an enigmatic thing. It is difficult to come to grips with a mature, intelligent adult novel. (Remnick 2000, 86)

Perhaps it will help us to understand the current situation at the end of the third millennium by reviewing what it was like at the end of the first and the second millenniums.

THE SITUATION IN 1000 AD

Lacey and Danzinger (1999) give us a rather speculative but historically based portrait of the world of an Englishman and his wife and the life they lived at the turn of the first millennium. The brain capacity of a man or woman living in the year 1000 AD was exactly the same as our own. The best way to get a sense of what it was like in England in those days is to listen to the Irish poet Seamus Heaney expressing on tape (Heaney 1999) that great epic from the end of the first millennium, *Beowulf.* In his version, he describes the story of encountering horrible experiences with monsters and overcoming and defeating them, being exhausted by the encounter and then having to live on, physically and psychically exposed, in an era of exhausted aftermath. The parallel between that situation around 1000 AD and the one which existed at the end of the second millennium (2000 AD) cannot fail to impress the listener. (Note that I advocate listening to *Beowulf* rather than attempting to read it, since it was originally recited, although it was one of the few epics of the time that were eventually written down.)

The people at the end of the first millennium learned how to entertain themselves. Their knowledge was retained without computers because they learned by observing, imitating, and memorizing, a phenomenon I have experienced even today in the third world in my acquaintance with illiterate young men who were raised in what can only be called a medieval atmosphere.

At the end of the second millennium, and lasting approximately the first three hundred years of the third millennium (2000–2300 AD), there was a terrible pestilence due to runaway bacterial infestations subsequent to a pandemic originally produced by terrorists and anarchists. A similar pestilence occurred in 962 AD and a great fatal fire in London. As an aftermath of these catastrophes, the possibility of famine was ever-present and haunted the imagination around the year 1000 just as it did between the years 2100 and 2300.

Around 1000, creativity took the form of the Gregorian chants. Lacey and Danzinger (1999) write: "The chant was the product of practice and elaboration by the countless churchmen and women of the first millennium whose lives were given meaning by this inspiring and transcendent sound" (104), an obvious parallel to Schopenhauer's late nineteenth century view of the role of the arts in making the ubiquitous harshness of life endurable. As the terrorists brought chaos and collapse to the decadent Western civilization shortly after the end of the second millennium, so the Vikings played that role at the end of the first millennium, appearing repeatedly and relentlessly, and in that process tearing down whatever precarious security and culture had been built up during the year.

The parallels continue, as Lacey and Danziger (1999) point out: "If the late 20th century is scented with gasolene vapour and exhaust fumes, the year

1000 was perfumed with shit. Cow dung, horse manure, pig and sheep drop-
pings, chicken shit—" (119). Bathing was almost unheard of and there was no
sense of hygiene or the technicalities of modern medicine but:

> The believer in the year 1000 could point to the Bible, which con-
> tained no less than thirty-five miracles in which Jesus defeated illness
> through the power of faith, and every believer knew that the saints
> were keeping that miraculous tradition alive. (122)

And everyone was a believer in those days, even the "heretics" and "infidels,"
who were thought simply to have the wrong beliefs or transfixed by the devil.

Humans felt closer to the animals, seeing them as fellow occupants of a
world in which human and animal interests intermingled in the struggle for
survival. Lief Eriksson discovered Newfoundland in or about the year
1000 AD, and predictions and auguries abounded; belief in these persisted
even when cold reality proved them to be wrong. So much for the classical
Greek view of man as a rational animal. The Christian belief system spread
from region to region, ranging from Kiev to Hungary to Iceland, just as the
nations of Europe's fringe around 2000 AD clamored to join the European
economic community. In the year 1000 it was clear that Christianity was win-
ning the battle against paganism just as in the year 2000 global capitalism triumphed over communism.

Violence predominated and the greatest lords were the greatest perpe-
trators, the aristocrats forming a cadre that had been trained to kill. The warrior hero is predominant in epic sagas like *Beowulf*. Chess arrived from the
East around that time, reaching Spain and southern France thanks to the
Arabs. The development of the abacus was revolutionary, speeding calcula-
tion in a magical fashion in 1000 AD, as was the computer in 2000 AD and it
had a comparable impact on the progress of trade and business. Arabic
numerals appeared for the first time. Lacey and Danziger conclude: "Death,
disease, and discomfort were daily companions in the year 1000, and living
through the annual round of toil . . . represented a veritable triumph of the
human spirit" (194).

We contemporary folk have received a fortunate contribution from those
scholars who survived in scattered and isolated small academic establishments
like St. John's College in Annapolis, Maryland, or Santa Fe, New Mexico that
persisted, in the early part of the third millennium, in the study of the "great
books." They kept the interest in them and what they have to say about
humans alive, and provided teaching of them to selected students. Similarly,
medieval monks early in the second millennium such as those in the isolated
Irish monasteries (Cahill 1995), through their copying of manuscripts as a
form of self-teaching, inadvertently preserved the great classics that enabled a

rebirth of Western civilization in the mid-second millennium. So in 1500 AD the emergence from a dark era was enabled by the application of the preserved great classics of Plato and Aristotle, as well as the dramas of Sophocles, Aeschylus, Euripides, and others to the study of human mentation. Whenever the cultural focus is on human consciousness and human psychological processes rather than on technological achievement for the purpose of the untrammeled acquisition of material goods, there is a great upsurge in the quality of human life. We saw this again in the middle of the third millennium (2500 AD) as it gradually dawned on humans that the preoccupation with accumulation of wealth did nothing for the human spirit and catalyzed an endless series of senseless wars and self-destruction.

THE SITUATION IN 2000 AD

In the Bible, Job tells us that a child's days are very long but in old age they fly faster than a weaver's shuttle; indeed, old age is like a stone falling. There is a certain group of individuals, mostly successful males, who, as they move toward their eighth and ninth decades of life, become captious, carnaptious, curmudgeonly, and crabby. Such individuals also sometimes have prophetic powers, or think they do, and some even write nine hundred page long books with titles like *From Dawn to Decadence: Five Hundred Years of Western Cultural Life* (Barzun 2000).

The noted scholar Jaques Barzun (2000) attempted to trace the dawn of Western cultural life from 1500 AD to 2000 AD in a book he published at the age of ninety-two to the accolades of conservatives in the United States. He was convinced that his era, 2000 AD, was an Alexandrian time, one of cultural sunset, depleted energies, and moral confusion in spite of its seemingly inexhaustible technological advances.

He divided his book into four parts. The first (1500–1660) describes the religious revolution of the Reformation. The second (1660–1789) is occupied with the rise of monarchy as an institution and the development of the nation state. The third (1789–1920) describes the political and cultural consequences of the French Revolution. The fourth part (1920–2000) deals with the aftermath of the "Great War," which in Barzun's opinion, combines World War I and World War II (what the Russians call "The Great Patriotic War"), culminating in what he labels the decline of the "demotic" culture of the United States. As we might expect from this ninety-two year old academic, we are given a prophesy in which the end of the West in 2300 AD is described not as an apocalypse but as boredom. This prophecy of course could not have been more wrong, since by 2300 AD the terrorists with their cleverly planted bacterial bombs had managed to set off a pandemic and decimate the population of the West even as the population of Africa and Asia was being decimated by the AIDS virus and we were plunged into the new dark age.

Barzun finishes his book with a jeremiad directed against contemporary culture, claiming that the West in 2000 AD was irretrievably on the skids. Institutions had lost their legitimation, leadership was mediocre if at all, and because the interest in consciousness and self-exploration had disappeared in the second half of the twentieth century there was only a narrow understanding of the problems humanity faced and a disintegration of high culture into what, in his dismal view, was the century of the common man. He writes, "when people accept futility and the absurd as normal, the culture is decadent" (11). To follow Barzun's logic, around 2000 AD the population, in hopeless trouble, should have all been praying to St. Jude, a saint not just for those with St. Jude artificial heart valves, but the patron of lost causes and desperate situations.

In the middle of the second millennium (1500 AD) the awareness of and the claims of the individual, generally known as humanism, became predominant as pure religion gave way to a more secular world. The first major shift in our understanding of the human psyche from the Greek ideal of man as a rational animal seems to have occurred in the years when romanticism was the spirit of the age, roughly the last decades of the eighteenth century and the first half of the nineteenth century. Rousseau taught us that human beings are moved by passion and that thought or reason is the instrument of desires. Man is conceived by romanticism as a creature who feels and can think but his every thought is charged with some emotion. This requires closer and closer attention to the inner life of humans.

Late in the second millennium, with the invention of and the rapid predominance of the railroad, Barzun explains:

> Human beings . . . had to sharpen their reflexes under the threat of moving objects. It has been a continual re-education of the nervous system as ever new warnings by sight and sound command the body to halt, or step in the safe direction. The eye must gauge speed, the ear guess the nearness of the unseen. And besides sheer survival, the daily business of life calls for taking in and responding to an ever-enlarging array of lights, beeps, buzzes, and insistent rings. (540)

Now, at the close of the third millennium, we have learned to our dismay that the various methods of moving from place to place, even faster than thrice the speed of sound and recently through our new regularly scheduled rocket excursions to the moon and Mars, adds nothing to intellectual or spiritual worth. A person is the same fool or knave at either end of the journey, and a business deal or tourism done more quickly because of the speed of the transportation simply adds to the culture of materialism, to a world dominated by the bourgeoisie whom Flaubert defined as "one[s] whose every thought is low" (Barzun 2000, 558).

The modern railroad engine and the motor car appeared around 1900. Within a hundred years after that all the major cities in the industrial countries of the world were inundated with traffic and submerged in a cloud of hydrocarbon fumes from cars and factories. At times, going from one place to another became as slow and difficult a chore as it was before these inventions, and just as dangerous, as car-jackers, drunken drivers, and other drivers either sleepy or high on drugs or driving with one hand (the other clutching a cell phone and the driver deep in conversation) or traveling at a reckless speed, abounded on the road like the highwaymen and brigands of old. Even shortly before that time Schopenhauer maintained that existence would be unendurable without art and Pater attempted to extract from masterpieces of painting and literature some magic to enhance life. These views became popular but then flickered out toward the end of the twentieth century. They were replaced by the mechanical so-called joy of sex, the almost unendurably loud noise of the rock concert, and the drug culture.

The art and literature that so entranced predominant thinkers from about 1500 AD to 1900 AD were replaced by products that could not be appreciated unless they were found unsettling, disturbing, cruel, and perverse. Along with this went a general relaxation of conduct, "attack on authority, the ridicule of anything established, the distortions of language and objects, the indifference to clear meaning, the violence to the human form, the return to the primitive elements of sensation" (Barzun 2000, 727). We end the second millennium, he says, with a demotic civilization: violence and crime return, "assault in the home, the office, and on city streets" became "commonplace and particularly vicious. . . . Prisons were full and new ones continually being built to receive causeless killers, offenders against the drug laws, and the personnel of organized crime" (776). Even the public schools became a setting for violent acts in the United States, a country where the public was hopelessly inundated with guns of all kinds, to the great delight and profit of the gun manufacturers who held congress in thrall. Barzun concludes, "To appear unkempt, undressed, and for perfection, unwashed, is the key signature of the whole age" (781). He describes how one went to a shop and bought jeans ready-made with spots and patches, cut short and unraveled at the edges. Public education was a widely acknowledged failure and TV "sound bites" replaced political debate.

THE SITUATION IN 3000 AD

We all know what happened after that. The first centuries of the third millennium saw a general man-made devastation of the world's population take place. Gradually in the middle of the third millennium there was a resurgence of the study of consciousness and a renewed interest in trying to find a solution to man's untrammeled aggressive drive by forming a clearer conception of how the human self is constituted. The old idea from the twentieth century that one must have a midlife crisis and find one's self was shown to be an error because the self is not found but made. This is what Nietzsche was attempting to express, although he garbled his message by employing a most unfortunate overdramatic language.

In the nineteenth century the philosopher Mendelssohn equated *Bildung* with Enlightenment, the former representing the idea of education as the cultivation of taste and good judgement. This controversial idea was in the air at the time of Hegel (Pinkert 2000). One of its most striking characteristics is that it transcended the idea of the old orders of society; it had nothing to do with one's birth status, but mainly involved how an individual directed and formed his or her self. In those centers of learning that remained in scattered isolated places during the middle of the third millennium there was a revival of study of the concept of *Bildung*, making one's self actively into a cultivated educated person. One can be passively educated, but *Bildung* requires self-activity, self-development, and self-direction. In Hegel's day it assumed the concepts of the Enlightenment, the age of reason, and a kind of spiritual revolution. The neohumanists of Hegel's time such as Von Humboldt argued that education should be aimed at *Bildung*, producing a person of cultivation and taste who was self-directed. They wanted a study of classical Greek, rather than Latin as conservative politicians of the time advocated, because classical Greek is closer to the roots of European culture.

By the latter part of the nineteenth century, it was clear to most sophisticated thinkers that God was dead and life would have to be lived without dogmatic bedrock. It was this discovery that led to the foundering and eventual decadence and decline of western culture at the end of the second millennium. In the late third millennium view, our modern view of *Bildung*, the individual has to consciously choose his or her basic project, based on both an understanding of the unconscious roots of this choice and an understanding of what Hegel called *Sittlichkeit*, the prereflective self in which the individual is situated in a family, society, and state, providing each person with a concrete orientation, an implicit grasp of who he or she is, and an impetus to each individual's choice of basic project.

These reflections in the middle of the third millennium led most fortunately in two directions, to a renewed study of and prestige for creativity and to the revival of psychoanalysis as a legitimate and crucially important enterprise. It was a common second millennium misconception that in order to be creative an individual had to suffer from an emotional illness. Early third millennium studies (Chessick 1999b, 2005a) indicated that this ubiquitous belief was untrue. Psychoanalytic observation of a large number of creative individuals repeatedly demonstrated that the amelioration of their neurotic difficulties releases and enhances their creative capacities. The successful interpretation and working through of a psychoneurotic conflict results in a movement of ego capacities to a more conflict free zone of functioning and one can see in many case histories how patients' psychopathology often actually ruins the products of their creative efforts. The removal of this psychopathology liberates their creative capacities and enables the patients at the same time to develop a more successful and fulfilling existence.

But only in the middle of the third millennium, with the renewed emphasis on humanism and the qualities of human consciousness, was it possible for creativity and psychoanalysis to gain respect again. Clearly, in order to better understand the thought processes of the psychoanalyst one must have the best possible understanding of creativity and how psychopathology interferes with it. This will enable us to gain a better understanding of how countertransference or psychopathology of the psychoanalyst interfere with the proper formulation of interpretations and generate enactments that can stalemate or destroy the psychoanalytic process. At this point, I will digress, and in the next part of this chapter further explore the relationship of emotional illness and creativity. Then I will return to my fantasy about the revival of psychoanalysis late in the third millennium.

II

The Creative Process and Psychopathology

The experience of art is neither subjective nor objective but rather a dialectical interchange between the object of art and the subjective viewer, or the musical performance and the audience. What transpires is a fusion of horizons that changes both the work of art and the viewer, a procedure similar to the experience of psychoanalysis, in which there also is a creative fusion of horizons changing both the patient and the analyst. So there is no such thing as a "correct" interpretation of a work of art, nor is there a completely free subjectivity in it. The same is true for a psychoanalytic interpretation. The viewer or listener completes the work of art by his or her interpretation, but at the same time the work of art completes the viewer by helping to realize or actualize his or her potential.

The parallel between the process of creativity and the process in the mind of the psychoanalyst as he or she formulates an interpretation was already recognized by twentieth century psychoanalysts such as Arlow (1980), and even Freud (1908) recognized the parallel between creative writing, fantasy formation, and day dreaming. Arlow (1980) stressed the major role of what he called "intuition" in the formulation of a psychoanalytic interpretation:

> Intuition consists of being able to organize silently, effortlessly, and outside the scope of consciousness the myriad of observations, impressions, facts, experiences . . . all that we have learned from the patient into a meaningful pattern. . . . All of these are perceived sometimes subliminally and are elaborated and conceptualized unconsciously, i.e., intuitively. There is something intensely aesthetic and creative about this mode of functioning. Scientific discoveries and artistic innovations of enormous complexity are known to have originated in precisely the same way. . . . Empathy facilitates intuition, in fact makes intuition possible. (201–202)

It is generally agreed that there is a substantial role of creativity in the work of the psychoanalyst and the psychodynamically oriented psychotherapist (Rothenberg 1987). For example, like Arlow, Emde (2006) points out how empathy can be "viewed as a creative act within the therapeutic relationship; it condenses multiple meanings, exercises tact and therefore, like the esthetic experience has evocative ambiguity" (142). Because the creative process is so important in the proper function of the psychoanalyst and always will be, it is worthwhile for us to pause and examine here what is known about that process and its vicissitudes.

Psychopathology of the artist interferes with and spoils the communication process, as dramatically illustrated in the bizarre self-imposed disruptions of Ezra Pound's magnum opus, *The Cantos*, fragmented by his arbitrary insertion of paranoid politics, crackpot economics, irrelevant letters, and obscure personal memories. Such disruptions in the artist's creativity due to psychopathology can be found in many, many other instances. For example, Walter Benjamin, one of the last great men of letters in the twentieth century, was not only unable to complete any manuscript but wandered aimlessly over Europe refusing several chances to escape the Nazis, until he felt hopelessly trapped and committed suicide. His magnum opus, which he carried in a briefcase with him like a security blanket, was reportedly lost.

The psychopathology of the artist, while on the one hand rendering the artist alienated and uncomfortable with the prevailing mythology of the civilization and filling him or her with the motive to express either this mythology or a new mythology in some artistic form, on the other hand mars the product due to either the intrusion of the artist's delusions and/or obsessional preoccupations into the creative endeavor or to the constriction of that endeavor by the artist's impaired ego functioning and fragmented sense of self.

Although Ernest Jones is reputed to have said neurotics are the torchbearers of civilization, psychopathology can steer artistic endeavors into a dead end.

The capacity for sublimation seems to be a critical issue for understanding the relationship between psychopathology and creativity. If an artist can wall off his or her psychopathology and somehow sublimate or transform his or her emotional conflicts and personal passions into creative work, these conflicts and passions can serve as a motor and drive the work forward, along with the selfobject function of the artwork or of the creative process itself (a selfobject function, as Kohut [1977] conceived of it, enhances one's sense of self, and firms up one's psychic integration). When coupled with talent, what emerges is a genuine work of art that speaks directly to the audience, is capable of many interpretations because it is multiply determined, and withstands subsequent generations of critics and variegated critical approaches. When this capacity for sublimation is not present, the psychopathology of the artist encloses his or her talent in a sort of straightjacket, restricting the creativity and, in the worst cases, disrupting it with obsessions and delusions.

From a psychoanalytic point of view, it is usually not difficult to recognize that such disruption has taken place. A careful study of the complete artworks of the artist usually reveals areas of constriction due to emotional difficulties. Within the areas that are not constricted, however, the artist may produce reputable work. For example, the poetry of Emily Dickinson, a reclusive, self-effacing woman who wrote many of her poems on little scraps of waste paper, still has a lasting and universal appeal. Emotional illness per se does not necessarily prevent the production of good art; it may simply constrict or disrupt it even to the point where, as in the *Cantos* of Ezra Pound, the whole work becomes a botched failure (as Pound himself admitted) with spots of beauty in it.

Psychopathology, unless it can be effectively dissociated or walled-off, complicates and obscures the truth that attempts to communicate itself through a work of art. First, it interferes with and constricts the creative process of the artist in many ways, sometimes even tragically causing the artist to destroy his or her own work entirely. Second, because of the defective aspects of the artwork that emotional illness engenders, it discourages us from tarrying before the work and interferes with our focus and capacity to directly experience the aesthetic phenomena expressed to us through the artist.

Creativity requires a relatively intact ego; when the ego deteriorates, artistic production deteriorates. Inherent genius along with the capacity for sublimation through artistic creativity is required for the production of great artworks that are not flawed. The driving force to creativity may be thought of as the universal human need to resolve intrapsychic conflicts and reduce anxiety (which is the driving force of all solutions, neurotic or healthy), or the universal human need to provide one's self with enhancing selfobjects as a "glue"

(Kohut 1977) to ensure cohesion of the self, or both. The artwork itself may form such a selfobject, or the mirroring appreciation of the audience may perform this function. But in the creation of a great artwork there is something more we experience, the shining forth of truth, beauty, and Being in new and unique modes of expression (Heidegger 1971). This has a profound civilizing effect.[2]

The traditional second millennium psychoanalytic view suggested there are two processes in artistic creation; inspiration, the feeling of being driven by a "muse" or outside agent, and elaboration, the purposeful organization and intent to solve a problem. The artist tries to endow with secondary public meaning what was meaningful originally only to himself or herself, an important task that the artist's psychopathology will impede. The much quoted phrase about temporary ego regression or regression in the service of the ego is alleged to describe what happens during inspirational creation, allowing the id to communicate more directly with the ego. This may or may not be an accurate conception of the creative process, but even Plato in the dialogue *Ion* called it a kind of productive insanity. The artist is able to perceive relations and images that most of us do not or cannot perceive. Creativity is an innate capacity, a rare characteristic of certain endowed individuals, involving both the tendency and the ability to perhaps playfully take apart and put together again, to break established patterns of relationships and replace them with new ones.

Recent psychoanalytic thinking suggests that creativity is not a reaction to childhood depression or narcissistic injury, but rather is due to the injury of nonrecognition of special talents and of the problems involved in adaptation to unusual endowments. Creativity is a solitary activity usually accompanied by withdrawal from complex emotional involvements with the external world except for that with selected selfobjects, for example, Freud and Fliess or Eugene O'Neill and his third wife (Kohut 1990, 324), and the replacement in the mind of typical everyday involvements by ideas, projects, fantasies, and personal, artistic, cultural, or religious striving. This produces a kind of self-insulating sanctuary that the artist lives in, at least for periods of time. Under these circumstances the artist is often mistakenly believed to be having neurotic difficulties in interpersonal relations, but actually he or she is temporarily living in a walled-off garden away from the turbulence and strife of the outer world and away from irksome emotional problems and involvements with people.

Contemporary psychoanalysts concentrate on the capacity of the artist to wall-off or transcend psychopathology. So, great art can even be produced by wicked individuals like Caravaggio or Wagner, or very disturbed individuals like Van Gogh or Virginia Woolf, when they can isolate off their psychopathology. If this fails, the creative process disintegrates and ego functioning deteriorates. Inner conflicts may increase the pressure to focus within, to enhance the power to symbolize, and to achieve liberation of expression. The pressure to create also comes from the necessity of all primates to communicate, deeply built into our species along with the need for mirroring, one of the earliest selfobject experiences.

The creative artist needs to cross three censor stations in order to transmit the meaning inherent in his or her work of art from the deep unconscious to the audience. These are the artist's own defenses or controls, the cultural barrier that the audience has (e.g., in every century the audience has complained about the cacophony of "new" music), and the psychological defenses and controls of the audience. Because these defenses change from time to time and the psychological needs of the audience change from one historical period to the other and from one culture to another, every period and culture is characterized by specific needs and patterns of defenses. This requires the creative artist to continually search for new means to keep communicating with that fluctuating cultural and intrapsychic state of the audience while continuing to create art. Thus, Hegel was wrong when he claimed that historically the creation of art was over and inevitably superceded by religion. A lot of great art has been produced since Hegel's era, but of course the creative products are vastly different just as our outlook on life has been vastly changed by the horrible events of the twentieth and into the twenty-first century.

Neurotics and creative artists differ not only in their basic psychopathology but in the way they succeed in coping with it. Freud said the artist, like the neurotic, withdraws from an unsatisfactory reality into the world of imagination but, unlike the neurotic, he or she knows how to find a way back from it and once more to get a firm foothold in reality. For example, the neurotic Mahler believed that what moves us in a work of art is precisely its mysterious and unfathomable elements. Feeling incapable of explaining his musical intention in words, he was nevertheless aware of expressing in his music powerful truths. He believed his music expressed his whole self and changed continuously as his self developed, and it went much farther. Mahler felt that creative artists are the people least able to answer the question of what is creative activity, and he insisted he could not even explain his compositions to himself let alone obtain an explanation for others.

OUR WORLD PICTURE

One of the biggest problems that face us when we talk about "art" is the contemporary issue of what constitutes art, a philosophical problem. Most critics today agree that art does not have to have a political message. Some philosophers claim that artworks are whatever artists make and there is no standard about how a work of art should look or whether it should communicate anything at all. But

I believe that art embodies knowledge and civilizing values phenomenologically given to us by that unique vehicle of aesthetic communication if we are open to it. Artistic and creative endeavors are found in all cultures and all eras, evidence for the universal need of humans even in primitive caves or in concentration camps to try to make contact with the stars. Art shows us, for any culture, what we respond to and what we are. Wittgenstein (1972) explained that for each of us, our world picture is a system of not easily removed or replaced convictions. It is a framework that we use for all discussions and proofs. Our world picture is tied to the practices we are taught as children when our parents say: "This is the way we do it." Our actions lie at the basis of our language games, and we rely on a memory bank of examples taught by our parents. Our world picture therefore rests neither on empirical knowledge nor on the scientific verification of hypotheses, for any sort of testing has to stop at or be based upon some underlying points of belief, axioms, or so-called "self-evident premises." Where do these come from? What we are taught as children we take on faith, and in so doing we form an organized structure, a world picture, a web of belief. The conclusions and premises from this structure give each other mutual support.

Our world picture is not easily shaken by conflicting empirical propositions. It is an important function of art in each culture to shape and communicate the prevailing world picture directly and to announce when it is changing or fragmenting! Our world picture is more like a methodology that one decides to adopt while ignoring conflicting evidence. The changeover to another system represents a conversion, and it is a shift moved more by loss of a war, persuasion, and dramatic unexpected aesthetic or spiritual experiences than by reason.

Art is inherently paradoxical in its meaning and always open to various interpretations. Although these interpretations are socially and historically grounded, they are personal; perhaps the best practical approach is to assume that if something is found in any given era to be displayed in an art museum and labeled as art or is performed by reputable musicians, it is art. This seems like a rather vague and unsatisfactory definition, but it is often sufficient for mental health professionals to use as a criterion to judge whether an individual's creative output is damaged by his or her psychopathology. In some interesting cases one can even trace deterioration of the artist's creative output over the years as the artist's psychopathology gains ascendancy over his or her personality. There are many examples of this in the history of the arts. There are also numerous examples of artists who, like Robert Louis Stevenson (see chapter 2) or Eugene O'Neill, when they have gained the proper selfobject function they require through a new marriage or relationship, then show a great creative flowering as their psychopathology is mollified or reversed through the corrective experience provided by a mirroring selfobject.

In trying to understand the relationship between emotional illness and creativity, I used both the phenomenologic and psychoanalytic investigative methods (1999b), which taken together demonstrate that there are no fixed rigid pathologic intrapsychic structural organizations and no such conditions as specific mental "diseases" (putting aside mental aberrations caused by established organic conditions such as brain tumors, etc.). The psychic state of patients in reasonably good physical health who manifest pathological psychiatric symptoms engages in a dynamic fluctuation and interplay. The ego moves back and forth, regressively and progressively, in its attempts to deal with unconscious conflicts, the superego, and external reality under the various conditions, vicissitudes, and developmental stages of life. A study of artists and their artworks is enormously rewarding by providing an understanding, in a dramatic form from gifted individuals, of this fluctuation, one that all of us engage in throughout our lives.

CASE ILLUSTRATION

I labeled Ezra Pound's work as metaphysical failure (1999b), a failure on his part to produce consistent poetry that reveals truths which cannot be attained by ordinary scientific methods. This manifestation of truth in artistic creations is to be found in the works of great playwrights, novelists, composers, and artists. Truth can be expressed in art even though the various concepts of truth are inherently ambiguous and the grasp of truth is often fleeting and ineffable. Furthermore, the experiencing of art as a manifestation of truth depends on one's sociocultural horizon so, as has become increasingly evident, we are always dealing with limited rather than absolute, essential, and eternal truths. But we *are* dealing with truth, the unveiling of Being, as Heidegger (1971) would put it.

Arshile Gorky was one of the more obscure of twentieth century painters, who, when he arrived in the United States, created an incredible false persona, pretending kinship to the Russian writer Maxim Gorky and claiming he studied in Paris and had a degree in engineering from Brown University, among other fictions. At one point Gorky published a poem by someone else, claiming that he wrote it; another time he prepared a portfolio allegedly of his own work in order to obtain a commission, in which he actually copied work by Picasso.

He was born in poverty as Vosdanig Adoian around 1903, in the Armenian town of Khorkom, near Van City in Ottoman Turkey, during a cruel Turkish persecution of the Armenians that eventually ended in the horrible slaughter of the Armenian people that shocked the "civilized" world near the end of the second millennium. Gorky's life story immediately brings to mind Deutsch's (1965) concept of the "as-if" personality; but, unlike most of these individuals, he disintegrated into fragmentation, psychotic depression, and suicide. There was, however, one significant difference between Arshile Gorky and the type of severe personality disorders one commonly sees in clinical practice: Gorky was an authentic genius. But he remained unassimilated, intransigent, chauvinistic towards women, absurdly proud and arrogant, and he deteriorated, after the development of rectal cancer necessitating a colostomy, into a life of violence, paranoia, and an overt borderline impulse disorder. No better example could be found of how an artist's psychopathology hampers the artist's creativity throughout life and wrecks any chance for finding the appropriate mirroring and audience that artists need to stabilize their sense of self and stimulate the full potential of their creative talents.

In Gorky's case, as he found himself increasingly isolated, he regressed to the search for an archaic selfobject, which he finally found in an eighteen-year-old girl whom he called Mougouch. His idea of a good wife or female companion was similar to that of Proust's behavior towards Albertine; she "was supposed to stay quietly in the bedroom and pretend she wasn't there" (Spender 1999, 79) and to obey him and serve him as he wished, sometimes described using the metaphor of a dumb horse pulling a cart. Needless to say, the women he encountered did not cooperate very well with this attitude until he was lucky enough to meet the devoted Mougouch, a very unusual person. Mougouch did not even know that her husband had been an Armenian called Vosdanig Adoian and she could not explain why she had never asked him for more accurate information about his past. But even she ran out of patience with him as he fragmented subsequent to his colostomy.

Trying to understand the psychodynamics of Arshile Gorky and trying to decipher his paintings, that seem to incorporate many of his memories from Armenia as well as other more transcendent themes, would constitute a lifetime of study. One should not lose sight of the fact that the genius of Gorky brought him as an autodidact from the slaughter in Armenia to the forefront of twentieth century art all at the same time he was trapped in a severely neurotic set of chains. He was one of the founding abstract expressionist painters in the United States.

The 1915 mass murder of the Armenians left an indelible mark on Gorky. He suffered through the hardships that characterized that situation, as well as the desertion of his father and the death of his mother from what was probably depression and anorexia after as refugees they had found some shelter in Russia. The indifference and arrogant misunderstandings of the art critics who viewed Gorky's work during his lifetime, the not really accidental incineration that he caused of his own studio, which he allowed to destroy a number of his significant paintings, and the narcissistic isolation in which he lived throughout his life were all factors leading to his self-destruction.

Gorky is quoted by Spender (1999) to have said, "Art is not in New York, you see; art is in you" (69). The true artist, Gorky believed, aims for "'the universal idea of art' which exists below the surface of the real" (69). So Gorky complained, "Too many American artists paint portraits that are portraits of a New Yorker, but not of the human being" (69). "See the excitement of the brush," said Gorky to a pupil who was watching him working, "as if the brush in his hand possessed a life of its own" (95). He was very insecure and sometimes accused his colleagues of stealing his ideas; for example, he had an ambivalent relationship with the more famous artist, Willem de Kooning, fuming as he observed the cleverness of de Kooning and his wife in promoting de Kooning, something Gorky could never do. He had to always be a teacher and assumed authority on all subjects to the point he really sounded ridiculous. But he had absolute integrity as an artist. Colleagues could not believe that Gorky was serious when he insisted "abstract art had the emotional power of a Renaissance work of art" (Spender 1999, 111). His work portrayed vivid abstractions in violent and magnificent color, which viewers either immediately responded to or turned away in confusion.

Because of his integrity and devotion to art, Gorky was able to create a small circle of interested and supportive friends who put up with his unpleasant personality traits to a remarkable extent and often gave him a place to live and food to eat. He believed that "the truth and the beauty of a work lay somewhere in between what lay on the canvas and the feelings which had gripped the artist while at work" (Spender 1999, 160). If one is unable to grasp this, then one is unable to appreciate Gorky's art, in which the artist "acts upon his material, takes it apart, reassembles and re-creates it" (ibid., 166). He suffered through the great U.S. economic depression of the early 1930's and, as the depression lifted, some of his major public work was destroyed by such characters as communist-hating generals who were convinced that abstract artists were all communists. (The Russian pseudonym Arshile Gorky did not help either!).

Toward the end of the 1930s, he felt a terrible isolation which no amount of subsequent friendliness on the part of the surrealists or anyone else could eradicate. Although he was an extremely difficult man to live with, he had an intense desire for a permanent relationship but "He had no talent for meeting people and persuading them to take an interest in his work" (ibid., 225). His depressions were at their worst when he was unable to paint. We do not know why he saved so little of his work from the fire in his studio in 1946; a couple of months after that he was operated on for cancer of the rectum and given a colostomy. He refused to let anyone help him in cleaning the colostomy, resenting all the time and bother this required. Waves of rage overtook him and he began to increasingly resemble a classical borderline personality disorder.

In spite of all his psychopathology and physical pathology, during the first ten months of 1947 Gorky completed roughly twenty-five major paintings that "includes a large proportion of the work which is valued today, and without these canvasses his reputation might easily have languished for lack of a major body of work to sustain it. It was a last, crushing effort of will" (ibid., 324). He became increasingly obsessed by the need to dominate his bodily functions and viewed the colostomy as an attack upon himself from within. He withdrew into noncommunicativeness, depression, and paranoia, although I gather there was no recurrence of the cancer itself. Near the end he began giving away his beautiful collection of artist's materials but no one, including psychiatrists who knew him socially, seems to have realized what that meant. Finally, "He descended from a reluctance to engage in any kind of physical contact to a psychological rejection of his wife's presence, a rejection connected with an increasingly tortured relationship with his own body" (ibid., 353) and he ended up with no control over his emotions. This remarkable man hanged himself at the age of forty-four.

THE REVIVAL OF PSYCHOANALYSIS LATE IN THE THIRD MILLENNIUM

Now I will return to the main subject of this chapter, my fantasy about psychoanalysis in year 3000 AD, the end of the third millennium. Creation requires an uncommon mind and strong will serving an original view of life and the world. It is now clear that the notion of creativity as being a consequence of mental illness that was held in the second millennium was wrong and that the abandonment of psychoanalysis at that time under the financial demands of managed care was a gigantic mistake. Both of these misfortunes could easily be understood as a consequence of how, as it spread over the earth, self-understanding was sacrificed for the pursuit of material gain. The arts were unable to overcome their state of fragmentation and despair at the rise of violence, injustice, and inequality in the world. In fact, one could argue that the only fortunate consequence of the self-destruction of the West by terrorist bacterial assaults and of Africa and Asia by the AIDS virus was the forced reorientation of humans when their very survival as a species was at stake, and the consequent collapse of the "me-first" ambiance in the middle of the third millennium, when consumerism no longer became the predominant passion of the human race. Here was a dramatic demonstration of what Wittgenstein insisted to be necessary before our world picture could be changed.

Critics of psychoanalysis could no longer deny that the human being was a biologically evolved creature driven by aggressive and sexual pulsations which attempted to unfold and discharge along the program of the pleasure principle, as Freud so eloquently described it. The horrors of the first three hundred years of the third millennium, coming after the "Great War" and the Holocaust in the second millennium, finally made it clear that Freud's description of human nature was accurate and that only a scientific study of how to strengthen the ego of each child so that it becomes the predominant rider of the id-horse, to develop the superego so that it is neither filled with lacunae nor sadistic and ferocious, would enable the species to remain on the earth without total self-destruction. It was finally realized that each child must become a wanted and precious addition to each family.

After almost a thousand years of neglect, psychoanalysis is now thriving all over the world as a function of the renewed interest in human mental process and the unconscious subdoxastic determinants of it, resulting at last in a major international focus on instincts and their vicissitudes that hopefully will result in the development of human beings who can live with each other in peace. As a consequence of this, there has been an evolution of training centers in psychoanalysis so that creativity is encouraged, new ideas are widely disseminated by written and electronic journals, and any attempts to preserve old ways or rigid ways of teaching and practice and publishing obscure jargon-filled writing along dogmatic lines are viewed with disfavor and suspicion as carry-overs from the blind rigidity of the psychoanalytic bureaucracy that predominated at the start of the second millennium.

Psychoanalysis from late in the second millennium has evolved by the year 3000 AD into a leading international organization for the dissemination and discussion of new ideas, new theories, new ways of teaching, and of all sorts of proposals to facilitate *Bildung*. Psychoanalysis hopes to produce what Nietzsche unfortunately called "the overman," which, in a soft reading (Chessick 1983) of Nietzsche, refers to the individual who is relatively at peace among his or her intrapsychic agencies and consequently able to live in peace with the environment and be generous to fellow humans. It is the representation in 3000 AD of Plato's concept from around 400 BC of the just soul in which the charioteer, (he thought of it as "reason") was in charge of the spirited and sensuous aspects of the soul, and all three were in balance and harmony. As Plato insisted thirty-five hundred years ago, there cannot be a just society unless the humans in it are modeled along this metaphorical pattern.

In a prescient passage at the start of the twentieth century, George Bernard Shaw tried to interest Henry James in using his plays to construct a scientific investigation of human beings for the purpose of bringing about much needed changes in human behavior—and this was even before the "Great War." This task is clearly more appropriate and hopeful if it is relegated to psychoanalysis, and James in 1915, in a famous letter to H. G. Wells, suggested an even more vital function for the arts. He wrote (Horne 1999), "It is art that makes life, makes interest, makes importance, for our consideration and application of these things, and I know of no substitute whatever for the force and beauty of the process" (555). What a remarkable contrast to the orientation that prevailed for the next thousand years, in which it was thought that the frenzied accumulation of material goods and keeping up with technological progress by purchasing every new gadget and up-graded old gadget that was developed, and every other silly thing everybody else had, became a mass obsession since that was thought to be the way to happiness and the construction of a successful life!

In that frenzy, the investigation of the conscious and the unconscious was neglected in favor of empirical biological brain studies (which are of course also important) and the arts became fragmented and peripheral to human life. No wonder those individuals who were unfortunate enough to live a thousand years ago at the end of the second millennium became increasingly disappointed, unable to be empathic with each other, rigid in their thinking and orientation, and increasingly filled with rage, a rage that manifested itself in universal wars, and during peacetime in senseless killings and shootings on the road and even in the schools as their children were caught up in it. The self-destruction of the species, begun in the second millennium with the two-phased "Great War" and reaching global proportions in the first part of the third millennium, was the inevitable result.

At last there is the final recognition that no amount of accumulated biological knowledge of the nervous system can possibly bridge the gap between mind and brain or, in other words, explain the "qualia" (Searle 1997) of consciousness, an aporia that constitutes the so-called "hard mind-body problem" (Chalmers 1996). Therefore, study of the mind will have to be developed and concentrated on using a language and technique different than that used in the biological sciences, just as was true in Freud's day. Psychoanalysis has finally been given legitimacy as a new type of discipline combining energetics, hermeneutics, and the natural sciences. The true depth and revolutionary nature of Freud's discovery has finally come into fruition as the spirit of humanism and compassion has revived.

11

What Constitutes Progress in Psychoanalysis?

> The disposition and activity of our and every age is to apprehend the science that exists, to make it our own, and, just in that process, to develop it further and to raise it to a higher level. By making it our own we make out of it something our own, different from what it was before. . . . Every philosophy, precisely because it is the exposition of one particular stage of development, belongs to its own time and is caught in that time's restriction.
>
> —Hegel (1833, 10–11, 49)

Some of the pertinent concepts of Hegel are relevant to the study of both the phenomenology and history of the development of psychoanalysis. Hegel's investigation is called "phenomenology" because it attempts to stand back with as few preconceptions as possible and let the manifestations of the development of self-consciousness, as he thought of it, show progress toward the Absolute Spirit (or Mind, depending on how one translates his use of *Geist*) becoming conscious of itself. Similarly, it is possible to let the development of psychoanalysis appear and show whatever way contemporary pluralistic psychoanalysis has come into being. Our current uncertainty is in contrast to Hegel's philosophy, for he was convinced that there was an inevitable dialectical development of consciousness towards the achievement of absolute eternal Truth. Our uncertainty then raises the question of whether or not the changes that have taken place in our field over the last fifty years really represent an approach to the truth or whether they simply represent a lateral movement, or even whether theory matters at all. A psychoanalyst's opinion about the answer to this question will have a profound effect in determining whether or not he or she maintains and follows one or the other of the multiplicity of contemporary changes and theories on the assumption they represent progress in the technique and practice of psychoanalysis.

The method of phenomenology (see chapter 4) hopes to get directly to what Husserl (1970) called the lived world, in contrast to abstractions, theories, and postulated agencies. One attempts to stand back and with as few preconceptions as possible observe the historical development of a subject such as psychoanalysis, allowing the manifestations of this development to appear before the person attempting phenomenological investigation. When one applies phenomenological study to the history and development of psychoanalysis, one finds that the current situation of a plurality of theories and orientations takes on a different coloration and tells something about our clinical ignorance regarding the whole psychoanalytic process.

Hegel tried albeit tendentiously to introduce this phenomenological approach in his study of the development of human consciousness. This chapter selects and refers to some of the salient points made by Hegel in his philosophy that have pertinence to the phenomenology of the history and development of psychoanalysis. It will apply these points to the field of psychoanalysis in an effort to learn more about the confusing plurality in the field and to question the viability of the entire subject. Also the views of the well-known continental psychoanalyst Andre Green (2000, 2005a, 2005b) must be considered. Green maintains that the polite compromises in the field today, the attempt to accept and even endorse the massive pluralism in theory and practice that exists, constitutes "a pretense of tolerance, search for willy-nilly common sharings that are not very convincing and appear as life jackets to avoid sinking" (2005a, 126). Green claims this pretense and search for willy-nilly common sharings that are not very convincing prevents the collapse of the entire field. He does not explain how it prevents this collapse. This would imply that, in extreme contrast to Hegel's belief in the inevitable development of consciousness to higher and higher levels of truth, the whole process of development leading to contemporary pluralistic psychoanalysis does not represent progress. It is instead for the purpose of preventing the extinction of the discipline by finding room for everybody.

HEGEL'S THOUGHT

Presented here are a few basic concepts of Hegel's thought, only those that might be found to be pertinent to an examination of the phenomenology of the development of psychoanalysis.[1] A centerpiece of his thinking is that there exists really ultimately only one system of philosophy, not a plurality of isolated systems, and this system extends from the Greeks all the way through historical development culminating in the thought of Hegel! Thus for Hegel, and this is probably the most important point, the history of philosophy *is* philosophy. That is to say, the dialectic method he uses is to suggest that in philosophy each phase is a retrospective comment on what is implied in the previous phases, comments which he believed were necessitated by what went before. For Hegel this is a rigorous and continuous process, and for him it terminates in Absolute Mind or Absolute Spirit becoming conscious of itself after a developmental progression that is inevitable. This concept of *inevitable* progression is one of the most controversial in Hegel's thought. Many scholars claim that in his publications he does a great deal of intellectual twisting and turning to try to convince himself and his readers of the inevitability of each historical transition in the self's consciousness of itself. Very few philosophers are in agreement with his claim of the inevitability of this progression any more.

For Hegel, self and object are not distinct; they are structures arising in experience and each contributes to the developmental actualization of the other. Hegel goes on to say that the self-conscious mind, both of man as a species and of each individual human, evolves in a parallel way. This means that both the self-consciousness of the collective mind as experienced by our species as a whole and the self-consciousness of mind as it is experienced in the development of each individual both occur in a (for him inevitable) series of unfolding levels in which each level is incorporated in the next. For Hegel, the mind is an inner force shaping outer observable forms and going through stages that affect our perception of such outer observable forms. The mind of the individual and the consensus in the consciousness of the species keeps changing and does not afford us an eternal objective disinterested judge.

This approach rejects traditional scientific empiricism with its allegedly permanent classifications such as are found in DSM IV today as too formal and rigid. Truth, he says, can only be reached by an historical approach showing the evolution of what is thought to be truth up to a particular stage of its development and always as the necessary outcome of a series of conflicts and discrepancies and their corrections. Hegel believes the final result is a self-consciousness of Absolute Spirit. In this, thought and its object are transcended and Absolute Spirit's self consciousness is communicated first through art and then religion and finally philosophy.

Hegel was the first philosopher to focus on the problem of alienation, Dostoevsky's "underground man." This was an unknown problem to the eighteenth-century philosophers of the Enlightenment, who thought they lived in a congenial and reasonable world. But for Hegel the state of "otherness" or alienation is a driving force for an advance to higher levels of philosophical consciousness, not, as it is for some other thinkers, representative of a dead end in human history. What he means is that the discomfort experienced at any level of self-consciousness because of the incompleteness of that level drives the individual and the species continuously to advance to higher levels until Absolute Sprit's consciousness of itself is reached. It is somewhat analogous to the creative drive found in alienated and uncomfortable individuals like Beethoven, whose work culminates in more and more sophisticated compositions until the unparalleled transcendental final quartets were created.

In one of Hegel's most famous conceptions, when a philosopher attempts to understand what is going on in his own epoch he or she can only review it, for it is already changing. Thus his famous saying: "The owl of Minerva spreads its wings only with the falling of the dusk" (1820, 13). Applying this to the phenomenology of the development of psychoanalysis, when we look at this development we can only review where it has been because it is already changing. The point is that we cannot use this phenomenological approach to influence or change the direction that psychoanalysis is going, only to understand it.

PROGRESS

In *The Philosophy of Right* (1820), Hegel presents his picture of the inevitable development of a rationally organized and free community, and he points out that our wants and desires are shaped by our society and by the social and historical forces of our times. By way of contrast, one hundred fifty years later, Greenberg (2005), in the current state-of-the-art *Textbook of Psychoanalysis* (Person, Cooper, and Gabbard 2005), claims, "History suggests that there is something about the psychoanalytic process that makes it more likely that we will come up with interesting questions than we will arrive at convincing answers" (220–221). Greenberg says that the emphasis on technical flexibility is very appealing today because there is such a predominant trend toward questioning of authority throughout our culture, but he warns of the temptation "To view change as evidence of progress, a sign that we are moving toward more effective technique and toward deeper understanding of therapeutic action. But despite historical ebbs and flows, there is still no consensus on the issue among contemporary analysts" (222). He warns us that holding fast and rigidly to a specific technique or theory as a matter of principle can be just as much an expression of the theorist's unconscious fantasies as the effort to modify technique because "the analyst's personal motives—unconscious as well as conscious, fantastic as well as realistic—shape every clinical decision and every observation. No prescription can immunize us from expressing our own unconscious wishes in our technical choices" (222).

A fundamental difference is manifest here between the thinking of Hegel and the thinking of Greenberg in that Hegel claims there is an inevitable progress toward Truth in the history of philosophy, whereas Greenberg questions whether there has been any such progress in the history and development of psychoanalysis. Most psychoanalysts today would agree that it is not inevitable that there should be such a progress. The question of how much and what sort of progress has occurred, however, remains very controversial.

Hegel took history seriously. He agreed with Schiller that the very foundations of the human condition could change from one historic era to another. He wanted to plunge into the phenomenology of the mind, that is to say, an investigation of the successive stages of how consciousness appears to itself. As each form of consciousness reveals itself to be less than genuine knowledge, one gets what he calls "determinate negation." This causes the mind to move on inevitably, says Hegel, to higher forms of knowledge of reality, a process of continuous overcoming. This dialectical progression is outlined in his (1807) famous *Phenomenology of Spirit*, but Hegel's attribution of it to "the cunning of reason" coming from one Absolute Mind or Spirit is, to say the least, very obscure, highly metaphysical (although tempting), and debatable (Fox 2005).

For Hegel (1837): "Spirit is at war with itself. It must overcome itself as its own enemy and formidable obstacle" (69). A similar battle for attaining a higher and deeper level of understanding a patient will certainly be familiar to every psychoanalytic clinician. Or, as Fox (2005) puts it, "Ultimately consciousness must endure the chastening experience of its own humiliation and comeuppance in order to reach mature wisdom" (107). Hegel (1812) maintains, for example in his *Science of Logic*, that apparently stable structures collide, disintegrate and form a new synthesis (*Aufhebung*) in which the old still resides in the new.

So Hegel began with the same approach as Freud, a study of our lived experiences, our being-in-the-world, and he explained that what makes a form of experience seem necessary is the social context of it. In a passage that is crucial to our understanding of the phenomenology of psychoanalysis, Fox (2005) writes: "Each philosophical construction gives voice to a perspective . . . that seems truthful to its author, living at the time and place it is recorded. Hence, every outlook must be understood as a standpoint that arises from within a particular sociocultural context" (25). So ideas and theories and systems, whether philosophical or psychoanalytic, are ways of dealing with the times, attempts to grasp the world in any epoch.

Freud, as well as Hegel and each great philosopher, had a vision or intuition about the nature of things, and such a vision or intuition lies at the center of every philosophical, psychoanalytic, and metapsychological system. Fox (2005) writes:

> Hegel also believed that new ideas, conceptions, and theories that seem to appear in consciousness as if from nowhere are actually the products of a slower process of germination and gestation. They may

be launched in a special creative moment, but to be of any lasting significance, they require refinement and reexpression [sic] in the
medium of rational cognition and through meaningful discourse. (58)

Nietzsche (1886) more psychoanalytically said, "Most of the conscious thinking of a philosopher is secretly guided and forced into certain channels by his
instincts" (201) and he regards every great philosophy as "the personal confes-
sion of its author and a kind of involuntary and unconscious memoir" (203).

In rejecting the system offered by Freud or Hegel, or reinterpreting it on
the basis of one's clinical convictions or even in an idiosyncratic way that suits
one's personal prejudices (for example, the "young Hegelians" versus the "old
Hegelians," the "right Hegelians" versus the "left Hegelians" or, in our field,
Kleinians versus Kohutians, Fairbairnians versus Jungians, and so on and so
on) one also rejects their central vision and substitutes a different central
vision (for example, Marx's "standing Hegel upside down" or Lacan's very controversial "return to Freud") about how things are. This substitution is what
has happened in the current plethora of psychoanalytic theories and also in
the turn in the United States philosophy departments from idealist continental philosophy to so-called analytic philosophy. The very basic questions asked
by these opposing orientations to the world are different. For example, continental philosophy asks, "How is truth disclosed in aesthetic and phenomenological experience," whereas so-called "analytic philosophy" asks, "What can
be known through the employment of logical analysis alone?," a dichotomy
which is only now being recognized and patched over by seminal thinkers like
Quine (1953). The crucial decision each of us must make is whether a new
system and the new vision on which it is based represent progress in human
knowledge. And this decision as well as the decision to adopt a new system is,
like all other human decisions, multiply determined and rooted in the individual's unconscious doxastic factors.

For Hegel and Freud there are three developmental voices of the phenomenology of mind. First, there is the merely conscious participant who is
only aware of the content of his or her consciousness. This proceeds to the self
conscious participant who attempts to articulate not only consciousness but
the form of consciousness itself, the theory behind it, its intentions and its
goals. Finally, and this was more emphasized by Hegel, there appears the
philosophical voice of reason, via the "cunning of reason," insight that eventually leads us through rational reflection to change for the better the way we see
ourselves and the world. In another version of this Freud (1927) wrote:

The voice of the intellect is a soft one, but it does not rest until it has
gained a hearing. Finally, after a countless succession of rebuffs, it suc-
ceeds. This is one of the few points on which one may be optimistic

about the future of mankind, but it is in itself a point of no small importance. . . . The primacy of the intellect lies, it is true, in a distant, distant future, but probably not in an *infinitely* distant one. (53)

I wonder if Freud, the quintessential realist, would still say that today.

SELF-CONSCIOUSNESS, THE SENSE OF SELF

For Hegel, a sense of self exists only by being acknowledged and it emerges out of a struggle with the world. Therefore, contra Descartes, there exist preconditions for the self and it is an interpersonal construction. In this manner Hegel is extremely modern and consistent with current psychoanalytic studies of infant and child development. For Hegel self-consciousness emerges out of the struggle with the world. It is not an immediate intuition and in that sense, we create each other. This is Hegel's famous concept of *Sittlichkeit* (from *Sitte*, custom), the complex of norms, rituals, rules, and practices that make up a society and make each one of us a part of society, a set of behaviors through which we define ourselves and our morality. It is a fatal distinction and error, he says, to try to separate this from individual autonomy. Hegel's standpoint is primarily a Greek notion, that we are created by our society and not set-off against it.

Left to itself, Hegel writes, reflection functions as understanding (*Verstand*) and posits perpetual oppositions. This leads to a continuing process of self expression and self manifestations as they collide, change, and develop through history. For Hegel this is a teleological process, the self-unfolding of an essence, the actualization of an eternal Idea, that of self-thinking thought (i.e., the Absolute Spirit). So the history of philosophy is the Absolute Spirit gaining knowledge of itself, and it is the task of philosophy to make this process clear. For Hegel, dialectical thought gives a deeper penetration of the nature of reality than the "understanding" (*Verstand*) used in the natural sciences can do, by overcoming the rigidity of the concepts that are assumed in the natural sciences. The task of "reason" (*Vernunft*), according to Hegel, must be to again and again form a higher synthesis of our plurality of concepts.

It was the psychoanalyst R. D. Laing (1969) who first made use of some of these ideas in his conception that mental illness, especially schizophrenia, could be seen as an attempt not only to reconstitute the rigid false self, but also to resume a development toward a higher integration and synthesis of the aspects of the personality which were sidetracked at an early time of life. So for Laing, schizophrenia had the potential to increase one's health rather than destroy it. Few psychiatrists agree with this approach today, but there are a number of isolated case reports that seem to support it, including some in my own clinical experience. Similarly, Heidegger (1962) from his study of Hegel formed his concept of "authentic awareness" as constituting a return out of forgetfulness and error. It is interesting that Hegel's good friend Hölderlin, who eventually became schizophrenic, disagreed with Hegel's concept of the Absolute Spirit and insisted that nature is not an emanation of Spirit but an unfathomable and inexhaustible invitation to creative activity. This constitutes yet another metaphysical theory.

TRUTH AND BELIEFS

For Hegel, phenomenology represents the attempt always to go beyond current concepts and understanding and to observe, in the unfolding of thought studied in an historical fashion, principles that better explain this unfolding. Truth, claims Hegel, is approached by affirmation and denial and contradiction, the whirl of passing stages in the development of thought, and we need an itinerary of our conceptions. Taken individually, some of our experiences and systems and the concepts that are fundamental to them seem wild and crazy, but eventually they can be gathered in a durable framework of overarching truth, says Hegel. So, in his famous statement in the preface to the *Phenomenology of Spirit* (1807), he says:

> Appearance is the arising and passing away that does not itself arise and pass away, but is "in itself" . . . and constitutes the actuality and the movement of the life of truth. The True is thus the Bacchanalian revel in which no member is not drunk; yet because each member collapses as soon as he drops out, the revel is just as much transparent and simple repose. Judged in the court of this movement, the single shapes of Spirit do not persist any more than determinate thoughts do, but they are as much positive and necessary movements, as they are negative and evanescent. (27–28)

He attempts to cure dogmatic dualisms by his dialectical method, he explains our current meanings as based on the linguistic community, and he maintains that the fundamentals of human thought change over history and also the fundamentals of human nature change over history. Human life becomes a self-expression clarifying what we are. This is a uniquely original orientation for its time, establishing Hegel as one of the world's greatest thinkers.

All foundational beliefs have changed historically, and history is a succession of human perspectives, both concepts and beliefs, which fundamentally differ. This succession for Hegel is dictated by a dialectical development culminating in Hegel's contemporary philosophic standpoint. In this sense the relationship of the mind and the world is what Hegel calls dialectical. For him, phenomenology is a study of the evolution of specific forms of knowledge, a critical enterprise in which each form is shown to be inadequate and each negation is what he calls a determinate negation giving rise to a new form of knowledge. So in order to understand the thought of any epoch, one must use an approach which is detailed and historical. Hegel stressed how conceptions of art, politics, and morality are not disembodied but are embedded in forms of social life and modes of practice within social life generally.

Psychoanalysts should note that, according to Hegel, there is an internal relation between practice and conceptual self-understanding. He (1820) writes:

> Whatever happens, every individual is a child of his time; so philosophy too is its own time apprehended in thoughts. It is just as absurd to fancy that a philosophy can transcend its contemporary world as it is to fancy that an individual can overleap his own age, jump over Rhodes. (11)

In the light of Hegel's concept of each philosophy as a child of its time, we may ask, "Has there been a development that can be seen in the phenomenology of psychoanalysis as viewed historically, toward a greater and greater approximation to truth, or have we just witnessed a transition from epoch to epoch in which both philosophy and psychoanalysis reflect the particular societal circumstances and customs of the time?" The quote from Greenberg given previously implies the latter and if Greenberg is correct psychoanalysis will keep shifting historically in a lateral rather than a progressive fashion. Each age has its own set of values and according to Hegel this is determined by the phenomenological status or ontological structure of that age. This structure, providing each age with standards of truth and propriety, is determined by the developmental stage or form of consciousness of the age. Since this is always imperfect, contradictions are recognized and overcome and so new underlying concepts and assumptions eventually form a new ontological structure.

IS PSYCHOANALYSIS PROGRESSING?

It is true that, as Inwood (1983) puts it, Hegel is (and has already been) all things to all men due to the obscurity of his writing, but he does pose a fundamental question for psychoanalysts. This question is, Has the conceptual and consequent technical shift in our field from a one person psychology to a two person psychology, that is, the shift from the neutral psychoanalyst conceived as a relatively objective observer, to the intersubjective process in which the psychoanalytic situation is created by the interaction of two human beings rather than primarily a manifestation of the transference from earlier developmental times of the patient, a representation of progress towards truth? Or is it simply a manifestation of the shift from the more authoritative epoch in the nineteenth century to the relativistic and pessimistic epoch in the twentieth and early twenty-first century?

For Hegel, the philosophy of an era pervades ideas and norms in the institutions of that era, and the business of philosophy is just to bring to consciousness what men have believed about thinking; it is a descriptive enterprise. The same pervasion of contemporary ideas and norms is found in psychoanalysis, as a phenomenological investigation of psychoanalysis reveals. This is of course familiar to anyone who has studied the field. I have repeatedly called for a genealogical study of the development of psychoanalysis (1999b, 2000a) that links the particular form of psychoanalysis which is predominant in a given culture with the history and customs of that culture. This would be in marked contrast to the idea that there is a correct form of psychoanalysis that should be universally applied and it implies that no such correct form or overarching theory can ever be realized. If Hegel's optimistic approach is valid, on the other hand, the correct form (Truth) will eventually be reached. But, as Hegel might say, the form of psychoanalysis employed in any given culture, whether it be France, South America, Japan, or the United States, et cetera, is, like the customs, beliefs, practices, and philosophy that predominate in that culture, a product of that culture. There are no absolute theoretical standards by which these different forms of psychoanalysis can be evaluated.

In psychoanalysis, as in philosophy, from a phenomenological point of view there is a dialectic of self-understanding and self-actualization that occurs employing forms that are shaped through a cultural tradition. So any individual's self-actualization and the appearance of any psychoanalytic system must be understood in its social and historical meaning. Hegel stresses the social and cultural aspects of the self's consciousness of itself just as we should stress the societal and cultural aspects of all systems of psychoanalysis, and recognize that self-understanding alters and develops in a dialectical process of experience.

This approach to psychoanalysis is parallel to that of Hegel, who emphasizes the inevitable collective striving of humanity for understanding its own essence. He employs the concept of *Sittlichkeit* to demonstrate that the Enlightenment moralists had little understanding of the hold tradition has on us. They had an ahistorical view of humans, both abstract and fictional (Wood 1990). Hegel (1840) observes that human history is "this slaughter-bench, on which the happiness of nations, the wisdom of states, and the virtues of individuals were sacrificed" (24). He tries to rise above this irrefutable fact about history by striving to recognize in it, despite the horror of it all, a progressive actualization of Absolute Spirit in human history and an inevitable unfolding of Spirit's understanding of itself. This, to say the least, is a tenuous argument even though it forms the essence of Hegel's metaphysical idealism.[2]

In spite of Hegel's magnificent and supreme endeavor, the world is too complex and cannot fit into any supreme philosophical or metapsychological system. But if one follows the lead of Hegel, any study of a psychoanalytic system would require us to ask what are the dynamic forces that make it what it is, what is its mode of understanding of the world and of itself, what are the basic shared assumptions, both conscious and unconscious. In his view, all knowledge is perspectival and each person is a child of his or her time. Knowledge is never apriori. It emerges out of collective effort and is historically situated, not the result of pure reason. Nobody can jump over their historical moment. The philosopher can only describe this and he or she cannot change it.

THE PHENOMENOLOGY OF PSYCHOANALYSIS

For Hegel (1833), a personality develops through action which alters the self in unforeseen ways. There is a dialectic between self-knowledge, self-actualization, and praxis, in which striving for a set of goals founded on knowledge of one's self leads to new self-knowledge, new goals, altered striving, et cetera. The approach of phenomenology reveals that this dialectic is also true of the history of psychoanalysis. Hegel claims to expose the pretenses and illusions that characterize both philosophy and, by implication for us, psychoanalysis (see Beiser 1993). These are: (1) that laws and values which were thought eternal are actually culturally relative; (2) that ideas thought to be innate are actually relative; (3) that institutions thought to have supernatural origin are actually culture-bound; (4) that entities reified as independent of human consciousness are actually products of the unconscious; (5) that intuitions that were thought due genius are also products immersed in their historical background; and (6) that one cannot create a presuppositionless philosophy or an eternally true and commonly agreed upon psychoanalysis. A philosopher, like a psychoanalyst, cannot leap beyond his or her age, for the thoughts, ideas, and concepts by which we think about the world undergo constant development and transformation and even the object of thought is not given to us but is created by our thinking about it. In a view the exact opposite of that of Plato, "meaning" becomes a collective effort over time.

It is very important to point out once more that Hegel was not a relativist. He did believe that Truth was universal and eternal and could be reached by

the gradual process of his dialectical method and would be revealed by a phenomenological investigation of the development of consciousness. However
we cannot extrapolate from Hegel's belief to the development of psychoanalysis because his belief in an eternal Truth is a metaphysical belief for
which there is no evidence one way or the other.

   Hegel called the cathedral at *Köln* in its sublimity a leftover from an earlier historical period. Some have tried to apply this attitude to the edifice
known as *The Standard Edition*, twenty-four volumes of collected works of
Sigmund Freud. These magnificent edifices represent the spirit of their age
but tend to be thought of as obsolete as cultures come and go. It is my understanding that in psychoanalytic institutes the collected works of Sigmund
Freud are no longer regarded as the basic foundation to be studied in becoming a psychoanalyst; it is hard for me to understand this but, when one turns
to Hegel's thinking, it becomes more explainable. Similarly, and again in contrast to Hegel, I once spent an entire week in a hotel room in *Köln* that had a
direct view of the cathedral, and I did not find it in any sense to be obsolete,
but rather stimulating to meditation and self-reflection. If one tarries before it
long enough, it leads one to an understanding that there is more to humans
than materialism, as manifested in the spiritual side numinously demonstrated
by this magnificent architectural work, the product of a whole community.
Here is an example of how, if given a chance and if we tarry long enough in
front of it, an aesthetic experience can lead to a new or alternative vision of the
world, to new and sometimes even transcendental knowledge that empirical
sciences and analytic philosophy cannot by their very nature attain. Great art,
architecture, and music never become circumscribed to their own historical
era, but have something to offer to everyone always. But one must be open to
it. The same is true of the collected works of the great thinkers of the past, the
great conversation from Plato and Aristotle historically through Nietzsche,
Freud, Wittgenstein, and Heidegger. Each presents an alternative vision of the
world, opening up new possibilities of knowledge for us.

   German idealists like Hegel claim that the human subject is never passive
but always active with respect to what it experiences. Therefore we never perceive what it is as it is in independence of us but rather, what we perceive is a
function of the subject, of who we are, and of the way that we shape the contents of our experience. I have spoken of this in the psychoanalytic context as
the formation of the core of the psyche at a very early age of life through
which everything else that follows becomes perceived and reenacted. Hegel
claims (Rockmore 1993), as we have seen, that no one, not even a philosopher,
can jump over his or her historical moment:

   We are all rooted in our own context, from which we cannot extricate ourselves and which, hence, limits thought, our thought, includ-

ing philosophical thought . . . we can only know on the basis of the world in which we live, from the angle of vision of our own cultural and historical world. (133)

Everyone agrees that there were rapid changes in psychoanalytic theorizing in the thirty-six years between the publication of *Studies on Hysteria* and the appearance of Glover's (1931) seminal paper "The Therapeutic Effect of Inexact Interpretations" and an accelerating accumulation of changes since that time. Glover claimed that these changes represent advances. But it is equally possible to argue that they are lateral changes and a function of the changing culture. And this is a very important debate for us to consider. Similarly, each of us must decide about such controversial issues as whether to follow the contemporary pluralistic shift to various theories of relational psychoanalysis, intersubjectivity, self psychology, and many other theories and techniques, or whether the analyst should practice a more traditional type of psychoanalysis.

In the Freudian psychoanalytic view, his vision of the world, conflict and fantasy are embedded in normal development. There is no escape from human weakness, lust, aggression, and destructiveness, and life is a constant struggle against the maladaptive reactivation of infantile conflicts. The psychoanalytic situation is structured to promote the reactivation of these infantile conflicts and fantasies in the transference for the purpose of study and the patient's achieving insight into them and resolving them in new ways, utilizing the ego of the patient who now is an adult. The work of Freud and Anna Freud eventually led to the structural theory and the focus on ego psychology and the mechanisms of defense. At this point Klein and Fairbairn and others in England and Horney, Hartmann, and others in the United States all rode off in their own directions, more or less obscuring Freud's vision and offering their own. This trend toward dispersion and diffusion continues today at an even more dramatic pace.

Can any of these proposed new versions of psychoanalysis, to whatever extent they are based on a different fundamental vision about humans, ever be proven in one way or another as superior to Freud's original vision? Or do they simply serve to fragment the field and hopelessly confuse the public, and if so, why this accelerated fragmentation at this time? In Kohut's terms, does it represent a manifestation of narcissistic wounding as the application of Freud's psychoanalysis to every form of mental and social illness in the mid-twentieth century did not live up to the enthusiastic promises made for it and led to the eclipse of psychoanalysis by psychopharmacology?

There is a failure in our field to distinguish change from progress. When we assume we are simply improving on the work of our predecessors, this (as Greenberg writes), "discounts the influence both of our personal theories and of the constraints imposed on psychoanalytic practice (and even on analytic thinking) by cultural trends. When we fail to distinguish change from progress, we lose touch with insights that may have arisen at a different time and under the sway of different premises" (2005, 222). This quotation could come directly from Hegel.

A GLOOMY THIRD ALTERNATIVE

In contrast to Hegel's conviction that there is a dialectical progress towards absolute and eternal Truth, there is an even more gloomy point of view than just arguing that psychoanalytic progress is simply a lateral and culturally determined movement. For completeness it must be considered next. Fonagy (Person, Cooper, and Gabbard 2005) asks:

> But do theories matter at all? Do they really influence clinical work with patients? This is a difficult question to answer. Evidently, analysts from very different persuasions, with very different views of pathogenesis, are convinced of the correctness of their formulations and are guided in their treatments by convictions. Since we do not yet know what is truly mutative about psychotherapy, it might well be that for many patients the analyst's theory of their etiology is not so crucial. (140)

Every psychoanalyst will have to explicitly or implicitly decide for himself or herself whether each of the changes in technique they have chosen and are practicing, and their adoption of different theoretical assumptions based on different visions of the truth about humans from Freud's original conceptions, represent progress and development in psychoanalysis towards a greater and greater approximation of truth and correctness. Or do they simply represent changes that reflect the changes in the culture and civilization that constitute the environment in which the particular psychoanalyst is carrying out the technique and practice of psychoanalysis? Or do theories even matter at all?

APORIAS

Hegel (1883) asks, "What are we to make of this contradiction between the unity of truth and the multiplicity of philosophies? What is the result of this long labour of the human spirit and how is it to be understood? In what sense are we to treat the history of philosophy?" (66). How, Hegel asks, can we seriously inquire whether certain beliefs are knowledge unless we have already made a presumption about what knowledge really is? So, any examination of knowledge must also be an examination of the standard or criterion by which claims to knowledge are assessed. It is only through a study of the phenomenology of the development of psychoanalysis that we can see how these fundamental premises have imperceptibly shifted over the years, from Freud's insistence that psychoanalysis was simply another branch of natural science to many contemporary theories that are based on the current predominance of Nietzschean perspectivalism, of relativism, of hermeneutics, of the need for political correctness, and on the general contemporary discouragement about whether any form of essential Truth either in philosophy or ethics or morality can be found.

It is possible that we shall never have answers to objective or scientific questions about what constitutes the "true" psychoanalysis. The ideal of objectivity is not self-evident, but rather came along with the primordial foundation of modern science. Compare for example the ancient definition of science, which was understood as "theoria," a mental intuition from what is observed without any thought of how it could be experimentally used, manipulated, or changed. But modern science is ruled by a technological spirit, one of success, of effectiveness of its methods. This gives us confidence that in principle nothing can escape the clutches of research any longer and everything can be brought to reveal itself. Yet this revelation has to do with the horizon employed. "Horizon" literally means "boundary line," "limit." Held (2003) explains: "A horizon determines what *can* arise in it in general." He goes on to point out that our current ideal of scientific objectivism causes us to "forget the subjective genesis of all horizons; in other words, by favoring the objective side of knowledge, science becomes an aggressively one-sided understanding of truth" (61).

There are many contemporary efforts to explain all of the phenomena of consciousness and human mentation solely by recourse to neurophysiology or computer science, with the extreme of such theories labeled in philosophy as eliminative reductionism. This is a highly controversial approach and unresolved in the very controversial philosophy of the mind-brain problem today, as discussed in chapter 9. We all agree, of course, that mentation always has a neurophysiological basis, but the hotly debated question is whether our subjective consciousness contains emergent phenomena such as the qualia of consciousness, that cannot be predicted from or clearly related to any specific neurophysiological processes. These issues raise the unresolved question of whether human understanding of the origin and nature of consciousness and the infinite subtlety of human relations and the dynamics of human psychic functioning can ever be confined to the horizon assumed by modern science. Hegel teaches us that we should turn to the arts, religion, and philosophy as the highest manifestations of humanity, affording us a more complete knowledge of sophisticated psychic functioning and in a way perhaps offering knowledge to some extent outside the horizon of empirical science. But one must tarry and be patient; in art as well as in the psychoanalytic process, truth reveals itself in its own way and in its own time. The complete *Standard Edition of the Psychological Works of Sigmund Freud* is based on a vision of the world; psychoanalysts wandering away from the basic premises offered there must realize they have adopted a different vision of the world. My point is that Freud's vision should be the foundation stone of psychoanalysis, the central core of our profession, until it can be demonstrated that a different vision approaches the truth more effectively and is not just another lateral move to please contemporary political and financial powers and fit into a changing culture.

12

Understanding the Human Mind in the Contemporary World

The Enlightenment, with its dream that reason and science could both understand and improve the world, could have died that very day, if its corpse were not already stinking up the quiet muddy fields of France and Russia. All the science, the crystal skyscrapered cities, the machines, the electrical networks, the rationalizations of time, the armies, the bureaucracies, the plans, the colonies and the commerce so artfully managed, the missionaries, the explorers, the revolutions, the manifestos, and the world systems, all the schemes and all the ideals, all the hard-booted engineers and all the covenants, all the best intentions and learning had all amounted to an artillery shell in the chest.

—*Einstein in Love* (Overbye 2000, 364)

Philosophy begins when we have lost our way and no longer feel secure about our place in the world and our way of life. As Heidegger (1956) pointed out:

The question about the nature of something awakens at those times when the thing whose nature is being questioned has become obscure and confused, when at the same time the relationship of men to what is being questioned has become uncertain or has even been shattered. (43)

It is the task of philosophy to explicate and criticize the fundamental beliefs and concepts that underlie any given culture such as ours. Because of all this, a philosopher is not at peace with the world. Stroud (2001) says:

> Philosophy depends on undying curiosity, and the pursuit of a limit-
> less enquiry. It arises out of a wish, or an attempt, to grasp the world
> as it is, as it is open to our view. . . . Philosophy is thought or reflec-
> tion, that is done purely for the sake of understanding something,
> solely to find out what is so with respect to those aspects of the world
> that puzzle us. (31–32)

The life of thought, its vitality and creativity, requires a process of moving
beyond itself and a critique of the ideals and presumptions that hold it in
place. Heidegger proposed that thought was an experiment belonging to
questions and uncertainties, one that does not anticipate a body of results or
forge a systematic account of the way things "really" are. For Heidegger, thinking is constituted by the ways of encountering other peoples thinking. It is a
process of strife and engagement, but one that does not foresee its own establishment as supreme and final.

The parallel between this philosophical concept of thinking and Freud's
orientation to his psychoanalytic clinical work is apparent. For Freud, psychoanalysis had as its main purpose an understanding of the human mind and the
more understanding that was achieved, the more the psychoanalytic process
gained therapeutic value as an ancillary consequence. The human mind in psychoanalysis, philosophy, music, and art must be understood historically. The
practice of psychoanalysis requires a certain stance of receptive patience; it cannot be hurried. Each patient unfolds at their own pace. Harries (2001) explains:

> Both Plato and Aristotle insist on this connection between philoso-
> phy and freedom: not only does the pursuit of philosophy require free
> time—only a person of leisure can be a philosopher—but it is pre-
> cisely because the philosopher does not approach things and issues
> with a particular end in mind that he is able to see them with more
> open eyes. (65)

The similarity to Freud's psychoanalytic attitude advocating free-floating
attention to the patient's material is obvious here.

There is a fundamental disagreement among both philosophers and psychoanalysts over what it means to be human. The stance called humanism
postulates that the human being can be described in the abstract, independently of time and place, and is endowed by nature with certain attributes like
the capacity for self-knowledge and the ability to make free rational choices.
In this sense modern humanism carries on the legacy of the Enlightenment
and assumes that humans are naturally free, equal, self-aware, and gifted with
reason. It follows that the more they exercise reason the more they know and
the better they are able to master their environment and control their destiny.

From this point of view ignorance and superstition are the enemies of humankind and, as we spread knowledge and technology over the world, freedom will spread along with it and life will become improved.

Anti-humanism defines humans not as given essences but as subjects who get created in different forms in particular historical times and places. So anti-humanists like Foucault (1973), claim there is no such thing as "man"; the era of "man" is over. This means that humans are simply precipitates of their society and their culture and they are constituted not by nature but by the ideology and linguistic and interpersonal structures that operate through them. Such theorists emphasize the limitations of Enlightenment thinking, often quoting from Marx, Nietzsche, and Freud, whom Ricoeur (1970) calls practitioners of the "hermeneutics of suspicion," searching for the subdoxastic factors determining our presuppositions and beliefs.

Much of philosophy today, especially in the United States and England, has become empty, boring, and sterile, and the issue of whether philosophers should actively work to make social change remains unresolved. But twentieth-century Continental philosophy tried to refigure the history of Western thought and uncover within it overlooked or suppressed conflicts, values, and meanings. It generated a whole new body of problems and movements of thought and comprised an encounter with the Western philosophical canon as represented currently by "analytic philosophy" in the United States and Britain (Cutrofello 2005). It put into question many of the major Western philosophical ideas and texts.

For example, as Sartre wrote in *Being and Nothingness* (see Levy 2002) our world is "hodological," a term he borrowed from the psychologist Kurt Lewin, meaning that the space of our world is mapped by human needs and interests. Thus distance and place are primordially measured in terms of lived experience. The world as we experience it is irreducibly meaningful, that is to say one can not strip everything mental away. There is no such thing as a description of something from no perspective whatever. Sartre claimed that we have no essence and we must choose and define ourselves; we are chance creations of blind forces of nature.

For Sartre: "Being-for-itself" is the kind of being we humans are in contrast to "Being-in-itself," which is simply re-arranged even when we destroy countries in war. "Being-for-itself" is defined by the ability to question itself and to distance itself from itself. This produces a fissure, since "Being-for-itself" can treat itself as an object by what Sartre calls the process of negation. A third form of being, "Being-for-others" occurs when another person looks at one; by this, one becomes an object in someone else's world and is imbued with a character and labeled as a kind or type of person. This is how we acquire a personal identity, says Sartre—by means of the gaze of another. For Sartre, this constitutes a sinister dialectic at the basis of all human relations.

For Sartre, "Being-for-itself" is profoundly alone. This view stands in sharp contrast to that of Heidegger (1962), who said that *Dasein* is always "being-with" others. But Sartre sees the "Being-for-itself"as existing in isolation and alienation, and in his (1968) later work he claims that the "practico-inert" functions to keep us that way, since scarcity requires us to be rivals. Only when imminent danger to the group occurs does group solidarity form, to a degree proportional to the peril. After the peril is resolved, things inevitably go back to the way they were, says Sartre.

IS THERE AN ESSENCE TO MIND AND TO THE WORLD?

The philosophers Jürgen Habermas (1971) and Karl Otto Apel (1998) both in their own way attempted to develop some kind of transcendental standards that ground philosophical inquiry, in opposition to the relativism and nihilism that pervade our time. In contrast to Sartre and Foucault and others in Continental philosophy, it is still possible to maintain, as I do, that there is an "essential I." For example, Carter (2002) explains that the "essential I" may be characterized by boundlessness, and agency. Boundlessness represents the fact that there is no place in your experience where your consciousness is not. Agency represents a set of concepts, intuitive beliefs, the unconscious, including ways of interpreting information that are programmed into the brain by both the genes and the environment. This is not as far from the efforts of Descartes as some modern philosophers seem to think it is. The subjectivity of consciousness and the fact that it provides each individual with a sense of their existence as a particular conscious person is still one of the great mysteries, the so-called "hard problem" in mind-brain research: How do physical processes in the brain give rise to the subjective private stream of consciousness that grounds our sense of individual existence? I discussed the mind-brain problem in chapter 9, and briefly review it here.

Some thinkers, such as Chalmers (1996), believe that consciousness is a fundamental element of the universe. McGinn (1993) argues that this question or "hard problem" is unanswerable due to our cognitive limitations. He (2002) thinks that the mind-brain problem is unsolvable because we lack the intellect. He writes:

> We are suffering from what I call "cognitive closure" with respect to the mind-body problem. Just as a dog cannot be expected to solve the problems about space and time and the speed of light that it took a brain like Einstein's to solve, so maybe the human species cannot be expected to understand how the universe contains mind and matter in combination. (182)

This position has become known as the "mysterian" position.

Other philosophers vehemently disagree with this point of view. At the present time, under the domination of computers and brain studies in our current society, they lean toward functionalism or eliminative materialism (see Lyons 2001). But their opponents believe that one cannot reduce complex psychology to neurophysiology and that consciousness basically represents the emergence of a surprising effect of brain functioning, the emergence of our subjective qualia. A large number of scholars tend to emphasize the peculiar nature of felt experience known as qualia, and the fact that each of us has access to his or own mental experience in a way that no other person does. Paintings and visual images, for example, possess a kind of subjectivity that seems to defeat materialistic or scientific explanations. Qualia represent the here-and-now subjective conscious experiences that each of us individually has and that distinguishes us from robots or zombies. Qualia constitute what might be called our interior life. How do molecules and electricity produce something aware of itself?

DEVELOPMENT OF THE MIND

Many of these disputes about what it means to be human are based on differing views about the development of the mind. For example, Cavell's (1993) book on the "psychoanalytic mind" stresses (2) Davidson's antisubjectivist view, which has many ramifications involving the psychoanalytic process. Cavell claims (46) that Freud's model of cognition assumes the infant has the capacity for veridical perception of specific objects and for recalling those objects in moments of need. She insists both philosophical argument and infant research agree that this model is mistaken and there can not be representation of absent objects before the age of about eighteen months. She also claims Freud's hallucinatory wish-fulfillment theory of infants is disproved by Piaget. She correctly says Freud's idea of the mind is subjectivist, seeing it as a kind of inner eye before which ideas occur as presentations: "The idea of a pre-linguistic imagistic form of thinking plays a central role in Freud's early account of repression" (47). So for Freud the prelinguistic images come first and then one's introduction into language provides a lens through which the thinker perceives his or her thoughts.

Cavell (102) claims that the infant has no thoughts before communication and that concepts are forged through dialogue, not discovered as Plato believed. So the mind, for Cavell, is continually in the making and the other person is indispensable. She disagrees with Stern's argument that there is a sense of self before self-consciousness and claims this is simply a projection that adults make back onto the infant. For Cavell there is no unknowable self behind the veil of language; Stern and Lacan are wrong and there is no self independent from other selves (114–117). Subjectivity for her is simply a relational property that logically presumes objects external to the subject. Cavell asserts (128) that (contrary to Kohut's self psychology) the mother does not mirror the baby's self but projects a self onto him or her. The baby learns through interactions with the mother a view of the world and how to communicate. For Cavell, the "fort-da game" (Freud 1920) is an attempt to take in the discovery of interpersonal reciprocity. She concludes, "The human infant requires something extrinsic or external to it, something from outside its brain and skin in the way of interaction with an external world, before it can have or be anything we can call a self" (230). For Cavell, self-reflective awareness comes only with thought as does the ability to imagine things. She continues, "One may complain that my version of the Oedipal [sic] Complex is a far cry from Freud's passionate family romance. The complaint is just" (230). Love for Cavell is a condition of mind and thought formation.

Rosenblatt (1997) points out that the Davidsonian approach espoused by Cavell is consistent with current psychoanalytic thought because the focus of psychoanalysis has shifted from internal drives to the intersubjective field. But he raises the question of how much, if any, social interaction is required for the genesis of thought and whether prelinguistic interaction is sufficient or language is necessary. He explains, "If thought has its origins in language, then it follows for Cavell that the pre-linguistic infant does not think" (189). It is highly debatable whether the preverbal infant has no concepts and of course Cavell is in disagreement with Stern (and me), who claim there is indeed an initial subjectivity. This subjectivity consists, during Piaget's psychomotor stage, of an awareness of action sequences in an interaction with the environment that includes "a primordial awareness of an action self without a necessary self-reflective awareness of self as agent" (Rosenblatt, 190). This basic subjective core differentiates with development and then language acquisition interacts with this awareness in a mutually reinforcing way as the infant enters what Lacan calls the symbolic order.

Rosenblatt criticizes Cavell's "all-or-nothing attitude about propositions" (190). For her, the unconscious is a repository of repressed verbal propositions that were once conscious. She disregards the nonpropositional consciousness consisting of mental processes and experiences that may be repressed, "for example, affective states, pictorial images, etc." (190) and, I would add, what has recently been known as procedural memory that is preverbal and includes a series of actions, psychomotor sequences, and interactions with the environment. The logical outcome of Cavell's theory is to oppose Freud's concept of primary process mentation and his theory of primal repression. Rosenblatt concludes that Cavell's "psychoanalytic mind" "does not resemble what most psychoanalysts encounter in their consulting rooms" (192).

So Cavell, along with the growing school of relativists and intersubjectivists, denies the presence of an ineffable, unutterable, inner core known only to the person and argues there is no sense of self before linguistic capacities develop. This is a major premise of her approach. The philosophers Nagel (1974) and Wolheim (1993) have suggested to the contrary that there are indeed certain inner realities that are unshared, hidden, and communicated, for example, in works of art. Freud was very interested in this but Cavell does not discuss it. Kuhns (1995) writes, "The life of art sequesters a hidden inner that finds its externalization in that mysterious aesthetic presence which itself hides an inner, only partially accessible presence-as-symbol of consciousness" (395). For him art is the royal road to the mind or at least that aspect of the mind which is the most mysterious and isolated yet unavailable to others. This is analogous to Freud's recognition of dreams as the royal road to the unconscious. Kuhns points out the overdetermination of all dreams and symptoms and the inexhaustibility of interpretation "that suggests an ever receding, always superabundant inner process and content that is never fully explicated, nor could it ever be fully known" (395). There is a psychoanalytic parallel to this in Winnicott's (1965) "private self."

Neu (1995) concludes that in Cavell's book, "Much of 'the psychoanalytic mind,' at least as I believe Freud understood it, is lost" (289). Cavell rejects Freud's instinct theory and gives no credence to preverbal thoughts and fantasies ascribed to the infant, including instinctual wishes that fuel dreams and basic core fantasies woven around early experiences ascribed to the infant. In spite of all this, writes Neu, "It is difficult to get away from the sense of an inner quality, a subjective (even if unspeakable) character of experience. Such subjectivity seems the essence of nonpropositional consciousness (pictorial as well as infantile). . . . Cavell's Davidsonian model makes rationality the mark of the mental" (290), for Davidson's "principle of charity" presumes rationality and a shared belief as a condition for successful interpretation.

Cavell seems to wander into a position which, because it denies Freud's instinct theory, makes it difficult to understand what drives the mind. Typical of her presentation is the oddly desexualized account of the Oedipus complex. These important psychical representatives of the instincts in the unconscious on the border of the mental and the physical are crucial to the whole structure of Freud's theory (Green 2000). Cavell leaves the infant with nothing but inchoate mental states, that consist of affects rather than emotions, programmed reactions, and no intentional actions, no meaningful instincts or concepts, no recognizable experience, and so no inner life at all.

Cavell acknowledges that this intersubjective turn in philosophy ~~n-ports the interactional or relational school of psychoanalysis. She ; Freud's idea of pre-linguistic phenomena that lie beyond the edge sayable, considering it to be a leftover from obsolete Cartesian meta'

Yet these prelinguistic phenomena are the source of both creativity and psychopathology; psychoanalysis, in my opinion, has as an important goal the attempt to bring that preverbal material into some kind of articulation. Whitebrook (1996) agrees: "To radically devalue the importance of the prelinguistic realm in psychoanalysis would be to submit to precisely the conceptual coercion from philosophy and impoverishment of psychoanalytic experience that Freud was determined to avoid" (990). As I have emphasized in previous chapters, the relativistic stance tends to lose or place on the back burner much that has been traditionally central to the psychoanalyst; Whitebrook concludes: "Cavell is so eager to stress the social and interpersonal side of development that what the child brings to the interaction almost drops out of the equation" (991).

Freud coined the term *Zwischenreich*, "in-between realm" (Anzieu 1986) to refer to the territory between the mental and the somatic. Even Cavell has to admit somewhat paradoxically that the child learns a lot before the acquisition of language, forming what she calls a background of preintentional understanding. This seems very much beyond the edge of the sayable that Cavell criticized Freud for pursuing, but exploring it is crucial to the practice of psychoanalysis. Furthermore, she and many psychoanalytic schools disregard the anarchic and infantile aspects of dreams almost completely because they are attempting to maintain an essentially rational and cognitive conception of the human mind and preserve a focus on current relationships. Whitebook insists that all this is very far away from Freud, "who at the end of his life, could still speak of the id as 'the core of our being'" (994). And it is.

One is reminded of Bertrand Russell's (1945) discussion in his *History of Western Philosophy* of Aristotle's *Nichomachean Ethics*. Russell shrewdly points out that Aristotle has nothing to say to a person whom, as all of us have experienced from time to time, is overwhelmed by powerful emotions. The Aristotelian advocacy of the rational person's golden mean falls apart in the seething cauldron of human experience, as we slide down the razor blade of life. The psychoanalytic mind of Cavell is also a long distance from Kohut's (1971, 1977) fragmenting self, one repeatedly overwhelmed by waves of uncontrollable lust and aggression. As Russell says of Aristotle's *Ethics*: "What he has to say is what will be useful to comfortable men of weak passions; but he has nothing to say to those who are possessed by a god or a devil, for whom outward misfortune drives to despair" (184).

THE IRRATIONAL AND
NONCOGNITIVE ASPECT OF HUMANS

Let us explore this background of preintentional understanding further. If we wish to turn from rationalistic concepts of the psychoanalytic mind such as those of Cavell and Davidson to the psychoanalytic mind as we experience it in the consulting room, where should we look for some kind of articulate depiction of what the mind is really like? Of course Freud's inimitable writings come to our attention immediately. His predecessor Nietzsche, much more radical and extreme than Freud, presented a concept of the mind almost diametrically opposite to that of Davidson. Freud claimed never to have read Nietzsche, but obviously he was much influenced by him, because the words of Nietzsche were on the tongues of everyone in Freud's Viennese milieu. Nietzsche used myths to stand for human drives and needs and claimed that passion and suffering were represented by Dionysus, the god of wine and sensuality and the dark unconscious states that these inspired. The ability to give these feelings logical shape and form was a gift of Apollo, the god of the cool Greek white marble sculptures manifesting rational and willed organization.

Nietzsche claimed the famous Greek plays of Aeschylus and Sophocles originated in the wild orgiastic rites of Dionysus, the memory of which was preserved by a chorus performing alone by means of chant, song, and rhythmic frenzy. Nietzsche believed this transported the audience to a state of religious ecstasy. The experience of music from the chorus, he said, made the tragic end of all our lives endurable by drawing every individual into the current of life which flows through and beyond the single individual. Some authors place Nietzsche's (1873) *The Birth of Tragedy* at the core of his work, emphasizing his extreme concentration on music and the power of the dark and Dionysian side of humans. As Nietzsche said, the degree and kind of a man's sexuality reaches up into the topmost summit of his spirit.

The Apollonian or detached rational grasp of the world exists side by side with the conflicting passionate Dionysian force of unreflected being; clarity and form clash with orgiastic ecstasy. Nietzsche's artistic and philosophical project for his short productive life was to try to find the way to bring out the Dionysian forces without taming them. Unfortunately, Nietzsche was a prodigious source of ideas which were too many, contradictory, and left him in a position where he could be read in any way the reader wishes to interpret him and utilize his writings (Chessick 1983).

Nietzsche insisted that the essence of the mind was based not on reason or logic but on dark vital instinct. He borrowed Schopenhauer's extraordinary emphasis on the importance of music and art in achieving a state of transcendence from the everyday realities of the struggle for survival. He criticized Socrates for rupturing the power of music and replacing it with dialectics. The Socratic turn, said Nietzsche, ushered in a rationalism that wanted nothing further to do with the depths of being. Rationalization for Socrates, said Nietzsche, overwhelmed the life forces of myth, religion, and art. Due to Socrates, "Human life breaks away from the obscure roots of its instincts and passions as if being had to justify itself to consciousness. Life strained toward the light, and dialectics triumphed over the dark music of fate" (Safranski 2002, 64).

This tendency in our civilization continues even in the psychoanalytic movement, which is gradually moving away from an emphasis on drives and passions and into a point of view where the self has no dark essence but is formed completely by linguistics or at least by interpersonal relationships. The immortal Ideas (Forms) of Plato are forgotten; the concept of Plotinus that the soul in essence is a true spark of the Divine, a fallen star, God or demon, imprisoned in the body but able in a divine frenzy to rise by its own intellectual powers of contemplation to the realm of its fellow gods, is ignored. This Neoplatonic notion is that the soul or spirit or psyche, metaphorically thought of as the soul vehicle, is the link between the sensible and intelligible realms. The connection between the world of experience and the world of transcendent being seems almost entirely foreign to contemporary attitudes and thoughts. Dante remains unread, appreciated only for his dramatic depiction of hell.

Nietzsche goes on to introduce the concept of sublimation, borrowed without attribution by Freud. Cultures, Nietzsche said, sublimate Dionysian energies but the Dionysian lurks before and under civilization as a colossal power. For Nietzsche, writing in his usual rhetorical style, what he has discovered are the "terrible foundations of being." Among these are what I have described in psychoanalysis (2000a) as "archaic sadism," a Dionysian aspect of humans that is rabidly bellicose and shockingly cruel, a tiger-like desire to annihilate, as Nietzsche put it. Indeed, as Kernberg (2000b) says, "Psychoanalysis is the only science that has evidence of the intensity of aggression" (328).

In a reflection of great relevance to contemporary psychoanalysts, Nietzsche considered it absolutely amazing that out of the entire hierarchy of nature, from the inanimate to the vegetative and the animal, consciousness emerged in humans. Only in humans does the awareness of awareness come in to play. At the same time Nietzsche (1873–1886) maintained:

> The tremendous coming and going of men on the great wilderness of the earth, their founding of cities and states, their wars, their restless assembling and scattering again, their confused mingling, mutual imitation, mutual outwitting and downtreading, their wailing in distress, their howls of joy in victory—all this is a continuation of animality. (158)

For Nietzsche, as for Schopenhauer, all nature, including human nature, is the epitome of ferocity.

The expression "Dionysian" was Nietzsche's way to describe the barbaric precivilized destructive and sexual drives at the root of the psychoanalytic mind. He saw culture as a way of keeping these essential Dionysian energies channeled by wrapping people in illusions, offering solace in religion and philosophy, or extolling the Socratic love of knowledge and science that has dominated the modern era. But one should not neglect the importance of art, myth-making, and religion to the human condition. In his mother's view, Nietzsche was nothing but a failed professor who moved restlessly from one dingy place to another, unmarried, and in poor health. She still had to send him socks and sausages. Yet this failed professor, at an early point in his thinking, offers us a very important alternative to the rational mind:

> What is the power of art? Art creates a magic circle of images, visions, tones, and ideas that hold us spellbound and transform anyone who enters the circle. The power of art is a life force to the extent that it provides insight into the dark tragic web of life, but creates a clearing of livability. Since human life is challenged by consciousness and carries within it the potential for creating hostility with itself, artistic power is also a counterforce that protects life from any possible self-destruction. (Safranski 2002, 286)

There is a fundamental ambiguity to the Dionysian aspect of humans that Nietzsche recognized and left in place in his writings, regarding it as part of the absolute reality of our psyche; perhaps this is a precursor to what the Kleinians later meant by the universal "psychotic core" they postulate in each of us.

THE PSYCHIC NEEDS OF HUMANS

Deep human needs are not being met by our materialistic culture and naturalistic world view. I believe also that this world view and the culture based on it is on a self-destructive course. Adams (2001) points out:

> While we have grown materially richer and more powerful, and we have enjoyed many benefits from our wealth and power that must be preserved, we have generated a profound human identity crisis, undermined the sectors of the culture that support the human enterprise and nourish the human spirit, deconstructed the context that gives meaning to our lives, and left ourselves confused and adrift, often depressed and dependent on drugs to keep going. (24)

The Enlightenment shook up the old certainties but put nothing substantial in their place. Stern (2002) explains how Hegel was clearly responding to the sense of dislocation this caused; "reason was seen as leading to skepticism, science to mechanistic materialism, social reform to bloody revolution, humanism to empty amoralism and crude hedonism, and individualism to social fragmentation" (14). Hegel, who may be thought of as the founder of modern Continental philosophy, took a position which was distinctive in his era, as discussed in the previous chapter. He did not become an irrationalist or a member of the counter-Enlightenment who questioned the critical power of reason. Nor did he become a Romantic, turning to art and aesthetic experience as a cure for the ills of modernity. He attempted "to give philosophy the exalted role of restoring our sense of intellectual and spiritual well-being, albeit a philosophy that thinks in a new, non-dualistic, way" (15). Hegel already recognized that the scientific outlook, although it accomplished many important achievements, still left some matters unresolved, and that scientific models and explanations cannot alone provide us with a proper way of understanding ourselves and the natural world.

The question is whether the critical problems we now face are from the nature of the barbaric culture in which we are currently immersed, or from the nature of humans itself, or both. Nietzsche correctly predicted the explosion of this culture, which occurred in 1914. Furthermore, things seem to be getting steadily worse. For example, Henninger (2002) reminds us that one cannot imagine unless they were actually there thirty years ago "how transfixed much of America was by public television's thirteen-part broadcast of Sir Kenneth Clark's 'Civilization.' The title alone gave one the sense each week of entering into something noble and good, not least because viewers back then believed that each of them was still part of it, of civilization. . . . Watching and reading about what's going on outside the assumed security of our homes and offices, it isn't hard to notice what a fragile and vulnerable thing civilized life can suddenly become" (A 10).

As the late William Phillips (2002), for more than forty years the editor of *Partisan Review*, a magazine of small circulation but with a great deal of influence, remarked sadly in his old age: "The future has not turned out so well" (83).

Schopenhauer (1818), who had a view of humans similar to that of Freud, insisted that only compassion for the general human plight in which we are all immersed has the capacity to eventually unite humanity. He viewed mind as an evolved survival mechanism and not suitable to detach from the phenomenal world in order to practice metaphysics. For Schopenhauer, as later for Freud, thinking is distorted and corrupted by will, so passions and not reason set the goals of human endeavor. For humans the mind is simply a tool to get drive gratification. Schopenhauer believed that the artist communicates insight into the true nature of things, and gives us knowledge of timeless reality (some sort of derivation of Plato's Forms) behind all perception. He argued that a sense of transcendent harmony wells up in the presence of great art. So the philosopher and the artist engage in seeking truths beyond science.

Schopenhauer:

> regarded human beings, by and large, as selfish, cruel, greedy, stupid, aggressive and heartless in most of their dealings with one another, and bloodthirsty in their attitudes toward the animal kingdom. The world seemed to him an appalling place, teaming with violence, crime, poverty, political oppression . . . and every individual life ending in the inescapable smash-up of death. The world of Nature was no better: literally in every instance thousands of screaming animals are being torn to pieces alive. (Magee 2000, 166)

He claimed that sexuality pervades the entire personality of all humans and he gave the sexual climax an extremely important role in producing a transient removal from the misery of human life. In a view similar to that of Nietzsche:

> He believed that understanding an individual's sexuality was essential to understanding that individual. The fullest expression of the individual's personality is in a loving sexual relationship, in which, perhaps paradoxically, the barriers and limitations of selfhood are transcended, the individual loses his sense of self and experiences oneness with the other person in the sexual act. (Magee 2000, 170)

Schopenhauer was much more emphatic about the role of art and especially music in taking us out of ourselves. Being absorbed in a work of art enables us to forget ourselves temporarily and time seems to have stopped. Works of art, thought Schopenhauer, are close to what Plato described in his theory of Forms, in which everything that exists is the embodiment of some universal eternal Idea. This makes Plato and Schopenhauer colleagues in the class of two-world theory philosophers.

The second world for Schopenhauer, existing underneath the representational world of everyday experience, was his metaphysical concept of "will." He believed that music especially was the voice of the metaphysical will, a super-art. The basic division of thinkers into those like Schopenhauer and Plato who believe there is something essential and hidden underlying the world of everyday experience, offering various versions of Kant's *noumena*, and those who believe that what we experience is all there is, such as the relativists that predominate in philosophy and psychoanalysis today, is still a valid dichotomy and one worthy of discussion and attention. In chapter 3, I referred to what the psychiatrist-philosopher Karl Jaspers (1932a, 1932b, 1932c) called "ciphers." These suggest the presence of a transcendent realm but by no means establish such a realm, in contrast to Schopenhauer's claim that he had established it with his notion of "Will" or Nietzsche's claim that underlying everything is the "Will To Power."

Is There An Essential Subjective Core
or Nature to Humans?

We are left even today with the fundamental question of the nature (if any) of humans and whether or not this nature can be changed, altered, or harnessed in such a way as to improve the human lot. For example, Wagner shifted under the influence of Schopenhauer from first believing in the hopeful political goal of improvement of the human lot to his conviction that, as Magee (2000) puts it:

> Tyranny and the abuse of power were perennial, as were cruelty, selfishness, greed, stupidity, and the failure of compassion, together with lovelessness and betrayal. These were not merely a part of the current order of things, about to be swept away, they were permanent features of life on this planet, and were reproduced over and over again in every age. The belief that this was going to change radically to a new order of things in which love, happiness and self-fulfillment were the order of the day was just a pathetic illusion. (186)

Reaching this conviction, Wagner used his own supreme musical creativity to advocate turning away from what he called the world of day—the central theme in his magnificent opera *Tristan Und Isolde* (Chessick 1990b), a depressing solution.

Marxists believed they had the solution, insisting that by abolishing private property and destroying the capitalistic system they would bring out what they thought was the essence of humans as a species-being, humans basically caring for each other. That caring, Marx thought, has been repressed by the emphasis on greed that lies at the basis of the capitalistic system. The experiment in the Soviet Union clearly failed, which does not mean Marx was wrong, since that experiment was not the kind of inevitable end of history he advocated. On the other hand, there is no convincing evidence that Marx was right. The issue remains undecided.

The solution to the human condition offered by Schopenhauer and Wagner was to turn one's back on this world and seek night and death. The solution offered by Freud was to use the quiet voice of reason in the hope of slowly, patiently, chipping away at human self-delusion and narcissism. The solution of a number of philosophers has been to change the culture in the hope that somehow this would change the essence of humans. Other philosophers have denied there is any essence to humans at all and that, as Lacanians believe, man is the marionette of his culture.

This is a matter of extreme importance to psychoanalysts because we are also trying to bring about fundamental changes in people. Can we, for example, replace a destructive malevolent introject that has been driving an individual to self-defeating behavior and maladaptation, with a benign introject from the therapist? It is rather doubtful, and we often have to be content with an identification plastered over what we might call a psychotic core in our neurotic patients. The sicker the patient, the more this is true and one observes, even in famous cases like Freud's "Wolf-Man," the return of deeply malevolent and psychotic phenomena under stress after psychoanalysis even by one as experienced as Freud himself. Elsewhere, I have tried to demonstrate this in case presentations (1984).

Gedo (Gedo and Gehrie 1993) proposes that there are two etiologies that explain the stubborn persistence of a psychotic core:

> Either the person suffered in childhood a state of disorganization that, when it returns in adulthood, has to be classified as a 'psychosis,' or the behaviors in question were acquired in the course of more or less expectable development as inevitable identifications with impaired caretakers. . . . It makes a great deal of difference whether such identification took place at the earliest stages of development or somewhat later; if it occurred early enough, its results may constitute the very foundations of the self-organization—a 'primary identity' that cannot be abandoned without a catastrophic sense of inner collapse. . . . Conditions of this kind are often irremediable—at least in my hands—and define one of the current limits of analyzability. (283)

If we believe we have reached a limiting point in the nature of humans—their archaic sadism and sexual lust—and in the unbudgeable malevolent introjects of seriously emotionally disturbed patients, none of this amenable to fundamental change, what are the consequences for us? How should this affect our treatment plans and even the way we live our own lives? Can we carry on psychoanalytic treatment in an atmosphere where we secretly believe there is no hope for major change in the subjective human core, hoping at least for amelioration, sublimation, and better psyhic integration? What should we tell the patient? These are the really important unresolved questions in philosophy and psychoanalysis today and ought to, but currently do not, provide the central themes of our publications and meetings. We are not looking squarely, dispassionately, and objectively at the human condition and we are not learning from the study of history the lessons that we ought to learn. It is this challenge that I offer to the next generation of psychoanalysts; if you succeed then, as I have hopefully imagined in chapter 10, psychoanalysis will once again occupy a central place in the sciences of humans as it should indeed come to be.

How Do We Know What We Know?

The late Continental philosopher, Hans-Georg Gadamer, preferred communicating with others through conversation. He proposed (as explained in chapter 10) that great art shows us the way things are even though the truth may be shattering. For both Gadamer and Heidegger, truth "happens" when one approaches an artwork. One says to one's self in the presence of great art, as Gadamer put it, "*So ist es!*," implying yes, that is how things are. Gadamer was deeply influenced by his teacher, Heidegger. In explaining aesthetics, Gadamer (Palmer 2001) in a reported conversation said:

> When a work of art truly takes hold of us, it is not an object that stands opposite us which we look at in hope of seeing through it to an intended conceptual meaning . . . the work is an *Ereignis*—an *event* that 'appropriates us' into itself. It jolts us, it knocks us over, and sets up a world of its own, into which we are drawn, as it were. Heidegger . . . recognized the tension that characterizes a work of art when it 'sets up a world' and at the same time sets this world into a resting form and fixes it there. . . . Heidegger calls this the struggle between world and earth in the work of art. . . . It is in the sheer being-there of the work of art that our understanding experiences the depths and unfathomability of its meaning. (71–72).

Gadamer used the term *Zurückkommen* (coming back) to serve as the mark of an eminent text; and so we tarry in front of the work of art if it is truly a great work. This tarrying (*Verweilen*), he says, is fundamental. Gadamer describes us as "an aesthetic culture that is withering away" (77). There is certainly no place for tarrying in today's television, which intensely and relentlessly bombards consumers with mindless "sound-bite" advertising. For example, Johnson (2002) is concerned from an examination of TV programs in the summer of 2002 that perhaps American culture has given up: "We'll never be as clever or cosmopolitan as the Europeans, so we've reached a collective, unconscious decision to surrender to our inner morons" (1). Describing television fare for that summer, Johnson concludes that what was offered, "celebrations of cerebral vacancy," supports the theory that "You'll never go broke underestimating the intelligence of the public" (4). Yet Gadamer (Palmer 2001) optimistically believed, "tarrying is something that will always exist" (77). He said, "By studying poetry, the visual arts, architecture, and music I come to understand what Heidegger means by 'nearness to being'" (114).

McGinn's (2002) "mysterian" position on the mind-brain problem described in chapter 9 is consistent with the epistemological position of Rockmore (2001), who predicts that at the end of this new century we will be reading Hegel rather than the twentieth century U.S. and British philosophers. Both Hegel and Kant agreed that there is a mind-independent external world. Kant pointed out that all cognition begins but does not end with experience. Hegel, continuing this line of thought, explained that what we perceive is altered by the way it is perceived so there is no way to distinguish between the object as it is in itself, the object as a mere object of thought, and the object as it appears in experience. For Hegel, as we have seen in the previous chapter, knowledge is historical and based on the standards and norms and values in a particular society at a given historical moment. So any claim is accepted or rejected in terms of a wider set of views prevailing in a given historical time or place. There is no such thing as grasping facts independent of a conceptual framework. Hegel called attention to the intrinsic historicity of claims to knowing and the knowing process.

Traditional psychoanalysts agree. The knowing process is based on perception of the world through a psyche that has been previously programmed to work in a certain way. Traditional psychoanalysts subscribe to the existence of an inner life of unconscious fantasy, with libidinal and aggressive drives, defenses and compromise formations. So:

> The memories that constitute our life history are created, in Arlow's conception, through the mingling of external perceptions with unconscious fantasies, as experienced against the background of the individual's past development, itself a mingling of earlier perceptions and unconscious fantasies into encoded memories. (Wallerstein 2002, 157)

This internal world is populated by intrapsychic object relations, self and object representations, and affective valences. Meyers (2000) explains:

> These intrapsychic object relations are internalized from early interpersonal relations and in turn affect later external object relations. . . . In the transference, as the patient looks for gratification, he or she is repeating early needs and defenses, repeating early internal object relations, as well as looking for the growth of the self. (451)

In our field of psychoanalysis, Hegel's point of view is clearly correct; subjectivity is inevitable. But, as Meyer says, "I do not believe the transference is constructed by patient and analyst; it is preformed. The internal world of the patient exists before and outside of analysis" (452–453). Furthermore, the traditional Freudian energic constructs may be at least heuristically conceived of as working through the subjective orientation formed by the role of unconscious fantasy in the constitution of psychic reality and providing the motivation for normal and abnormal behavior. There is a parallel and mutual confirmation between Hegelian thought about the cultural and historical antecedents and determinants of what at any current time is regarded as truth, and the thought of modern traditional psychoanalysts such as Arlow (1969b, 1985b), who view the individual's infantile core as constituting the antecedents and determinants of that individual's current behavior and beliefs.

Pine (1990), in an approach similar to mine (1992a) that was reviewed in chapter 1, although he does not give primacy to Freud's drive theory, uses four explanatory theories in his psychoanalytic work. These are based on urges (drive psychology); modes of defense and adaptation (ego psychology); relationships and their internalization, distortion, and repetition (object relations); and issues of differentiation, autonomy, and self-esteem (self psychology, but not quite that as developed by Kohut). Pine points out that a patient's life "is largely of his or her own making. Barring the prototypic situation of a safe falling off a roof onto a person's head, a patient's 'fate,' including 'accidents,' and certainly ongoing inner experiences and object relations, seems to entail endless experiences of, or repetitions of, what he or she brings along intrapsychically" (29). Pine emphasized that: "A focus on wish, fantasy, and character rather than on what others do to the patient leads to the most effective psychoanalytic work" (29–30).

Pine claims that once the internal representational world is established, involving a set of expectations, response readiness, and a conception of how the self and other will mutually interact, later relationships are assimilated into this and new events do not alter the inner world. In fact once these internal representations have been set up they themselves become a force to keep it that way. "They tend to be self-sustaining, to be maintained by the individual—sometimes, it seems, at all costs" (90). I refer to this as a core psyche the patient develops early in life through which he or she then experiences everything after that. The tendency to repeat these early experiences only serves to confirm the patient's conviction that what he or she is experiencing through the pair of glasses put on early in life (as described in chapter 1) is "reality."

IMPLICATIONS FOR PSYCHOANALYTIC TREATMENT

The bulk of psychoanalytic work consists of helping the patient to become insightful about this core set of fantasies and internal representations and how they came to be, and showing the patient how the compulsion to repeat has simply confirmed the patient's distorted view of reality. This is the process of working through, because it has to be experienced again and again in the analytic situation and discussed over and over in terms of the transference, interpersonal enactments, and outside activities of the patient. Slowly and gradually the patient discovers his or her internal core, maladaptive compromise formations become ego alien, and, if the process is successful, the patient joins the analyst in the effort to correct the situation.

Working against this is the tremendous anxiety stirred up if the early compromise solutions should be removed, for these represent a protection formed early in life to help the patient deal with overwhelming anxieties and even fear of annihilation or psychosis. They were the best possible solutions the ego of the child could find at that time. This is one of the reasons why the patient clings so tenaciously to what are obviously self-defeating and self-destructive beliefs, activities, and behaviors. We are confronted, especially in preoedipally damaged individuals, with a long and tedious process that taxes the patience of the analyst and puts great stress on the analysand. Motivation is everything; if the patient is weakly motivated the procedure will fade into obscurity. On the other hand, if the patient does not have the capacity to withstand the anxiety it may lead to a rupture of the treatment or a forced transformation of the treatment from a psychoanalysis into a supportive psychotherapy and/or pharmacotherapy.

I have discussed the overlap in the fields of psychoanalysis and philosophy on the matter of what constitutes the human, on how the mind develops, and how both fields require a receptive stance to whatever is studied. I have contrasted the humanist versus the antihumanist positions on the question of whether there is an essential nature to humans and discussed the ramifications of these views in the field of psychoanalysis. In contrast to the currently popular two-person psychoanalytic movement, Freud's psychoanalysis maintains that there is an essential "I" which we should not lose sight of. Whether or not there is a universal human nature as part of it, the essential subjective "I" formed at the beginning of life shows itself in the transference regardless of the here-and-now situation, and dominates it in a well conducted psychoanalysis. By way of contrast to this Freudian view, I have reviewed Cavell's and Davidson's rationalistic and anti-Freudian propositions, maintaining that concepts are formed only through dialogue. This stance eschews the idea of an essential preverbal core and implies attributing primary importance to the two-person dialogue as constituting the emerging data of the psychoanalytic process. I have attempted to outline arguments against this view, hoping to focus psychoanalysis again on the great Freudian discovery of the transference.

I have explored the views of Nietzsche, Schopenhauer, and Freud, all thought of by Ricoeur (1970) as practitioners of the "hermeneutics of suspicion," on the irrational and noncognitive aspects of humans. I have tried to explain how this is inextricably bound up with all our perceptions, concepts, and so-called "knowledge" and convictions about "reality." The materialistic or scientific attempt to explain everything in the human mind by reducing it to biology and neurophysiology that is predominant today has left humans with serious unmet needs. This issue and the question of whether humans can be fundamentally changed at all, and if so how, I have proposed should be the central theme of psychoanalytic meetings and discussions. Obviously, change will be necessary if there is to be an improvement in the human condition and an end to the insanity called "war." I have attempted to develop the ramifications of the humanistic view for the practice of psychoanalytic therapy and I have proposed that this view, which underlies the practice of traditional psychoanalysis, remains our most viable and hopeful approach to understanding humans.

It will soon be time for me to sign off from the great conversation over the ages that I have described elsewhere (1999b) and mentioned previously in this book in chapters 6 and 8. I have not been talented enough to contribute to that conversation but I have been lucky enough to be an auditor of it as it has been recorded to unfold from the times of Thales and Parmenides and Heraclitus to the present day in the world of music, art, poetry, literature, philosophy and, more recently, in Freud's psychoanalysis.

Immanuel Kant repeatedly stated that he had a sense of wonder at the starry skies above and the moral law within. I conclude by posing a different question: humans have largely solved the problem of the existence of the starry skies above in modern astrophysics and cosmology. Humans have solved the problem of the origin of the moral law within with the help of Freud and psychoanalysis. Why, then, is it that a species able to solve the most difficult problems that confronted the greatest philosophers who ever lived, cannot solve the crucial problem of their need to kill each other. As Schopenhauer said: "*Homo homini lupus*": Man is a wolf to man. Must it always be this way?

Notes

CHAPTER 1

1. Plato in *Sophist* also speaks of *gigantomachìa perì tēs ousiás* (the battle of the giants concerning Being). See Hamilton and Cairns (1973, 990).

CHAPTER 2

1. Translated by Dr. Chessick.

CHAPTER 3

1. An outstanding series of lectures on the *Divine Comedy* is available from The Teaching Company, 4151 Lafayette Center Drive, Suite 100, Chantilly, VA 20151–1232

2. Botticelli, S. 2002. *The Drawings for Dante's Divine Comedy*. London: Royal Academy of Arts.

CHAPTER 5

1. American Academy of Psychoanalysis and Dynamic Psychiatry. Winter meeting in New York, December 10, 2005, Columbia University.

2. Since the time of this writing the patient did successfully resolve her problems, complete her analysis, marry, and begin a family of her own. There were no more "accidents."

CHAPTER 6

1. In chapter 3, I already discussed a variety of available translations (Ciardi 1954, 1970a, 1970b; Mandelbaum 1982, 1984, 1986; Merwin 2000; Milano 1961; Musa 1984, 1985, 1986; Norton 1941; Pinsky 1997; Sayers 1951; Sinclair 1959, 1961a, 1961b; Singleton 1970a, 1970b, 1973a, 1973b, 1975a, 1975b; Sisson 1981; White

1948) of Dante's poem. Extremely detailed scholarly commentary on each Canto is found in Singleton (1970b, 1973a, 1975a). Sisson's (1981) commentary is a bit scanty; for the ordinary reader the Mandelbaum (1982, 1984, 1986) volumes or the Musa (1984, 1985, 1986) volumes offer adequate explanatory notes.

2. For details see Ciardi (1970a) p. 399.

CHAPTER 7

1. Kohut (1977) suggests that certain idealizing or mirroring transferences may drop away by themselves when the patient no longer needs them. Interpretation of these transferences, especially if it is premature, may be experienced by the patient as a serious lack of empathy on the part of the analyst.

CHAPTER 8

1. An excellent set of audiotaped lectures on the seven major tragedies of Shakespeare given by the famous critic Harold Bloom is available from Recorded Books, 270 Skipjack Road, Fredrick, MD.

2. Discerning persons, gourmets.

CHAPTER 10

1. This chapter is divided into two parts. The first is a fantasy about the future of psychoanalysis and the second is a discussion of creativity in psychoanalysis.

2. The civilizing effect of immersion in the arts is the central premise of a wonderful series of lectures by William Kloss: *A History of European Art*, an audiovisual presentation produced in 2005 by The Teaching Company, Chantilly, VA.

CHAPTER 11

1. Hegel is very difficult reading and requires years of study. For introductory material it is usual to start with his lectures on the philosophy of history, especially the introduction (Hegel 1840b), and his (1833) lectures on the history of philosophy. His masterpiece (1807), *The Phenomenology of Spirit*, probably cannot be digested without the help of either a class or some explanatory texts. Hegel's (1840a) *Philosophy of History* is a fascinating interpretation of the evolution of Spirit in history, applies and explains his famous dialectical method of thesis, antithesis, and synthesis (not his terms, and ones he would label as much too simplistic), and sometimes goes into detail on some of the key concepts of the phenomenology of Spirit.

2. A leading British analytic philosophy journal once prefaced an issue with a blank page, identifying it as a picture of the Absolute Spirit (Solomon and Sherman 2003).

References

Abend, S. 2001. Expanding psychological possibilities. *Psychoanalytic Quarterly* 70:3–14.

Adams, E. 2001. Reinstating humanistic categories. *The Review of Metaphysics* 55:21–39.

Adler, G. 1980. Transference, real relationship and alliance. *International Journal of Psycho-Analysis* 61:547–58.

Adorno, T. 1973. *Negative dialectics*. London: Routledge.

Alexander, F. 1964. Social significance of psychoanalysis and psychotherapy. *Archives of General Psychiatry* 11:235–44.

Alighieri, D. 1290. *La vita nuova (Poems of youth)*. Trans. B. Reynolds. New York: Penguin Books, 1969.

Allison, G. 2000. The shortage of psychoanalytic patients: An inquiry into its causes and consequences. *Psychoanalytic Inquiry* 20:527–40.

Alterman, E. 2002. Stop the presses: Unhappy anniversary. *The Nation* 274:10.

Althaus, H. 2000. *Hegel: An intellectual biography*. Trans. M. Tarsh. Cambridge, UK: Polity Press.

Anzieu, D. 1986. *Freud's self analysis*. New York: International Universities Press.

Apel, K. 1998. *From a transcendental-semiotic point of view*. Manchester, UK: Manchester University Press.

Arlow, J. 1969a. Unconscious fantasy and disturbances of conscious experience. *Psychoanalytic Quarterly* 38:1–27.

———. 1969b. Fantasy, memory, and reality testing. *Psychoanalytic Quarterly* 38:28–51.

———. 1980. The genesis of interpretation. *Psychoanalytic explorations of technique*. Ed. H. Blum. New York: International Universities Press.

———. 1985a. Some technical problems of countertransference. *Psychoanalytic Quarterly* 54:164–74.

———. 1985b. The concept of psychic reality and related problems. *Journal of the American Psychoanalytic Association* 33:621–35.

Arlow, J., and C. Brenner. 1988. The future of psychoanalysis. *Psychoanalytic Quarterly* 57:1–14.

Arnold, M. 1882. *Culture and anarchy and other writings*. New York: Macmillan. New York: Cambridge University Press, 1993.

Aron, L. 1999. The patient's experience of the analyst's subjectivity. *Relational psychoanalysis: The emergence of a tradition*, S. A. Mitchell and L. Aron. Hillsdale, NJ: Analytic Press.

Askay, R. 1999. A philosophical dialogue between Heidegger and Freud. *Journal of Philosophical Research* 24:415–43.

Atlas, J. 2000. *Bellow: A biography*. New York: Random House.

Atwood, G., and R. Stolorow. 1984. *Structures of subjectivity: Explorations in psychoanalytic phenomenology*. Hillsdale, NJ: Analytic Press.

Bacon, F. 1993. In *Conversation with M. Archimbaud*. London: Phaidon Press.

Balter, L. 1999. Constant mental change and unknowability in psychoanalysis. *Psychoanalytic Study of the Child* 54:93–129.

Bartley, R. 2002. I'm O.K., you're O.K.! Enron's O.K.? *Wall Street Journal*, Jan. 21, 2002, p. A13.

Barzun, J. 2000. *From dawn to decadence: Five hundred years of western cultural life*. New York: HarperCollins.

Batchelor, J. 2000. *John Ruskin: No wealth but life*. London: Chatto & Windus.

Beiser, F. 1993. *The Cambridge companion to Hegel*. New York: Cambridge University Press.

Bell, I. 1992. *Dreams of exile: Robert Louis Stevenson: A biography*. New York: Henry Holt.

Benardete, S. 2001. *Symposium*. Reprinted in *Plato's Symposium* and originally found in *The Dialogues of Plato*. Ed. E. Segal. New York: Random House, 1986. Chicago: University of Chicago Press, 2001.

Bergin, T. 1967. *Perspectives on the "divine comedy."* Bloomington: Indiana University Press.

Bergmann, M. 2001. Life goals and psychoanalytic goals from a historical perspective. *Psychoanalytic Quarterly* 70:15–34.

Berlin, I. 1997. Two concepts of liberty. *The proper study of mankind*. Ed. H. Hardy. London: Chatto & Windus.

Bettelheim, B. 1983. *Freud and man's soul*. New York: Knopf.

Binswanger, L. 1963. *Being-in-the-world: Selected papers of Ludwig Binswanger*. Trans. J. Needlman. New York: Basic Books.

Binyon, L. 1961. *The portable Dante: The "divine comedy."* New York: Viking.

Bion, W. 1963. *Elements of psycho-analysis*. New York: Basic Books.

———. 1967. *Second thoughts: Selected papers on psycho-analysis*. New York: Jason Archson.

Blackburn, S. 2005. *Truth: A guide*. New York: Oxford University Press.

Bloom, A. 1987. *The closing of the American mind*. New York: Simon and Schuster.

Bloom, H. 1998. *Shakespeare: The invention of the human*. New York: Riverhead Books.

Blum, H. 1998. An analytic inquiry into intersubjectivity: Subjective objectivity. *Journal of Clinical Psychoanalysis* 7:189–208.

Boesky, D. 1990. The psychoanalytic process and its components. *Psychoanalytic Quarterly* 59:550–84.

Bollas, C. 1987. *The shadow of the object: Psychoanalysis of the unknown thought*. New York: Columbia University Press.

Bordieu, P. 1984. *Distinction: A social critique of the judgement of taste*. Trans. R. Nice. Cambridge, MA: Harvard University Press.

Boss, M., ed. 1963. *Psychoanalysis and Daseinanalysis*. New York: Basic Books.

———. 2001. *Martin Heidegger: Zollikon seminars*. Trans. F. Mayr and R. Askay. Evanston, IL: Northwestern University Press.

Boudon, R. 2005. *The poverty of relativism*. Trans. P. Hamilton. Oxford: Bardwell.

Boyer, B. 1993. Countertransference with severely regressed patients. In *Countertransference: The therapist's contribution to the therapeutic situation*, ed. L. Epstein and A. Finer, chapter 15. Northvale, NJ: Jason Aronson.

Brandchaft, B., and R. Stolorow. 1984. The borderline concept: Pathological character of iatrogenic myth? In *Empathy II*, ed. J. Lichtenberg, M. Bornstein, and D. Silver. Hillsdale, NJ: Analytic Press.

Brenner, C. 1985. Countertransference as compromise formation. *Psychoanalytic Association* 54:155–63.

———. 1995. Some remarks on psychoanalytic technique. *Journal of Clinical Psychoanalysis* 4:413–28.

Brookner, A. 1983. *Look at me*. New York: Vintage, 1997.

Budd, M. 1995. *Values of art: Pictures, poetry and music*. New York: Penguin.

Bush, M. 1969. Psychoanalysis and scientific creativity: With special reference to regression in the service of the ego. *Journal of American Psychoanalytic Association* 17:136–90.

Cahill, T. 1995. *How the Irish saved civilization: The untold story of Ireland's heroic fall from the fall of Rome to the rise of medieval Europe* (Hinges of History). New York: Doubleday.

Canby, V. 1991. Review of the double life of Veronique. *New York Times*, May 26, 1991.

Canguilhem, G. 1994. *A vital rationalist*. New York: Zone Books.

Caper, R. 1995. Comments on "notes on psychoanalytic theory and its consequences for technique." *Journal of Clinical Psychoanalysis* 4:465–70.

Carter, R. 2002. *Exploring consciousness*. Berkeley: University of California Press.

Cassidy, D. 1992. *Uncertainty: The life and science of Werner Heisenberg*. New York: Freeman.

Cavell, M. 1993. *The psychoanalytic mind: From Freud to philosophy*. Cambridge, MA: Harvard University Press.

Chalmers, D. 1996. *The conscious mind: In search of a fundamental theory*. Oxford: Oxford University Press.

Chediak, C. 1979. Counter-reactions and countertransference. *International Journal of Psycho-Analysis* 60:117–29.

Chessick, R. 1974. *The technique and practice of psychotherapy*. New York: Jason Aronson.

———. 1977. *Great ideas in psychotherapy*. New York: Jason Aronson.

———. 1980. *Freud teaches psychotherapy*. Indianapolis, IN: Hackett Publishing.

———. 1983. *A brief introduction to the genius of Nietzsche*. Washington, DC: University Press of America.

———. 1984. A failure in psychoanalytic psychotherapy of a schizophrenic patient. *Dynamic Psychotherapy* 2:136–56.

———. 1985. *Psychology of the self and the treatment of narcissism*. Northvale, NJ: Aronson.

———. 1988. Prolegomena to the study of Paul Ricoeur's book Freud and Philosophy. *Psychoanalytic Review* 75:299–318.

———. 1990a. Self analysis: Fool for a patient? *Psychoanalytic Review* 77:311–40.

———. 1990b. On falling in love: The mystery of Tristan and Isolde. In *Psychoanalytic explorations in music*, ed. S. Feder, R. Karmel, and G. Pollock, 465–83. Madison, CT: International Universities Press.

———. 1992a. *The technique and practice of listening in intensive psychotherapy*. Northvale, NJ: Jason Aronson.

———. 1992b. *What constitutes the patient in psychotherapy*. Northvale, NJ: Jason Aronson.

———. 1992c. The death instinct revisited. *Journal of the American Academy of Psychoanalysis* 20:3–28.

———. 1993. *The psychology of the self and the treatment of narcissism*. Northvale, NJ: Jason Aronson.

———. 1994. What brings about change in psychoanalytic treatment? *Psychoanalytic Review* 81:279–300.

———. 1995a. Postmodern psychoanalysis or a wild analysis? *Journal of the American Academy of Psychoanalysis* 23:47–62.

———. 1995b. The effect of Heidegger's pathological narcissism on the development of his philosophy. In *Mimetic desire: Essays in German literature from romanticism to post modernism*, ed. J. Adams and E. Williams, 103–18. Columbia, SC: Camden House.

———. 1996a. *Dialogue concerning contemporary psychodynamic therapy.* Northvale, NJ: Jason Aronson.

———. 1996b. The application of postmodern thought to the clinical practice of psychoanalytic psychotherapy. *Journal of the American Academy of Psychoanalysis* 24:385–407.

———. 1996c. Archaic sadism. *Journal of the American Academy of Psychoanalysis* 24:605–18.

———. 1998. Empathy in psychoanalysis and psychotherapy. *Journal of the American Academy of Psychoanalysis* 26:487–502.

———. 1999a. Contingency and the unformulated countertransference. *Journal of the American Academy of Psychoanalysis* 27:135–49.

———. 1999b. *Emotional illness and creativity.* Madison, CT: International Universities Press.

———. 1999c. The phenomenology of Erwin Straus and the epistemology of psychoanalysis. *American Journal of Psychotherapy* 53:82–95.

———. 1999d. Passionate love. *Journal of the American Academy of Psychoanalysis* 27:515–21.

———. 1999e. Happiness and reverence for human life. *Academy Forum of American Academy of Psychoanalysis* 43:6–10.

———. 2000a. *Psychoanalytic clinical practice.* London: Free Association Books.

———. 2000b. Psychoanalysis at the millennium. *American Journal of Psychotherapy* 54:277–90.

———. 2000c. What is psychoanalysis? *Journal of the American Academy of Psychoanalysis* 28:1–23.

———. 2000d. Psychoanalysis at the end of the third millennium. *Journal of the American Academy of Psychoanalysis* 28:587–608.

———. 2001a. Dante's *Divine Comedy* revisited: What can modern psychoanalysts learn from a medieval psychoanalysis? *Journal of the American Academy of Psychoanalysis* 29:245–65.

———. 2001b. The secret life of the psychoanalyst. *Journal of the American Academy of Psychoanalysis* 29:403–26.

———. 2001c. The contemporary failure of nerve and the crisis in psychoanalysis. *Journal of the American Academy of Psychoanalysis* 29:661–80.

———. 2001d. Review of *The Metaphysical Club*, by L. Menand. American Journal of Psychiatry 158:2100–103.

——— . 2002a. Transference and countertransference revisited. *Journal of the American Academy of Psychoanalysis* 30:83–97.

——— . 2002b. Psychoanalysis as science and art. *Journal of the American Academy of Psychoanalysis* 30:257–74.

——— . 2002c. Confusion of tongues, psychoanalyst as translator. *Journal of the American Academy of Psychoanalysis* 30:361–82.

——— . 2002d. What is phenomenology? *Journal of the American Academy of Psychoanalysis* 30:673–89.

——— . 2003a. The Zollikon lectures. *Journal of the American Academy of Psychoanalysis* 31:343–48.

——— . 2003b. The effect on countertransference of the collapse of civilization. *Journal of the American Academy of Psychoanalysis* 31:541–62.

——— . 2005a. What grounds creativity? *Journal of the American Academy of Psychoanalysis and Dynamic Psychiatry* 33:3–27.

——— . 2005b. The human mind in the contemporary world. *Journal of the American Academy of Psychoanalysis and Dynamic Psychiatry* 33:299–321.

——— . Forthcoming. *Case report: Battle of the giants—A desperate struggle in psychoanalytic therapy to keep the patient alive.*

Chisholm, R. 1957. *Perceiving: A philosophical study.* Ithaca, NY: Cornell University Press.

Chodorow, N. 1999. Toward a relational individualism: The mediation of self through psychoanalysis. In *Relational psychoanalysis: The emergence of a tradition*, ed. S. A. Mitchell and L. Aron. Hillsdale, NJ: Analytic Press.

Chomsky, N. 1972. *Language and mind.* New York: Harcourt Brace Jovanovich.

——— . 2000. *New horizons in the study of language and mind.* New York: Cambridge University Press.

Churchland, P. 1984. *Matter and consciousness: A contemporary introduction to the philosophy of mind.* Cambridge, MA: Massachusetts Institute of Technology Press.

Ciardi, J., trans. 1954. *Dante Alighieri: The Inferno.* New York: Mentor Books.

——— . 1970a. *Dante Alighieri: The Divine Comedy.* New York: Norton.

——— . 1970b. *Dante Alighieri: The Paradiso.* New York: New American Library.

Coen, S. 2000. The wish to regress in patient and analyst. *Journal of the American Psychoanalytic Association* 48:785–810.

Collingwood, R. G. 1939. *An autobiography.* London: Oxford University Press.

——— . 1940. *An essay on metaphysics.* Oxford: Clarendon Press.

——— . 1942. *The new Leviathan: Or man, society, civilization and barbarism.* London: Oxford University Press. Rev. ed., 1993.

——— . 1946. *The idea of history.* Oxford: Clarendon Press. Rev. ed., 1993.

Cooper, A. 1986. Some limitations on therapeutic effectiveness: The burnout syndrome in psychoanalysts. In *Psychoanalytic Quarterly* 55:576–98.

Crain, C. 2002. License to ink. *The Nation*, Feb 11, 25–29.

Crick, Joyce, trans. 1999. *Sigmund Freud: Interpretation of dreams*. New York: Oxford University Press.

Crystal, A. 2001. *A company of readers*. New York: Free Press.

Curtis, H. 1980. The concept of therapeutic alliance: Implications for the "widening scope." In *Psychoanalytic explorations of technique: Discourse on the theory of therapy*, ed. H. Blum, 159–92. New York: International Universities Press.

Cutrofello, A. 2005. *Continental philosophy: A Contemporary introduction*. New York: Routledge.

Dante. 1293. *La vita nuova*. Trans. B. Reynolds. New York: Penguin.

Dennett, D. 1991. *Consciousness explained*. Boston: Little Brown.

Deutsch, H. 1965. Some forms of emotional disturbance and their relationship to schizophrenia. In *Neuroses and character types*. New York: International Universities Press.

Dewald, P. 1964. *Psychotherapy*. New York: Basic Books.

———. 1976. Transference regression and real experience in the psychoanalytic process. *Psychoanalytic Quarterly* 45:213–30.

Doi, T. 1993. *Amae* and transference-love. In *On Freud's observations on transference-love*, ed. E. Person, A. Hagelin, and P. Fonagy. New Haven, CT: Yale University Press.

Doré, G. 1976. *The Doré illustrations for Dante's Divine Comedy*. New York: Dover Publications.

Dreyfus, H., and P. Rabinow. 1983. *Michel Foucault: Beyond structuralism and hermeneutics*. Chicago: University of Chicago Press.

Eliot, T. 1950. Dante. In *Selected essays of T. S. Eliot*. New York: Harcourt Brace.

Emde, R. 2006. Mobilizing fundamental modes of development: Empathic availability and therapeutic action. In *Contemporary psychoanalysis in America: Leading analysts present their work*, ed. A. Cooper, 137–62. Washington, DC: American Psychiatric Publisher.

Emerson, C. 1997. *The first hundred years of Mikhail Bakhtin*. Princeton, NJ: Princeton University Press.

Epstein, L., and A. Finer, eds. 1993. *Countertransference: The therapist's contribution to the therapeutic situation*. Northvale, NJ: Jason Aronson.

Erle, J. 1993. On the setting of analytic fees. *Psychoanalytic Quarterly* 62:106–8.

Feinsilver, D. 1999. Counter identification, comprehensive countertransference, and therapeutic action: Toward resolving the intrapsychic-interactional dichotomy. *Psychoanalytic Quarterly* 68:264–301.

Fenichel, O. 1945. *The psychoanalytic theory of the neuroses*. New York: Norton.

Ferenczi, S. 1988. *Clinical diary of Sándor Ferenczi*, ed. J. Dupont. Trans. M. Balint and N. Jackson. Cambridge, MA: Harvard University Press.

Fergusson, F. 1966. *Dante*. New York: Macmillan.

Fodor, J. 1975. *The language of thought*. New York: Crowell.

Follesdal, D. 2001. Hermeneutics. *International Journal of Psycho-Analysis* 82:375–79.

Fonagy, P. 1999. Memory and therapeutic action. *International Journal of Psycho-Analysis* 80:215–23.

———. 2005. Psychoanalytic developmental theory. In *The American Psychiatric Textbook of Psychoanalysis*, eds. E. Person, M.D., A. Cooper, M.D., and G. Gabbard, M.D. Washington DC: American Psychiatric Publishing.

Fotion, N. 2000. *John Searle*. Princeton, NJ: Princeton University Press.

Foucault, M. 1973a. *Madness and civilization*. Trans. A. Smith. New York: Vintage.

———. 1973b. *The order of things*. New York: Vintage.

Fox, M. 2005. *The accessible Hegel*. Amherst, New York: Humanity Books.

Freeman, T. 1998. *But facts exist: An enquiry into psychoanalytic theorizing*. London: Karnac Books.

Freud, A. 1946. *The ego and the mechanisms of defence*. New York: International Universities Press.

Freud, S. 1895. Project for a scientific psychology. *Standard edition* 1:283–346. London: Hogarth Press.

———. 1900. The interpretation of dreams. *Standard edition*, vols. 4 and 5. London: Hogarth Press.

———. 1900a. The interpretation of dreams. Trans. A. A. Brill. New York: Modern Library.

———. 1908. Creative writers and day-dreaming. *Standard edition* 9:142–53. London: Hogarth Press.

———. 1912a. Recommendations to physicians practicing psycho-analysis. *Standard edition* 12:11–120. London: Hogarth Press.

———. 1912b.The dynamics of transference. *Standard edition* 12:97–108. London: Hogarth Press.

———. 1913. On beginning the treatment. *Standard edition* 12:123–44. London: Hogarth Press.

———. 1914a. On narcissism: Introduction. *Standard edition* 14:67–104. London: Hogarth Press.

———. 1914b. Some reflections on schoolboy psychology. *Standard edition* 13:241–44. London: Hogarth Press.

———. 1914c. Remembering, repeating and working through. *Standard edition*, vol. 14. London: Hogarth Press.

———. 1915. Observations on transference-love. *Standard edition* 12:157–71. London: Hogarth Press.

———. 1917. Mourning and melancholia. *Standard edition* 14:239–58. London: Hogarth Press.

———. 1918. History of an infantile neurosis *Standard edition* 17:7–122. London: Hogarth Press.

———. 1920. Beyond the pleasure principle. *Standard edition* 18:7–66. London: Hogarth Press.

———. 1926. The question of lay analysis. *Standard edition* 20:179–258. London: Hogarth Press.

———. 1927. The future of an illusion. *Standard edition* 21:3–58. London: Hogarth Press.

———. 1930. Civilization and its discontents. *Standard edition* 21:64–148. London: Hogarth Press.

Friedman, H. 2001. Sources of opposition to relatedness in psychoanalysis. *Psychoanalytic Inquiry* 21:640–57.

Friedman, L. 1976. Cognitive and therapeutic tasks of a theory of mind. *International Review of Psychoanalysis* 3:259–75.

Fromm-Reichmann, F. 1950. *Principles of intensive psychotherapy.* Chicago: University of Chicago Press.

———. 1959. *Psychoanalysis and psychotherapy: Selected papers of Frieda Fromm-Reichmann,* ed. D. Bullard. Chicago: University of Chicago Press.

Frosch, J. 1991. The New York psychoanalytic civil war, *Journal of the American Psychoanalytic Association.* 39:1037–1064.

Gabbard, G. 1995. Countertransference: The emerging common ground. *International Journal of Psycho-Analysis* 76:475–85.

———. 1997. A reconsideration of objectivity in the analyst. *International Journal of Psycho-Analysis* 78:15–26.

———. 2000. On gratitude and gratification. *Journal of the American Psychoanalytic Association* 48:697–718.

Gadamer, G. 1989. *Truth and method.* 2nd ed. Trans. J. Weinsheimer and D. Marshall. New York: Crossroad.

———. 1991. *Truth and method.* New York: Crossroad.

Gedo, J. 1979. *Beyond interpretation: Toward a revised theory for psychoanalysis.* New York: International Universities Press.

———. 1984. *Psychoanalysis and its discontents.* New York: Guilford.

———. 1988. *The mind in disorder: Psychoanalytic models of pathology.* Hillsdale, NJ: Analytic Press.

———. 1997. *Spleen and nostalgia: A life and work in psychoanalysis.* Northvale, NJ: Aronson.

————. 1999. *The evolution of psychoanalysis: Contemporary theory and practice.* New York: Other Press.

Gedo, J., and M. Gehrie, eds. 1993. *Impasse and innovation in psychoanalysis: Clinical case seminars.* Hillsdale, NJ: Analytic Press.

Gedo, J., and A. Goldberg. 1973. *Models of the mind: A psychoanalytic theory.* Chicago: University of Chicago Press.

Gill, M. 1954. Psychoanalysis and exploratory psychotherapy. *Journal of the American Psychoanalytic Association* 2:771–97.

————. 1978. Metapsychology is irrelevant to psychoanalysis. In *The human mind revisited*, ed. S. Smith, 349–96. New York: International Universities Press.

————. 1982. *Analysis of the transference*, vol. 1. New York: International Universities Press.

————. 1984. Psychoanalysis and psychotherapy: A revision. *International Review of Psycho-analysis* 11:141–79.

Giovacchini, P. 1968. Characterological faculties and the creative personality. *Journal of the American Psychoanalytic Association* 19:524–42.

Gitlin, T. 2002. *Media unlimited.* New York: Metropolitan.

Glover, E. 1931. The therapeutic effect of inexact interpretation: A contribution to the theory of suggestion. In *The technique of psycho-analysis.* New York: International Universities Press, 1965.

Goode, E. 2001. Patient suicide brings therapists lasting pain. *New York Times*, January 16, D1–D6.

Gottlieb, A. 2000. *The dream of reason: A history of philosophy from the Greeks to the renaissance.* New York: Norton.

Green, A. 2000. Conference proceedings. In *The Hartmann era*, ed. M. Bergman, 248–58. New York: Other Press.

————. 2005a. Theories of therapeutic action and their technical consequences. In *Understanding dissidence and controversy in the history of psychoanalysis*, ed. M. Bergman. New York: Other Press.

————. 2005b. The illusion of common ground and mythical pluralism. *International Journal of Psycho-Analysis* 86:627–32.

————. 2005c. *Key ideas for a contemporary psychoanalysis: Misrecognition and recognition of the unconscious*, trans. A. Weller. Hove: Brunner-Routledge.

Greenberg, J. 2005. Theories of therapeutic action and their technical consequences. In *Textbook of psychoanalysis*, eds. E. Person, A. Cooper, and G. Gabbard, chap. 14. Washington DC: American Psychiatric Publishing.

Greenberg, J., and S. Mitchell. 1983. *Object relations in psychoanalytic theory.* Cambridge, MA: Harvard University Press.

Greenson, R. 1967. *The technique and practice of psychoanalysis.* New York: International Universities Press.

————. 1978. Loving, hating, and indifference to the patient. In *Explorations in psychoanalysis*, 505–18. New York: International Universities Press.

Grubrich-Simits, I. 1996. *Back to Freud's texts: Making silent documents speak.* New Haven, CT: Yale University Press.

Grünbaum, A. 1984. *The foundations of psychoanalysis: A philosophical critique.* Berkeley: University of California Press.

Gunther, M. 1976. The endangered self: A contribution to the understanding of narcissistic determinants of countertransference. *Annual of Psychoanalysis* 4:201–24.

Gutting, G. 2001. *French philosophy in the twentieth century.* New York: Cambridge University Press.

Habermas, J. 1971. *Knowledge and human interests.* Trans. J. Shapiro. Boston: Beacon Press.

Hahn, E., ed. 1997. *The philosophy of Hans-Georg Gadamer.* Chicago: Open Court.

Hamilton, E., and H. Cairns, eds. 1973. *Plato: The collected dialogues.* Princeton, NJ: Princeton University Press.

Hanly, C. 1977. Commentary. *Journal of Clinical Psychoanalysis* 6:485–93.

Harries, K. 2001. Philosophy in search of itself. In *What is philosophy?* New Haven, CT: Yale University Press.

Hartmann, H. 1958. *Ego psychology and the problem of adaptation.* Trans. D. Rapaport. New York: International Universities Press.

Heaney, S. 1999. *Beowulf: A new translation.* London: Penguin Books.

Hegel, G. 1807. *Phenomenology of spirit.* Trans. A. Miller. London: Oxford University Press, 1977.

————. 1812. *The science of logic.* Trans. A. Miller. Atlantic Highlands, NJ: Humanities Press.

————. 1820. *Hegel's philosophy of right.* Trans. T. Knox. London: Oxford University Press, 1976.

————. 1830. *Lectures on the philosophy of world history.* Trans. H. Nisbet. Cambridge: Cambridge University Press, 1975.

————. 1833. *Hegel's introduction to the lectures of the history of philosophy.* Trans. T. Knox and A. Miller. Oxford: Clarendon Press, 1985.

————. 1837. *Reason in history.* Trans. R. Hartman. New York: Macmillan, 1988.

————. 1840a. *Introduction to the philosophy of history.* Trans. L. Rauch. Indianapolis, IN: Hackett, 1988.

————. 1840b. *The philosophy of history.* Trans. J. Sibree. New York: Dover, 1956.

————. 1896. *Hegel's philosophy of right.* Trans. T. Knox. New York: Oxford University Press, 1976.

Heidegger, M. 1956. *What is philosophy?* Trans. W. Kluback and J. Wilde. Albany, New York: NCUP.

———. 1962. *Being and time.* Trans. J. Macquarrie and E. Robinson. New York: Harper & Row.

———. 1968. *What is called thinking.* Trans. J. Gray and F. Wieck. New York: Harper & Row.

———. 1969. *Discourse on thinking.* Trans. J. Anderson and E. Freund. New York: Harper & Row.

———. 1971. The origin of the work of art. In *Poetry, language, thought,* trans. A. Hofstadter, 163–86. New York: Harper & Row.

———. 1977. *The question concerning technology and other essays.* New York: Harper & Row.

———. 1991. *The principle of reason.* Trans. R. Lilly. Bloomington, IN: University of Indiana Press.

Held, K. 2003. Husserl's phenomenology of the life-world. In *The new Husserl: A critical reader,* ed. D. Welton. Bloomington, IN: Indiana University Press.

Henninger, D. 2002. Civilization and slaughter. *Wall Street Journal,* October 18.

Hollander, R. 2001. *Dante: A life in works.* New Haven, CT: Yale University Press.

Holmes, G. 1980. *Dante.* New York: Hill and Wang.

Holt, R. 1973. On reading Freud. In *Abstracts of the standard edition of the complete psychological works of Sigmund Freud,* ed. C. Rothgeb, 3–79. New York: Jason Aronson.

———. 1981. The death and transfiguration of metapsychology. *Journal of the American Psychoanalytic Association* 25:835–72.

Horne, P., ed. 1999. *Henry James: A life in letters.* New York: Viking.

Husserl, E. 1970. *The crisis of European sciences and transcendental phenomenology.* Evanston, IL: Northwestern University Press.

———. 1977. *Cartesian meditations.* Trans. D. Cairns. The Hague: Martinus Nijhoff.

Ignatieff, M. 2001. The attack on human rights. *Foreign Affairs* 80:102–16.

Inwood, M. 1983. *Hegel.* London: Routledge and Kegan Paul.

Issacharoff, A. 1993. Barriers to knowing. In *Countertransference: The therapist's contribution to the therapeutic situation,* eds. L. Epstein and A. Finer, chap. 1. Northvale, NJ: Jason Aronson.

James, C. 1991. Review of the double life of Veronique. *New York Times,* Dec. 8, 1991.

Jaspers, K. 1932a. *Philosophy,* Vol. 1. Chicago: University of Chicago Press, 1969.

———. 1932b. *Philosophy,* Vol. 2. Chicago: University of Chicago Press, 1969.

———. 1932c. *Philosophy,* Vol. 3. Chicago: University of Chicago Press, 1969.

———. 1963. *General psychopathology.* Trans. J. Hoenig and M. Hamilton. Chicago: University of Chicago Press.

Johnson, P. 1998. *R. G. Collingwood: An introduction.* Bristol, England: Thoemmes Press.

Johnson, S. 2002. You thought TV couldn't sink lower, but this summer hit new depths. *Chicago Tribune* sec. 5, August 26, 2002.

Jowett, B. 1920. *The dialogues of Plato,* Vol. 1. New York: Random House.

Joyce, M. 1961. The Symposium. In *The collected dialogues of Plato,* eds. E. Hamilton and H. Cairns. Princeton, NJ: Princeton University Press.

Kant, I. 1781. *Critique of pure reason.* Trans. N. Smith. New York: St. Martin's Press, 1965.

———. 1790. *Critique of judgement.* Trans. W. Pluhar. Indianapolis, IN: Hackett.

Kantrowitz, J. 1996. *The patient's impact on the analyst.* Hillsdale, NJ: Analytic Press.

———. 1999. The role of the preconscious in psychoanalysis. *Journal of the American Psychoanalytic Association* 46:65–89.

Kernberg, O. 1975. *Borderline conditions and pathological narcissism.* New York: Jason Aronson.

———. 2000a. Psychoanalytic perspectives on religious experience. *American Journal of Psychotherapy* 54:452–76.

———. 2000b. Conference proceedings. In *The Hartmann era,* ed. M. Bergman. New York: Other Press.

Kim, J. 1982. Psychophysiological supervenience. *Philosophical Studies* 41:51–70.

Klein, M. 1946. Notes on some schizoid mechanisms. In *Envy and gratitude and other works 1946–1963.* New York: Delta, 1975.

Kohut, H. 1971. *The analysis of the self.* New York: International Universities Press.

———. 1977. *The restoration of the self.* New York: International Universities Press.

———. 1982. Introspection, empathy, and the semi-circle of mental health. *International Journal of Psycho-Analysis* 63:395–407.

———. 1984. *How does analysis cure?* Chicago: University of Chicago Press.

———. 1990. *The search for the self,* vol. 3. Ed. P. Ornstein. Madison, CT: International Universities Press.

Körner, J. 2002. The didactics of psychoanalytic education. *International Journal of Psycho-Analysis* 83:1395–1405.

Kraus, A. 2001. Phenomenological-anthropological psychiatry. In *Contemporary psychiatry.* Vol. 1, *foundations of psychiatry,* ed. F. Henn, N. Sartorius, H. Helmchen, and H. Lauter. New York: Springer-Verlag.

Kuhn, T. 1962. *The structure of scientific revolutions.* Chicago: University of Chicago Press.

Kuhns, R. 1995. Review of *"The psychoanalytic mind: From Freud to philosophy." Journal of Philosophy* 92:392–97.

Lacey, R., and D. Danzinger. 1999. *The year one thousand: What life was like at the turn of the first millennium; an Englishman's world.* Boston: Little, Brown.

Laing, R. 1969. *The divided self.* New York: Pantheon.

Langs, R. 1979. *The therapeutic environment.* New York: Jason Aronson.

Laplanche, J. 1992. *Jean Laplanche: Seduction, translation and the drives.* Ed. J. Fletcher and M. Stanton. Trans. M. Stanton. London: Institute of Contemporary Arts.

Lasch, C. 1978. *The culture of narcissism: American life in an age of diminishing expectations.* New York: Norton.

Laughlin, R. 2005. *A different universe: Reinventing physics from the bottom down.* New York: Basic Books.

Lewis, B. 2002. *What went wrong? Western impact and Middle East response.* New York: Oxford University Press.

Lewis, R. 2001. *Dante.* New York: Lipper/Viking.

Levy, N. 2002. *Sartre.* Oxford: One World.

Lipton, S. 1977a. The advantages of Freud's technique as shown in his analysis of the rat man. *International Journal of Psycho-Analysis* 58:255–74.

———. 1977b. Clinical observations on resistance to the transference. *International Journal of Psycho-Analysis* 60:215–16.

———. 1979. An addendum to "The advantages of Freud's technique as shown in his analysis of the rat man." *International Journal of Psycho-Analysis* 60:215–16.

———. 1983. A critique of so-called standard psychoanalytic technique. *Contemporary Psychoanalysis* 19:35–46.

Little, M. 1957. 'R'—the analyst's total response to his patient's needs. *International Journal of Psycho-Analysis* 38:240–54.

Loewald, H. 1960. On the therapeutic action of psychoanalysis. *International Journal of Psycho-Analysis* 75:3–20.

Lyons, W. 2001. *Matters of the mind.* New York: Routledge.

Macdonald, D. 1962. *Against the American grain.* New York: Random House.

Magee, B. 2000. *The Tristan chord: Wagner and philosophy.* New York: Holt.

Mahony, P. 2001. Freud and translation. *American Imago* 58:837–40.

Maltsberger, J., and D. Buie. 1974. Countertransference hate in the treatment of suicidal patients. *Archive of General Psychiatry* 39:625–33.

Mandelbaum, A., trans. 1982. *The "divine comedy" of Dante Alighieri: Inferno.* New York: Bantam Books.

———. 1984. *The "divine comedy" of Dante Alighieri: Purgatorio.* New York: Bantam Books.

———. 1986. *The "divine comedy" of Dante Alighieri: Paradiso.* New York: Bantam Books.

Marx, K. 1844. *Early writings.* Trans. T. Bottomore. New York: McGraw-Hill, 1963.

Mayer, E. 1998. Changes in science and changing ideas about knowledge and authority in psychoanalysis. In *Knowledge and authority in the psychoanalytic relationship,* ed. O. Renik, 143–85. Northvale, NJ: Aronson.

McGinn, C. 1991. *The problem of consciousness*. Oxford: Basil Blackwell.

———. 1993. *Problems in philosophy: The limits of inquiry*. Oxford UK: Blackwell.

———. 2002. *The making of a philosopher: My journey through twentieth century philosophy*. New York: HarperCollins.

McLaughlin, J. 1981. Transference, psychic reality, and countertransference. *Psychoanalytic Quarterly* 50:639–64.

———. 1987. The play of transference: Some reflections on enactment in the psychoanalytic situation. *Journal of the American Psychoanalytic Association* 35:557–82.

Mead, G. H. 1962. *Mind, self, and society from the standpoint of a social behaviorist*, ed. C. Morris. Chicago: University of Chicago Press.

Melville, H. 2002. *Moby Dick*. New York: Norton. (Orig. pub. 1851.)

Menninger, K. 1958. *Theory of psychoanalytic technique*. New York: Basic Books.

———. 1988. *Whatever became of sin?* New York: Bantam.

Merleau-Ponty, M. 1962. *Phenomenology of perception*. Trans. C. Smith. London: Routledge & Kegan Paul.

———. 1967. *The structure of behavior*. Trans. A. Fisher. Boston: Beacon Press.

Merwin, W. C. 2000. *Dante Alighieri: Purgatorio: a new verse translation*. Borzoi Book Series. New York: Knopf.

Meyers, H. 2000. Discussion of Dr. Epstein's case. *Journal of Clinical Psychoanalysis* 9:451–56.

Milano, P. 1961. *The portable Dante*. New York: Viking Press.

Mitchell, S. 1997. *Influence and autonomy in psychoanalysis*. Hillsdale, NJ: Analytic Press.

Mitchell, S., and L. Aron, eds. 1999. *Relational psychoanalysis: The emergence of a tradition*. Hillsdale, NJ: Analytic Press.

Modell, A. H. 1978. The nature of psychoanalytic knowledge. *Journal of the American Psychoanalytic Association* 26:641–58.

———. 1990. *Other times other realities: Towards a theory of psychoanalytic treatment*. Cambridge, MA: Harvard University Press.

Monk, R. 1990. *Ludwig Wittgenstein: The duty of genius*. New York: Free Press.

Moran, D. 2000. *Introduction to phenomenology*. New York: Routledge.

Musa, M., trans. 1984. *Dante: The divine comedy*. Vol. 1: *Inferno*. New York: Penguin Books.

———. 1985. *Dante: The divine comedy*. Vol. 2: *Purgatory*. New York: Penguin Books.

———. 1986. *Dante: The divine comedy*. Vol. 3: *Paradise*. New York: Penguin Books.

Muslin, H., and M. Gill. 1978. Transference in the Dora case. *Journal of the American Psychoanalytic Association* 26:311–28.

Nacht, S. 1962. The curative factors in psychoanalysis. *International Journal of Psycho-Analysis* 43:206–11.

Nagel, T. 1974. What is it like to be a bat? *Philosophical Review* 83:435–50.

———. 1995. *Other minds: Critical essays 1969–1994.* New York: Oxford University Press.

Natterson, J. 1991. *Beyond countertransference: The therapist's subjectivity in the therapeutic process.* Northvale, NJ: Jason Aronson.

Neu, J. 1995. Review of "*The psychoanalytic mind: From Freud to philosophy.*" *Philosophical Review* 104:289–93.

Niederland, W. 1976. Psychoanalytic approaches to artistic creativity. *Psychoanalytic Quarterly* 45:185–212.

Nietzsche, F. 1873. The birth of tragedy. In *Basic writings of Nietzsche.* Trans. W. Kaufmann. New York: Modern Library, 1968.

———. 1873–1886. *Untimely meditations III: Schopenhauer as educator.* Trans. W. Kaufmann. Hollingdale. New York: Cambridge University Press, 1983.

Norton, C., trans. 1941. *The "divine comedy" of Dante Alighieri.* New York: Houghton Mifflin.

Ornstein, A. 1999. Discussion of Goldberg's paper "between empathy and judgement." *Journal of the American Psychoanalytic Association* 47:381–90.

Ornston, D. 1992. *Translating Freud.* New Haven, CT: Yale University Press.

Ortega y Gasset, J. 1925. *The dehumanization of art; and other essays on art, culture, and literature,* trans. H. Weyl. Princeton, NJ: Princeton University Press, 1968.

Orwell, G. 1968. *The collected essays, journalism and letters of George Orwell.* Ed. S. Orwell and I. Angus. New York: Harcourt, Brace Jovanovich.

Overbye, D. 2000. *Einstein in love: A scientific romance.* New York: Viking.

Palmer, R., ed. and trans. 2001. *Gadamer in conversation: Reflections and commentary.* New Haven, CT: Yale University Press.

Paniagua, C. 2001. The attraction of topographical technique. *International Journal of Psycho-Analysis* 82:671–84.

Person, E., A. Cooper, G. Gabbard, eds. 2005. *The American psychiatric textbook of psychoanalysis.* Washington, DC: American Psychiatric Publishing.

Petranker, J. 2001. Who will be the scientists? *Journal of Consciousness Studies* 8:83–90.

Phillips, W. 2002. William Phillips, quoted in *The Economist,* Sept. 21.

Pieper, J. 1952. *Leisure: The basis of culture.* Trans. A. Dru. New York: Pantheon.

Pine, F. 1985. *Developmental theory and clinical process.* New Haven, CT: Yale University Press.

———. 1990. *Drive, ego, object, and self: A synthesis for clinical work.* New York: Basic Books.

——. 1992. From technique to a theory of psychic change. *International Journal of Psycho-Analysis* 73:251–54.

——. 1998. *Diversity and direction in psychoanalytic technique*. New Haven, CT: Yale University Press.

——. 2001. Listening and speaking psychoanalytically—with what in mind? *International Journal of Psycho-Analysis* 82:901–16.

Pinkard, T. 2000. *Hegel: A biography*. New York: Cambridge University Press.

Pinsky, R., trans. 1997. *The inferno of Dante*. New York: Farrar Straus and Giroux.

Polanyi, M. 2000. The eclipse of thought. In *Dumbing down: Culture, politics and the mass media*. Ed. I. Mosley. Bowling Green, OH: Imprint Academic.

Pound, E. 1939. *ABC of reading*. Norfolk, CT: New Directions.

Quine, W. 1953. Two dogmas of empiricism. In *From a logical point of view*, chap. 2. Cambridge, MA: Harvard University Press.

——. 1960. *Word and object*. Cambridge MA: Massachusetts Institute of Technology Press.

Racker, H. 1968. *Transference and countertransference*. New York: International Universities Press.

Ragland, C., and S. Heidt. 2001. *What is philosophy?* New Haven, CT: Yale University Press.

Rangell, L. 1974. A psychoanalytic perspective leading currently to the compromise of integrity. *International Journal of Psycho-Analysis* 55:3–12.

——. 1989. Action theory within the structural view. *International Journal of Psycho-Analysis* 70:189–203.

Rawls, J. 1970. *A theory of justice*. Cambridge, MA: Harvard University Press.

Raymond, L., and S. Rosbrow-Reich. 1997. *The inward eye: Psychoanalysts reflect on their lives and work*. Hillsdale, NJ: Analytic Press.

Remnick, D. 2000. Profiles: Into the clear. *The New Yorker*, May 8.

Renik, O. 1993. Analytic interaction: Conceptualizing technique in light of the analyst's irreducible subjectivity. *Psychoanalytic Quarterly* 62:553–71.

——. 1998. The analyst's subjectivity and the analyst's objectivity. *International Journal of Psycho-Analysis* 79:487–97.

Richards, A., and A. K. Richards. 1995a. Notes on psychoanalytic theory and its consequences for technique. *Journal of Clinical Psychoanalysis* 4:429–56.

——. 1995b. Response to our respondents. *Journal of Clinical Psychoanalysis*. 4:543–64.

Ricoeur, P. 1970. *Freud and philosophy*. Trans. D. Savage. New Haven, CT: Yale University Press.

——. 1977. The question of proof in Freud's psychoanalytic writings. *Journal of the American Psychoanalytic Association* 25:835–72.

Rockmore, T. 1993. *Before and after Hegel: An historical introduction to Hegel's thought.* Berkeley: University of California Press.

———. 2001. Analytic philosophy and the Hegelian turn. *Review of Metaphysics* 55:339–70.

Rosenblatt, A. 1997. Review of *The psychoanalytic mind: From Freud to philosophy.* *International Journal of Psycho-Analysis* 78:188–92.

Rothenberg, A. 1987. *The creative process of psychotherapy.* New York: Norton.

Royal, R. 1999. *Dante Alighieri: Divine comedy divine spirituality.* New York: Crossroad.

Ruggiers, P., trans. 1954. *Michele Barbi's life of Dante.* Berkeley: University of California Press.

Russell, B. 1945. *A history of western philosophy.* New York: Simon and Schuster.

Ryan, M. 2000. Turning on the audience. In *Dumbing down: Culture, politics and the mass media.* Ed. I. Mosley. Bowling Green, OH: Imprint Academic.

Ryle, G. 1949. *The concept of mind.* New York: Barnes and Noble.

Safranski, R. 2002. *Nietzsche: A philosophical biography.* Trans. S. Frisch. New York: Norton.

Salvadori, G., and V. Lewis, trans. 1968. *Dante: His life, his times, his works.* New York: American Heritage Press.

Sandler, J. 1983. Reflections on some relations between psychoanalytic concepts and psychoanalytic practice. *International Journal of Psycho-Analysis.* 64:35–46.

Sandler J., and A. Dreher. 1996. *What do psychoanalysts want?* New York: Routledge.

Sartre, J. 1968. *Search for a method.* Trans. H. Barnes. New York: Vintage.

———. 1973. *Being and nothingness: A phenomenological essay on ontology.* Trans. H. Barnes. New York: Washington Square Press.

———. 1976. *Critique of dialectic reason.* Trans. A. Sheridan-Smith. London: New Left Books.

———. 1981. *The family idiot: Gustave Flaubert, 1821–1857.* Vol. 1. Trans. C. Cosman. Chicago: University of Chicago Press.

Sayers, D., trans. 1951. *The comedy of Dante Alighieri the Florentine: I. Hell.* Middlesex: Penguin Books.

Schafer, R. 1985. Wild analysis. *Journal of the American Psychoanalytic Association* 33:275–99.

Schlesinger, H. 2003. *The texture of treatment: On the matter of psychoanalytic technique.* Hillsdale, NJ: Analytic Press.

Schlessinger, N. 1984. On analyzability. In *Psychoanalysis: The vital issues,* vol. 2, ed. G. Pollock and J. Gedo, 249–74. New York: International Universities Press.

Schlessinger, N., and F. Robbins. 1974. Assessment and follow-up in psycho-analysis. *Journal of the American Psychoanalytic Association* 22:542–56.

Schopenhauer, A. 1818. *The world as will and representation.* 2 vols. Trans. E. Payne. Indian Hills, CO: Falcon Press, 1958.

Schwartz, S. 1999. Medieval antecedents of the therapeutic alliance. *Journal of the American Academy of Psychoanalysis* 27:275–84.

Searle, J. 1994. *The rediscovery of the mind.* Cambridge, MA: Massachusetts Institute of Technology Press.

———. 1997. *The mystery of consciousness.* New York Review of Books Press.

———. 1998. *Mind language and society: Philosophy in the real world.* New York: Basic Books.

Searles, H. 1965. *Collected papers.* New York: International Universities Press.

Shane, M., E. Shane, and M. Gales. 1997. *Intimate attachments: Toward a new self Psychology.* New York: Guilford Press.

Sinclair, J., trans. 1959. *The "divine comedy" of Dante Alighieri: Inferno.* New York: Oxford University Press.

———, trans. 1961a. *The "divine comedy" of Dante Alighieri: Purgatorio.* New York: Oxford University Press.

———, trans. 1961b. *The "divine comedy" of Dante Alighieri: Paradiso.* New York: Oxford University Press.

Singer, E. 1970. *Key concepts in psychotherapy.* New York: Basic Books.

Singer, I. 2000. *George Santayana, literary philosopher.* New Haven, CT: Yale University Press.

Singleton, C., trans. 1970a. *Dante Alighieri: The "divine comedy": Inferno 1. Italian text and translation.* Princeton, NJ: Princeton University Press.

———, trans. 1970b. *Dante Alighieri: The "divine comedy": Inferno 2. commentary.* Princeton, NJ: Princeton University Press.

———, trans. 1973a. *Dante Alighieri: The "divine comedy": Purgatorio 1. Italian text and translation.* Princeton, NJ: Princeton University Press.

———, trans. 1973b. *Dante Alighieri: The "divine comedy": Purgatorio 2. commentary.* Princeton, NJ: Princeton University Press.

———, trans. 1975a. *Dante Alighieri: The "divine comedy": Paradiso 1. Italian text and translation.* Princeton, NJ: Princeton University Press.

———, trans. 1975b. *Dante Alighieri: The "divine comedy": Paradiso 2. Commentary.* Princeton, NJ: Princeton University Press.

Sisson, C., trans. 1981. *Dante: The "divine comedy."* Chicago: Regnery Gateway.

Solomon, R., and D. Sherman. 2003. *The Blackwell guide to contemporary philosophy.* Malden, MA: Blackwell.

Spence, D. 1982. *Narrative truth and historical truth.* New York: Norton.

Spender, M. 1999. *From a high place: A life of Arshile Gorky.* New York: Knopf.

Spezzano, C. 1999. A relational model of inquiry and truth: The place of psycho-analysis in human conversation. In *Relational psychoanalysis: The emergence of a tra-dition*, ed. S. A. Mitchell and L. Aron. Hillsdale, NJ: Analytic Press.

Spillius, E. B. 1983. Some developments from the work of Melanie Klein. *International Journal of Psycho-Analysis* 64:321–32.

———. 2001. Freud and Klein on the concept of phantasy. *International Journal of Psycho-Analysis* 82:361–73.

Steiner, G. 1971. *In Bluebeard's castle: Some notes towards the redefinition of culture*. New Haven, CT: Yale University Press.

Steiner, J. 1993. *Psychic retreats: Pathological organizations in psychotic, neurotic, and bor-derline patients*. London: Routledge.

Steiner, R. 1984. Review of *Psychoanalysis and France*, ed. S. Lebovici and D. Wid-locher. *International Journal of Psycho-Analysis* 65:232–33.

Stern, R. 2002. *Hegel and the phenomenology of spirit*. New York: Routledge.

Stevenson, R. 1988. *The lantern-bearers and other essays*. Ed. J. Treglown. New York: Farrar Straus Giroux.

———. 1989. The enchantress. *Georgia Review* 43:551–68.

Stolorow, R., B. Brandchaft, and G. Atwood. 1987. *Psychoanalytic treatment: An inter-subjective approach*. Hillsdale, NJ: Analytic Press.

Stolorow, R., and G. Atwood. 1992. *Contexts of being: The inter-subjective foundations of psychological life*. Hillsdale, NJ: Analytic Press.

Stone, L. 1981. Notes on the noninterpretive elements in the psychoanalytic situation and process. *Journal of the American Psychoanalytic Association* 29:89–118.

Stroud, B. 2001. What is philosophy? In *What is philosophy?* chap. 1.New Haven, CT: Yale University Press.

Sullivan, H. 1947. *Conceptions of modern psychiatry*. Washington, DC: William Alan-son White Psychiatric Foundation.

———. 1953. *The interpersonal theory of psychiatry*. New York: Norton.

Symons, J. 2002. *On Dennett*. Belmont, CA: Wadsworth/Thompson Learning.

———. 1995. *The construction of social reality*. New York: Free Press.

Taylor, C. and P. Finley. 1997. *Images of the journey in Dante's "divine comedy."* New Haven, CT: Yale University Press.

Thomas, K. 2001. The life of learning: Why scholarship still matters—or ought to. *The Times Literary Supplement*, December 7, 12.

Tower, L. 1956. Countertransference. *Journal of the American Psychoanalytic Association* 4:224–55.

Turing, A. 1950. Computing machinery and intelligence. *Mind* 59:433–60.

Voorhees, B. 2000. Dennett and the deep blue sea. *Journal of Consciousness Studies* 7:53–69.

Wallerstein, R. 1988. One psychoanalysis or many? *International Journal of Psycho-Analysis* 69:5–21.

———. 1995. *The talking cures: The psychoanalysis and the psychotherapies.* New Haven, CT: Yale University Press.

———. 1999. *Psychoanalysis: Clinical and theoretical.* Madison, CT: International Universities Press.

———. 2002. The growth and transformation of American ego psychology. *Journal of the American Psychoanalytic Association* 50:135–69.

Waquet, F. 2000. *Latin: Or the empire of a sign.* London: Verso Publishers.

Ward-Perkins, B. 2005. *The fall of Rome and the end of civilization.* New York: Oxford University Press.

Weissman, P. 1967. Theoretical considerations of ego regressions and ego functions in creativity. *Psychoanalytic Quarterly* 36:37–50.

Whitaker, C., and T. Malone. 1953. *The roots of psychotherapy.* New York: Blakiston.

White, C. 2002. The middle mind. *Harpers* (March): 15–19.

White, L. 1948. Trans. *Dante Alighieri: The "divine comedy."* New York: Pantheon.

Whitebrook, J. 1996. Review of "*The psychoanalytic mind: From Freud to philosophy.*" *Journal of the American Psychoanalytic Association* 44:986–95.

Wile, D. 1972. Negative countertransference and therapist discouragement. *International Journal of Psycho-Analysis and Psychotherapy* 1:36–67.

Windschuttle, K. 2002. The cultural war on Western civilization. *The New Criterion* (January): 4–16.

Winnicott, D. 1958. Hate in the countertransference. In *Collected Papers.* New York: Basic Books. 194–203.

———. 1965. *The maturational processes and the facilitating environment.* New York: International Universities Press.

Winterer, C. 2001. *The culture of classism.* Baltimore: Johns Hopkins University Press.

Wittgenstein, L. 1972. *On certainty.* Ed. G. Anscombe and G. von Wright. New York: Harper.

Wolf, E. 1985. The search for confirmation: Technical aspects of mirroring. *Psychoanalytic Inquiry* 5:271–82.

Wolheim, A. 1993. *The mind and its depths.* Cambridge, MA: Harvard University Press.

Wood, A. 1990. *Hegel's ethical theory.* New York: Cambridge University Press.

Yorke, D. 1995. Freud's psychology: Can it survive? *Psychoanalytic Study of the Child* 50:3–31.

Index